COMMUNITY AND CRITIQUE

MOVEMENT RHETORIC/RHETORIC'S MOVEMENTS

Victoria J. Gallagher

MOVEMENT
RHETORIC
RHETORIC'S MOVEMENTS

Also of Interest

Activist Literacies: Transnational Feminisms and Social Media Rhetorics
Jennifer Nish

The Democratic Ethos: Authenticity and Instrumentalism in US Movement Rhetoric after Occupy
A. Freya Thimsen

Liturgy of Change: Rhetorics of the Civil Rights Mass Meeting
Elizabeth Ellis Miller

Peace by Peace: Risking Public Action, Creating Social Change
Lisa Ellen Silvestri

Rhetorica Rising: Feminist Rhetorical Methods for Social Change
Eileen E. Schell, K.J. Rawson, Curtis J. Jewell, Abigail H. Long, Sidney Turner, and Gabriella Wilson, eds.

Your Daughters Will Prophesy: Religion and Rhetoric in the Nineteenth Century Woman's Movement
Lisa Marie Gring-Pemble and Martha Watson

COMMUNITY AND CRITIQUE

The Rhetorical Activism of Black American Women's Memory Work

SARA C. VANDERHAAGEN

THE UNIVERSITY OF SOUTH CAROLINA PRESS

© 2025 University of South Carolina

The text of this book is licensed under a Creative Commons Attribution Non-Commercial No Derivatives 4.0. International (CC BY- NC- ND 4.0) license: https://creativecommons.org/licenses/by-nc-nd/4.0/.

Some rights reserved, including for text and data mining, artificial intelligence (AI) training, and similar technologies.

Published by the University of South Carolina Press
Columbia, South Carolina 29208

uscpress.com

Printed in the United States of America

Library of Congress Cataloging-in-Publication Data
can be found at http://catalog.loc.gov/.

ISBN: 978-1-64336-546-6 (hardcover)
ISBN: 978-1-64336-612-8 (paperback)
ISBN: 978-1-64336-613-5 (ebook)
DOI: https://doi.org/10.61162/9781643366135

The inclusion of this book in the Open Carolina collection is made possible by the generous funding of the University of South Carolina Libraries.

Parts of chapter 1 were originally published in a slightly different form in "Memory Work and Rhetorical Activism," in the *Oxford Handbook on African American Women's Writing,* edited by Simone C. Drake. Published online February 2, 2025. https://doi.org/10.1093/oxfordhb/9780197647424.013.0001. Reproduced with permission of the Licensor through PLSclear. This content is excluded from all forms of open access license, including Creative Commons, and the content may not be reused without the permission of Oxford University Press. Details of how to obtain permission can be found at https://global.oup.com/academic/rights/permissions/.

Much of the material from chapter 3 first appeared as the essay "'A Grand Sisterhood': Black Women Speakers at the 1893 World's Congress of Representative Women," *Quarterly Journal of Speech* 107, no. 1 (2021): 1–25. https://doi.org/10.1080/00335630.2020.1864660. Copyright (c) National Communication Association, reprinted by permission of Taylor & Francis Ltd, https://www.tandfonline.com on behalf of National Communication Association.

For Phoebe and Joanna,

That you might be faithful witnesses to the lives of those who have gone before and joyful workers for the liberation of those yet to be.

CONTENTS

LIST OF ILLUSTRATIONS

SERIES EDITOR'S PREFACE

The University of South Carolina series "Movement Rhetoric/Rhetoric's Movements" builds on the Press's long-standing reputation in the field of rhetoric and communication and its cross-disciplinary commitment to studies of civil rights and civil justice. Books in the series address two central questions: In historical and contemporary eras characterized by political, social, and economic movements enacted through rhetorical means, how—and with what consequences—are individuals, collectives, and institutions changed and transformed? How, and to what extent, can analyses of rhetoric's movements in relation to circulation and uptake help point the way to a more equal and equitable world?

In this well-researched and beautifully written book, Sara C. VanderHaagen examines the powerful role of Black women who used memory as a form of activism during the period between Reconstruction and the New Negro Movement. VanderHaagen defines "memory work" as the deliberate, public efforts by individuals or groups to use rhetoric to preserve, create, revise, deploy, and circulate accounts of the past to strengthen community bonds and effect change. She skillfully reads Black women's memory practices in their historical contexts and also in conversation with contemporary Black feminist thought and activism. As a result, *Community and Critique* provides readers a historically grounded and contemporarily relevant examination, one that foregrounds the intersectional experiences of Black American women and illuminates their substantial intellectual and strategic contributions to contemporary rhetorical praxis.

ONE

"To Embalm Her Memory in Song and Story"

Charting Black Women's Community and Critical Memory Work

This book is a story about how Black American women have created something where many believed there was nothing. Specifically, it is about how Black American women built a storehouse brimming with memories of Black people—especially women—in the United States in the face of forces constantly threatening to tear it down. Working with very little, these women laid the foundation, carefully erected the framing, constructed the walls and roof, and filled it with memories from which future Black people might draw to sustain themselves. Like the Spirit of God "hovering over the waters" in the ultimate act of creation, Black women began with a past they believed to be "formless and empty" and spoke shared memories into being.[1] Yet this book also tells the story of how, as they undertook their creative work, Black American women unearthed the history that was there all along. They simultaneously were creators and discoverers of their shared memories.

Writer, social reformer, and African-American clubwoman Victoria Earle Matthews described Black women's relationship to the past in her speech "The Awakening of the Afro-American Woman," which she delivered at the 1897 annual convention of the International Society of Christian Endeavor in San Francisco. As many other Black women did at the turn of the century, Matthews admonished a White audience to acknowledge the remarkable progress that women like her had made since the end of slavery. Although Matthews primarily focused on the pursuit of education and development of home life, she also reflected on the role of the past in understanding Black women's present. Black women, she informed listeners, "had no past to which they could appeal for anything." She argued that slavery "had destroyed, more than in the men, all that a woman holds sacred, all that ennobles womanhood." Black women "had nothing but the future."[2] Matthews did not say that the past was utterly empty but, rather, that it offered nothing of persuasive power—nothing "to which they could appeal." Unlike the White women whom Matthews addressed, Black women could find little uplifting history from which to draw inspiration. Black women were instead forced to turn to the future, which enabled them to accomplish more in less time than any other group of women in human history. Matthews drew rather modest, conservative lines around Black women's accomplishments, cozily ensconcing them in a comfortable domestic space. Yet she also noted that the act of Black women "awakening" to the great task of creating "a home for her race" was "glory enough to embalm her memory in song and story." Matthews continued, "As it is, it will be her sufficient monument through all time that out of nothing she created something, and that something the dearest, the sweetest, the strongest institution in Christian government."[3] The Black mother of Matthews's speech had humble yet meaningful goals focused on her family and the Black community. However, the memory of the Black mother's accomplishments extended far beyond the confines of home to become a "monument" and a memory to be praised in public through "song and story." Although these women may not have been able to draw on the available past to fuel their activism, they accomplished enough to become sources of inspiration for future Black women. It was up to women such as Matthews and her listeners to undertake the memory work required to honor their Black foremothers.

This book examines how Black American women such as Matthews engaged in memory work to uplift Black communities and to critique dominant White memories. I use the term *memory work* throughout the book to refer to the deliberate, public efforts by individuals or groups to use rhetoric to preserve, create, revise, deploy, and circulate accounts of the past to strengthen community bonds and effect change. This concept enables me to foreground the purposive, often strategic, rhetorical work of Black women who used memory as a form of activism. Black women rhetors engaged directly in what we might call *memory activism*, which publicly advocated for specific ways of remembering the Black past. They also engaged less directly—although no less significantly—in memory work designed to equip Black communities for activism in other contexts and other time periods. These women understood that different audiences created divergent rhetorical constraints. In turn, they attuned their rhetorical strategies to both the specific audiences and purposes they aimed to achieve.

To pinpoint the distinctive audiences and purposes of Black women's memory work, I identify its two key forms: community memory work and critical memory work. The first uplifts Black community memories, whereas the second corrects hegemonic memories. Through the concept of "memory work," this book explores how Black women used rhetoric to construct shared memories that could move their communities and those around them. I undertake a rhetorical analysis that places Black women's memory practices in their historical contexts and reads them in conversation with contemporary Black feminist thought and activism. This study triangulates three conceptual lenses—rhetorical studies, public memory studies, and Black feminism—to elucidate Black women's memory work during the period between Reconstruction and the New Negro Movement.

Community and Critique focuses explicitly on how Black American women used rhetoric to perform memory work. Some scholarship has examined White (usually Southern) women's efforts to promote racialized memories during the late nineteenth and early twentieth centuries, yet few studies have highlighted the sustained work of Black women in constructing memories—especially about and for their own communities.[4] This book seeks to rectify that imbalance and thereby address two related research needs: (1) the need for continued substantive engagement with Black women's rhetorical practices and intellectual traditions and (2) the need for research in public memory that foregrounds the intersectional experiences of Black American women.

First, this book extends recovery work to substantively engage Black women's rhetorical strategies, intellectual traditions, and memory practices. The book thus responds to a call by many Black feminist scholars to move beyond recovery toward deeper engagement with Black women's intellectual and rhetorical work.[5] Today's scholars are able to make this move only because of the pioneering work done by historians such as Evelyn Brooks Higginbotham, Darlene Clark Hine, and Nell Irvin Painter, who made great strides in recovering the history of Black women in the diaspora. Recovery work in history was followed by similar efforts in rhetorical studies.

Early monographs and essays in this area have expanded our understanding of individual Black women speakers and writers, especially of the nineteenth century. The publication of Karlyn Kohrs Campbell's 1986 essay, "Style and Content in the Rhetoric of Early Afro-American Feminists," offered a rationale and select examples for public address scholars, most in the field of communication, to study the distinctive discourse of Black women between 1830 and 1925.[6] Olga Idriss Davis's early essays outlined important considerations for embodying the role of the "Black woman critic" and studying the rhetoric of Black women.[7] Anthologies of Black women's rhetoric by Robbie Jean Walker (1992) and Shirley Wilson Logan (1995) recovered critical primary sources.[8] A small number of influential books have analyzed and theorized Black women's rhetoric, intellectual work, and activism. These books include Carla L. Peterson's *Doers of the Word: African American Women Speakers and Writers of the North, 1830–1880* (1995); Shirley Wilson Logan's *We Are Coming: The Persuasive Discourse of Nineteenth-Century Black Women* (1999); Jacqueline Jones Royster's *Traces of a Stream: Literacy and Social Change Among African American Women* (2000); and Deborah F. Atwater's *African American Women's Rhetoric: The Search for Dignity, Personhood, and Honor* (2009).[9] My work draws upon and extends the historical research and rhetorical analysis by these and other scholars, thereby contributing to the subfield that Ronisha Browdy named as "Black Women's Rhetoric(s)."[10]

Second, *Community and Critique* foregrounds the intersectional experiences of historical Black women in the study of public memory. When Black women are heeded at all, they have often been treated as objects or victims of others' memories rather than active shapers and producers of their own memories. A small number of rhetorical studies have examined Black women's work as theorists and practitioners of memory, including the research of Rosalyn Collings Eves and Patricia Davis, which explored Black women's memory work in cookbooks and historical reenactment, respectively.[11] This book builds on the work of Eves and Davis to demonstrate how Black women, individually and collectively, synthesized personal experience and historical fact to craft distinctive public memories that could sustain their communities and undermine hegemonic White fictions. It also extends my previous work in *Children's Biographies of African American Women* (2018), moving from a focus on Black women as subjects of memory to Black women as agents of memory. *Community and Critique* centers the memory work of Black American women to demonstrate the significant, if underexamined, role that they played in shaping our shared past.

To investigate Black women's memory work, this book pursues the following questions: How did Black American women living after the demise of slavery yet before the advent of the civil rights movement use rhetoric to create memories for themselves and for others? Whose memories did Black women preserve, and how were they portrayed? How did they articulate the motives for and purposes of their memory work? Finally, how did Black women's memory work relate to their advocacy and activism, both then and now?

Public Memory and Black Women's Memory Work

Although my assumptions about memory in this book are shaped by conversations within the richly interdisciplinary field of memory studies, I ground my analysis in the concept of "public memory" as it has been articulated in my own field of rhetorical studies. Memory studies is a well-established line of interdisciplinary humanistic inquiry.[12] The field boasts dedicated journals such as *Memory Studies*, national and international conferences, and numerous monographs and anthologies. According to sociologist and memory scholar Jeffery Olick and his colleagues, memory studies as an academic field stretches back at least a century.[13] Scholars of rhetoric entered modern conversations about public memory in the 1980s and 1990s to understand how persuasive symbol use by members of the public enables them to generate shared meaning about the past.[14] However, interests in memory as a rhetorical technique date back millennia, at least to the ancient Greeks, as Frances Yates and others have documented.[15] The field of rhetoric thus has a historic tie to questions of memory and offers a generative contemporary vantage point from which to consider how the process of memory is formed through the public use of strategic language. The conclusions drawn from such a vantage point, I argue, are useful for scholars of memory from many different fields, especially those who consider memory as a human-driven process rather than an object or series of products.

A rhetorical approach to public memory provides a fruitful framework for exploring the case studies in this book: representative historical case studies of Black American women's memory work. Choosing "public memory" rather than another animating term such as "historical memory," "collective memory," or "cultural memory" shapes my interpretation of the texts I examine. I have argued elsewhere that, deployed in this way, public memory functions as a hermeneutic rather than a descriptor for some objective category of phenomena.[16] Public memory highlights how people use rhetoric in public spaces to advance collective visions of the past that seek to accomplish something in the present and future. To put it slightly differently, public memory is "an actively reinterpreted resource for action in the present and future, negotiated by public discourse."[17] Using the lens of public memory illuminates how groups of people use language deliberately to construct, revise, and deploy accounts of the past to accomplish certain shared goals. Because public memory is a "highly rhetorical process" in which "memories are open to contest, revision, and rejection," deploying the critical tools of rhetoric enables us to better understand how this process occurs in specific texts and discourses.[18]

By viewing these case studies as instances of public memory, I can show not only how Black women's memory work functions rhetorically but also how it is publicly salient, how it fosters identification, and how it provides resources for people to act together. Houdek and Phillips explained that public memory, as defined by scholars in communication and rhetoric, "entails the acts and processes, through which memories move beyond the remembering individual and become shared, passed on, and in this way, form a broader network through which people gather a sense of collectivity."[19] This definition highlights that both rhetorical "acts" such as giving speeches, forwarding petitions, and writing biographies and rhetorical "processes" such as the transmission of Black hero stories from generation to generation should be considered part of the broader formation of public memory. It also draws attention to the movement of memories from individuals to the broader public. This emphasis on publicity is also central to rhetoric scholars. As Carole Blair, Greg Dickinson, and Brian L. Ott explained, the descriptor "'public' situates shared memory where it is often the most salient to collectives, in constituted audiences, positioned in some kind of relationship of mutuality that implicates their common interests, investments, or destinies, with profound political implications."[20] Part of my argument in this book is that Black American women's memory work, whether manifested in more straightforward rhetorical acts such as speeches or less obvious efforts such as editing biographical sketches, is publicly significant. Approaching these case studies as examples of public memory further advances that argument. Focusing on public memory also invites us to consider how people deploy rhetorical strategies to transform individual recollections into shared memories that foster identification. Personal recollections and firsthand memories are especially important for understanding the history of Black Americans, whose accounts have been intentionally suppressed and undermined by White hegemonic memories. Finally, public memory reveals how shared understandings of the past can, in Houdek and Phillips's words, "form a broader network through which people gather a sense of collectivity" and thereby establish a basis for people to act together. Although the memory work itself does not always constitute activism, it often lays the groundwork for future activism based on a common narrative.

In *Community and Critique*, I consider public memory as a rhetorical process, and I introduce the term "memory work" to pinpoint the rhetorical labor undertaken within that process. Rhetoric itself supplies many of the crucial tools for memory work. The Black women gathered in this book—many of them educated members of the Black middle class—knew these tools. Whether unable to read like Sojourner Truth, self-educated like Maria W. Stewart, or having earned a doctorate like Anna Julia Cooper, Black American women deliberately deployed rhetorical tools to accomplish their persuasive goals. By considering Black women's practices as memory work, I emphasize the sustained effort, rhetorical skill, and collective knowledge that they invested in influencing shared understandings of the past. I also use the term "memory work" to encompass rhetorical activities that both lay the groundwork for activism and constitute the activism itself. A speech to fellow African Americans at a religious gathering may not have directly advocated for specific social changes, but it may have marshaled the names of women leaders to encourage female listeners to view themselves as agents capable of working for change. A petition to Congress opposing a harmful monument, on the other hand, more directly agitated for changes in how we remember. As memory work, however, both rhetorical acts cultivate an orientation toward public activism. Typically, studies of memory foregrounding an activist function have focused on memories as resistance. Although I am certainly interested in forms of resistive memory, a central argument of this book is that memory work is more than just resistance. Memory work is more capacious than existing concepts such as "counter-memory" or critical memory, which articulate themselves directionally toward dominant memories. Memory work can be used to create space for survival, to build community, and to cultivate joy. As a chorus of contemporary activists have affirmed, the work of social change is and must be about all of these things simultaneously.[21]

The concept of "memory work" has not been widely theorized or applied in the field of rhetorical studies. It has been used sporadically by scholars in fields as varied as geography, history, and education.[22] In an early articulation of the concept, cultural historian Annette Kuhn described memory work as "an active practice of remembering which takes an inquiring attitude towards the past and the activity of its (re)construction through memory."[23] Kuhn's interests in memory and her development of the method she called "memory work" stemmed from her commitments as a feminist historian prioritizing what Joan Wallach Scott has called "the evidence of experience."[24] My use of the term "memory work" resonates with Kuhn's usage insofar as both articulate a feminist approach to inquiry, and both view memory as an active process of reconstruction. However, whereas Kuhn and others in this vein characterize memory work as an individual research method or practice, I use it to describe a form of intentional rhetorical practice undertaken by a collective. As such, the term "memory work" strikes a useful balance of scale between the perilously broad "public memory" and narrower concepts such as "counter-memory." It functions thus as a generative conceptual guide rather than a specific method.

The concept of "memory work" also trains our attention on the rhetorical agency of those doing the work—in this case, Black American women. Centering Black women as active agents performing memory work and thereby shaping public memory addresses the gap in scholarship on US memory, which has previously focused more on Black women as objects of memory than agents of memory.[25] Even scholarship that intentionally foregrounds the intersections of race and memory dramatically underplays the role of Black women. For instance, David Blight's influential *Race and Reunion: The Civil War in American Memory* acknowledged the existence of Black women during the late nineteenth and early twentieth centuries but virtually ignored their vigorous public efforts to shape memories of slavery, especially in the 1890s when they were actively speaking on the subject.[26] Historical studies of race and memory during other time periods, such as Renee C. Romano and Leigh Raiford's edited collection *The Civil Rights Movement in American Memory*, do feature essays focused on memories *of* African-American women but not primarily as *producers* of memory.[27] Other scholarship in this area focuses on commemorations of Black men from Crispus Attucks to Booker T. Washington to Malcolm X.[28] Historical studies dedicated to remembrances of Black women, such as Milton Sernett's *Harriet Tubman: Myth, Memory, and History*, are rare and do not necessarily pay sustained attention to Black women as agents of memory.[29] Edited collections and monographs in the field of rhetorical studies have also noted the intersections among rhetoric, memory, and race but do not center Black women in a deliberate and sustained fashion, whether as subjects worthy of remembrance or as agents advancing certain memories.[30] Using the term "memory work" builds agency into the book's conceptual framework and enables me to affirm Black women as rhetorical agents engaged in skilled and savvy efforts to influence public memory.

Situating Black Memory Work

Community and Critique represents an effort to understand Black American women's historical memory work on its own terms as much as possible. As Kent Ono has argued, this effort requires that I locate the discourse within a "contextual field," which refers to the "situating elements used to make sense of the rhetorical text, texts, intertexts, transtexts, paratexts, or even 'discourse formations' under study." A contextual field is "actively put into relation to a given rhetoric or rhetorical texts as a heuristic, specifically to generate analytic and hermeneutic possibilities and further imagine rhetoric's effectivity."[31] Two key contextual fields that guide my analysis are conceptualizations of Black American memory and the Black feminist tradition. Taken together, these bodies of thought illuminate the ways in which memory work in Black communities and by Black Americans serves distinctive rhetorical functions. Considering these contextual fields also reveals how Black women's memory work grows out of, and yet is a unique expression of, African-American memory more generally.

Before I proceed to discuss three key influences on my understanding of Black memory work, I will provide a note on terminology. Throughout *Community and Critique*, I generally use the terms "Black" and "Black American" to refer to African-descended people living in the United States. The more inclusive term "Black" typically denotes a racial group including people of any nationality or ethnicity who live in all but the northernmost regions of the continent of Africa or are descended from the people of that region. The term "Black" most strongly invokes the people or cultures of the African diaspora. Because my analysis focuses on African-descended women in the United States, I will use both "Black" and "Black American" to describe these speakers and writers. For variety and readability, I will also occasionally use the term "African American" to denote the same identity. I recognize that some people use "Black" to denote a racial category and "African American" to refer to an ethnicity and cultural group. I use the terms "Black" and "African American" interchangeably, because recent polling and personal experience indicate that people of African descent in the United States are evenly split on their preferences for these labels. A 2019 Gallup Poll of African-descended Americans found that seventeen percent of survey respondents preferred the term "Black," eighteen percent preferred "African American," and sixty-four percent claimed to have no preference.[32] As an adjective, such as in this section on "Black memory work," I prefer to use the term "Black" because of its simplicity and inclusiveness. Although I use the terms "Black" and "African-American" to denote a racial and social group, I do so recognizing that this group is both socially constructed and richly diverse.[33]

Although conceptualizations of memory and related terms have been intermittent and implicit in Black studies, as Christel N. Temple has observed, they have nonetheless produced important insights for scholars aiming to study memory practices that emerged from the African diaspora.[34] The most prominent treatments of Black memory have been developed by literary scholars in the Black studies tradition, such as Houston A. Baker, Temple, and Badia Ahad-Legardy. Because they also stem from a humanistic tradition focused on reading texts, their theorizations and analyses resonate with a rhetorical perspective.

Houston A. Baker Jr.'s "Critical Memory and the Black Public Sphere" offers an important reflection on memory's political and rhetorical functions. Baker outlined the "twin rhetorics" through which Black modernity engages with the past: nostalgia and critical memory.[35] Baker argued that these forms of memory, which both emerge from the Black public sphere, express different relationships to revolution. Nostalgia safely imprisons revolution in the past, whereas critical memory continues to fuel revolution in the present. Baker claimed that "the essence of critical memory's work is the cumulative, collective maintenance of a record that draws into relationship significant instants of time past and the always uprooted homelessness of now."[36] To illustrate the power of critical memory for the Black public sphere, Baker showed how Martin Luther King Jr. had been captured by nostalgia when he should instead be seen as "*a black political radical of the first order.*"[37] The tool of critical memory enables us to see King more fully by situating him in a relationship of continuity rather than a rupture with other Black political figures and movements. Baker's analysis highlights the fact that public memory as a rhetorical process is shaped by the ideological and political structures of the time in which it is produced and responsive to the people by whom it is produced. For instance, representing King as a champion of colorblind unity serves White politicians seeking to appease fearful White voters while appearing to appeal to Black voters. Baker's essay cautions readers to remain cognizant of how different forms of memory can create varied—and sometimes deeply dangerous—political results. I draw on Baker's work to conceptualize the idea of critical memory work that resists dominant White memories and to show how memory work connects to Black publics.

Although not as explicitly focused on memory as Baker's essay, Christel N. Temple's work applies to my project because of its Afrocentric approach to Black diasporic engagement with the past. I have drawn particularly from Temple's essay about the concept of "*sankofa*" and her book *Black Cultural Mythology*.[38] Both of these works plumb the deep cultural foundations excavated by Afrocentric thinkers. Long present in Black communities, Afrocentric philosophies began to play a more prominent role in the late twentieth century. The reclamation and celebration of African traditions in the US diaspora included not only words and language—especially from West African cultural groups—but ideas. A key African idea pertaining to memory is *sankofa*, which is both a word and an image that Temple describes as an "Adinkra communicator."[39] Adinkra is a visual system of communication used by the Akan people of West Africa to convey the central ideas and values of their culture. A "communicator" such as *sankofa* is not a mere symbol or word but a visual representation of a complex philosophy. The word *sankofa* is often translated as "go back and fetch it" or "it is not taboo to go back and retrieve what you have forgotten or lost."[40] The visual representation of this idea is a bird turning its head backward and opening its beak toward a round object on its back, perhaps an egg or a seed. Together, this word and image have given birth to a diasporic practice by Black Americans that builds collective bonds through acknowledgment of and education about the past. Temple argued that Black communities have deployed this communicator with "fascinating and creative agency" to "define [their] experience through the naming of schools, bakeries, beauty products, businesses, rites of passage programs, and more."[41] Although the Black women whose rhetoric is examined in this book did not explicitly invoke *sankofa* to describe their activities, their memory work resonates strongly with the tradition.

Christel N. Temple's theorization of Black cultural mythology also begins from an Africana foundation to develop a framework for understanding how Black diasporic communities have constructed mythologies that ensured their survival and flourishing. Although Temple's operative term is *mythology*, memory figures prominently in her framework. Her opening chapter defines Black cultural mythology as "a renewed approach to stabilizing cultural memory that collectively ensures the preservation and recollection of African American and broader diasporan legacy using conceptual tools to actively engage the culturally relevant past."[42] Temple argues that this approach is especially essential for Black diasporic communities in societies in which they are the minority and in which their place in the society is overdetermined by the history of chattel slavery, such as the United States.[43] The framework seeks to rehabilitate the concept of mythology within an Africana worldview so that it can help us understand the distinctive practices that Black communities have used to survive in a society that has persistently sought to alienate them from their history and their agency. Temple's ambitious project—especially her excavation and reframing of key thinkers in mythology—illustrates the importance of considering Black engagement with the past on its own terms as much as possible rather than subjecting it to misreading through a hegemonic White worldview. Temple's framework is furthermore valuable for my project, because it demonstrates that Black women such as Maria W. Stewart have served crucial roles in theorizing and contributing to Black cultural mythology. Although the broad contours and commitments of Temple's framework parallel the analysis in this book, her framework does not substantively engage with Black feminism. Therefore, instead of applying Temple's framework holistically, I use specific attributes of the framework, such as "hero dynamics" and "ancestor acknowledgment," to illuminate how Black women's memory work often aligns with Afrocentric memory practices.[44]

Finally, Badia Ahad-Legardy's conceptualization of "Afro-nostalgia" supplies a rationale for reading the positive, productive functions of Black memory work without ignoring its painful exigencies. Ahad-Legardy recuperates the idea of nostalgia on behalf of fellow African Americans, for whom such "'pretty' modes of memory" had been previously thought unavailable.[45] Afro-nostalgia serves as "a lens through which we can conceptualize the desires of the African-descended to discern and devise romantic recollections of the past in the service of complicating the traumatic as a singular black historical through line."[46] Ahad-Legardy's analysis challenges the idea that nostalgia is a luxury of the privileged—whether White people or the Black elite—to show that it is, in fact, an important aspect of Black American culture writ large. Like Christel N. Temple's formulation of Black cultural mythology, Ahad-Legardy's concept of Afro-nostalgia expands the understanding of how Black people relate to the past beyond the bounds of trauma. Afro-nostalgia thus becomes a positive cultural practice that "lace[s] the gaps of historical memory with pleasure-inducing affect—not by rewriting the past but by embracing nostalgia's imaginative capacity to rehabilitate the black historical past and refashion the present."[47] Although

Ahad-Legardy's analysis of Afro-nostalgia focuses on contemporary examples, the concept is generative for the study of historical examples as well. In fact, because it aims to show how nostalgia functions as "a means of historical pleasure" in Black life, it is especially relevant for thinking about how African Americans performed memory work when memories of enslavement were fresh and the manifestations of White supremacy more brazen.

Several key themes emerge from this Black studies scholarship that resonate with my goals. First, these thinkers seek to reorient Black American memory beyond the trauma lens to account for more robust and even joyful forms of engagement with the past. As Ahad-Legardy's work makes especially clear, such a reorientation seeks not to ignore trauma but to consider it within a larger affective landscape. Second, they consider the past as a resource to be shaped and used rather than an inert mass of objectively existing information. Considerations of memory from within Black studies largely reject the sharp distinction that some scholars—most prominently Pierre Nora—have made between history and memory to argue that the two exist in an interdependent relationship. This approach resonates with ideas that I have articulated here and elsewhere.[48] Third, these scholars affirm the existence of distinctive—though by no means monolithic—Black American memory practices. Christel N. Temple, in particular, seeks to accomplish this in a comprehensive fashion through her theorization of Black cultural mythology. Although my aims are not as sweeping as Temple's, her work provides an important underlying justification for my project's specific focus on Black American women's memory work. Fourth, these scholars insist that Black Americans have consistently acted as central agents of memory, despite being ignored or misunderstood as such. The very idea of agency as the capacity for creative, effectual action proves crucial in all of the aforementioned treatments of Black memory.[49] Fifth, their work emphasizes the significant role of "heroic" individuals in Black public memory, from Harriet Tubman and Sojourner Truth, to Martin Luther King Jr. and Malcolm X. These individuals demonstrate the possibilities of Black agency past, present, and future. Such figures are not without flaws, but their lives are deliberately presented as examples of survival, resistance, and radical imagination. The analysis in the subsequent chapters likewise recognizes the centrality of exemplary lives not as mere hagiography but as robust resources for memory work and future action. Finally, this scholarship points to an approach to time that emphasizes deep continuity among past, present, and future rather than rupture or the rejection of tradition. Moments of transformation exist, yet they are contextualized within a broader approach to time that seeks to connect those who have gone before with those yet to be.

Agency, Collaboration, and Memory in Black Feminist Frameworks

Any exploration of Black women's memory work must rely on the maps and signposts of Black feminist thought. Emerging from a long tradition of Black women thinkers, Black feminism draws our attention to Black women's unique intersectional identities and experiences and the actions that emerge from them. Using Black feminism as a guide keeps us on the right path while leading us beyond the boundaries of Whiteness. Some of the women who have contributed to the Black feminist tradition lived before the appearance of the term "feminist" or may not have applied it to themselves because "feminism" connoted White women.[50] Although most did not self-identify as feminists, Black women of the nineteenth century and early twentieth century anticipated and built the groundwork for contemporary Black feminist thought. Many of these women engaged in memory work—both in its community and critical modes—because of their commitments to uplifting and liberating Black women. Therefore, in this book, I approach Black women's memory work and the Black feminist tradition as symbiotic projects. Three central Black feminist ideas emerge as especially relevant to Black women's memory work: an emphasis on agency, collaborative activism, and reframing memory beyond critique. Attention to these themes guides my analysis in the case study chapters.

Agency is a grounding concept in Black feminist thought. Patricia Hill Collins described agency as "an individual or social group's will to be self-defining and self-determining."[51] Agency entails Black women defining their own identities and actions, resisting oppression regardless of whether such efforts were widely recognized by White oppressors, and producing valuable knowledge from their experience.[52] Black feminist scholars such as bell hooks, Alisa Bierria, Olga Idriss Davis, and Shardé Davis have echoed Collins's emphasis on self-determination and self-definition.[53] Philosopher Jennifer C. Nash has argued that these ideas are foundational to the "second-wave" Black feminism of the 1970s, including thinkers such as Alice Walker, June Jordan, and Audre Lorde. Nash said that such Black feminism is rooted in "a shared commitment to 'self-love, self-respect, and self-determination.'"[54] Furthermore, the Black feminist emphasis on agency seeks to provide what D. Soyini Madison called "tools of resistance," which facilitate critical engagement with hegemonic discourses.[55] Finally, Black feminist thought frames agency as Black women's ability to interpret and make sense of their own actions. For instance, Collins noted that her path-breaking work in *Black Feminist Thought* sought to challenge the "treatment of black women as objects of knowledge by valorizing African American women as agents of knowledge."[56] Likewise, Black feminist communication scholars Marsha Houston and Olga Idriss Davis advocated for research that treats Black women "as active agents who create and interpret their own and others' discourse" and values "experiential data [. . .] more than experimental data."[57] Although many of these scholars have pinpointed the importance of agency in contemporary configurations of Black feminism, an analysis of rhetorical texts from Black women of the past suggests that they also viewed testifying to and creating space for agency as a key rhetorical goal. Moreover, these women recognized that crafting memories for present and future Black women could provide resources for self-definition and action.

Black feminist thought also emphasizes the significance of collaborative, collective activism. From the mutual aid societies of the eighteenth and nineteenth centuries to the Combahee River Collective, to the contemporary Black Women Radicals and the #SayHerName campaign, Black women have advocated collectively for themselves and their communities. For this reason, *Community and Critique* underscores the simultaneous significance of both individual and collective rhetorical actions. By tacking back and forth between individual and collective rhetorical acts, my analysis aims to reflect the insistence of Black feminist thought on communal resistance and to reveal, as Brenda J. Allen put it, "the complexity and heterogeneity of Black women's communicative lives, even as we seek commonalities of experience."[58] Although my analysis often engages in close readings of individual rhetorical acts, such as speeches, these are considered within the context of shared experience and collective action. Reading Black women's memory work through Black feminism holds individual and communal agency in tension, which, in turn, enables me to avoid oversimplification and stereotyping on the one hand and simple tokenism on the other. The concept of memory work also contributes to this goal by encompassing both individual and communal rhetorical activity.

Finally, turning to Black feminist thought reframes our understanding of Black women's memory work beyond the function of critique. As I have noted, little scholarship on public memory has been centered on Black American women's public memory work.[59] Contemporary conversations about Confederate memorials and public school history curricula have prominently featured some Black women, such as journalist Nikole

Hannah-Jones, but almost exclusively as *critics* of hegemonic White memory. Black women have undoubtedly had many reasons to criticize White memories. However, to consider only this type of intervention risks misunderstanding Black women's memory work as only a *reaction* to Whiteness. Rather, Black women have also undertaken to recover, preserve, and promote memories of Blackness primarily for Black people.

Black women and the ideas they produce have often been restricted to the position of critique. Jennifer Nash explored this problem in an eloquent and compelling fashion in *Black Feminism Reimagined.* She explained that Black feminism has been reduced to a means of defending the concept of intersectionality as a stand-in for Black feminist thought more generally. Nash observed that the demand that Black women and Black feminist scholars—which, as she states, are not identical categories[60]—constantly protect and correct is itself deeply shaped by White supremacy. The same is true of Black women's memory work. If Black women's memory work is purely critical and corrective, then it is again beholden to Whiteness. As Nash noted, "If the tradition [of Black feminism] is designed merely to correct, rather than to exist as its own vibrant field of debate, then it is logical that black feminists find themselves mired in the impasse of the present, one marked by the intersectionality wars that again attempt to tether black feminism to one intellectual product—intersectionality—and to reduce and collapse 'black woman,' 'black feminism,' and 'intersectionality.'"[61] By examining both the community and critical memories fashioned by Black women, this project charts the complexity highlighted by Nash and aims to engage Black women's memory work on its own terms.

Contextualizing Black American Women's Community and Critical Memory Work

African-American women have historically engaged in what I describe as both community memory work and critical memory work. The intersecting but distinct forms of memory work performed by Black women differ primarily in terms of audience and purpose. Community memory work focuses on members of a particular group that self-identifies as a community. Communities, as Benedict Anderson explained, are not simply given but imagined.[62] Most of Black women's community memory work is oriented toward recovering, building, and imagining meaningful memories about and for Black Americans—especially for young people and children. This work reminds Black communities of their rich history—contrary to the narrative advanced by White supremacy—and aims to instill a sense of pride in that history. Community memory work is about serving Black people. Critical memory work focuses on correcting hegemonic White memories that have systematically erased or diminished Black people. It is intentionally oppositional and corrective. In some cases, it simply challenges White memories. In other cases, critical memory seeks to supplant White memories. In both cases, its primary audience is White people and often, more broadly, anyone benefitting from the privilege embedded in White memories. Houston Baker has described Black critical memory as "the very faculty of revolution," which "judges severely, censures righteously, renders hard ethical evaluations of the past that it never defines as well-passed."[63] Because of the unique audiences and goals of these two forms of memory, Black women have engaged distinctive rhetorical strategies suited to each.

The relationships between community memory work and critical memory work parallel the relationships between different spheres of Black life and activism. Like their respective purposes, the spheres in which community memory work and critical memory work occur are distinct yet intertwined. Although Black communities can be self-contained, they can also be linked to the White public sphere. Black spaces have historically provided respite from and served as incubators for activism in White spaces. As Darlene Clark Hine observed, "The primary launching site of every struggle was the community."[64] For hundreds of years, the memory work of Black women occurred within what Catherine Squires has called enclave or counterpublic spaces. Both of these alternative contexts arise when groups are excluded from the dominant public sphere, as Black women frequently have been. The inwardly focused community memory often occurs in an enclave that hides "counterhegemonic ideas and strategies in order to survive or avoid sanctions, while internally producing lively debate and planning."[65] The community memories gathered and stored within the safe walls of the Black family, church, or neighborhood often subsequently nourish critical memory. In contrast, counterpublic discourse engages in "debate with wider publics to test ideas and perhaps utilize traditional social movement tactics," much as critical memory addresses dominant publics to uproot problematic memories that have taken hold there.[66] Acknowledging these varied spheres is especially important when considering the historical, rhetorical activities of women—particularly women of color—which often occurred in spaces hidden from public view.

African-American women have written memory into public discourse for hundreds of years. In 1773, Phillis Wheatley published a poem titled "On Recollection," which praised Mneme—the Greek muse of memory—and the "ample treasure of her secret stores." The enslaved[67] poet Wheatley wrote of how "the heav'nly phantom [Mneme] paints the actions done / By ev'ry tribe beneath the rolling sun." One can easily imagine that Wheatley sought to include her own lost natal "tribe" in the realm of historical action. She spoke of memory's ability to bring reckoning—"Has vice condemn'd, and ev'ry virtue blest." Whereas Mneme blesses those who act uprightly, her appearance is "dreaded by the race, / Who scorn her warnings, and despise her grace."[68] Given her own Christian piety, Wheatley could have been speaking of recollections and judgment of individual sins; yet her mention of a "race" that might dread the unpredictable eruptions of memory into the present could also plausibly serve as a veiled critique of Whiteness and chattel slavery. Wheatley's theorization of memory in this poem evocatively suggests her understanding of its connection to both action and judgment. White intellectuals such as Thomas Jefferson dismissed Wheatley's verse as amateurish and derivative, and Black cultural critics from Edward Wilmot Blydon to Amiri Baraka scoffed at Wheatley's supposed lack of self-determination and race consciousness.[69] Yet others—especially Black women—recognized the significance of her contribution. For example, in *In Search of Our Mother's Gardens*, Alice Walker honored Wheatley's memory work, saying, "It is not so much what you sang, as that you kept alive, in so many of our ancestors, the notion of song."[70]

Many Black women since Wheatley have recognized the power of memory to carve out life-giving spaces for themselves, to create cohesive communities for African Americans, to instill race pride, to advocate for their rights, and to destabilize racist and sexist discourses that sought to diminish their humanity. Memory has served a particularly central role for African Americans, whose shared identity has been forged from a common diasporic experience—whether voluntary or involuntary. Many Black Americans were brought to the Americas by force and systematically deprived of the native languages, tribal affiliations, and religious practices that typically unite and sustain displaced people. When combined with carefully constructed racial hierarchies, that deprivation left many Black Americans with a sense that they had no history as a people, as a "race."

African Americans' supposed lack of recorded history seems to have been especially poignantly felt around the period of emancipation. In an 1863 speech to the Ohio Colored Teachers' Association, Sarah J. Woodson (later Early) invoked the historical erasure of Blackness to exhort young people to pursue education: "We inherit from our fathers nought but subjugation and dishonor. No history records the deeds of our great and good, no tongue ever heralded the praise of our brave and noble. No banner was ever inscribed with the insignia of our national existence; yet our history, humiliating as it may be, is not without precedent."[71] Woodson then followed other African Americans by comparing her people's story with that of the Israelites, "God's chosen people," enslaved in Egypt. A few years later in 1866, Sarah Parker Remond penned a letter to the *National Anti-Slavery Standard* that lamented the apparent impossibility of African-American history, saying, "What a record could the victims of this terrible hatred present against the dominant race. It will never be written. It never can be written."[72] These women grieved not that Black people had not acted; they grieved that no one would know. They lamented that the Black past had been systematically suppressed in public memory. Remarkably, women such as Woodson and Remond used this suppression as a motive for community activism and public advocacy. Black women understood the persuasive power of public memory, and they recognized the role that rhetoric played in constructing and circulating usable pasts.[73]

Black Women's Memory Work between Reconstruction and the New Negro Movement

As the examples of Wheatley, Woodson, and Remond make clear, Black women's memory work adapted to changing historical circumstances. The time period featured in this book is a crucial moment for both the development of US public memory and the growth of Black women's public activism, and—at the intersection of these two phenomena—the expansion of Black women's memory work. The beginning of this time period is marked by emancipation, which ushered in dramatic changes for African Americans, from legal freedom to Black male enfranchisement and representation in all levels of government. Emancipation also brought opportunities for commemorating new freedoms and remembering centuries of bondage.[74] The conclusion of this period is signaled by the New Negro Movement of the 1920s, also called the Harlem Renaissance, which "promoted a renewed sense of racial pride, cultural self-expression, economic independence, and progressive politics."[75] Like the sankofa bird, many Black artists, writers, and cultural leaders reached into the shared past for creative inspiration, making memory work a key piece of the movement. Black women were especially active in preserving and promoting memories during this decade. As Eric King Watts put it, the New Negro Movement was "the product of a special kairos."[76] In this section, I highlight several important historical changes between emancipation and the New Negro Movement that affected how Black women approached rhetorical activism and public memory work.

Black Americans living between 1865 and 1930 were engaged in both private labor and public movements to advance their rights and resist rampant racial violence. They faced intense racial hostility, from disenfranchisement to restrictive Jim Crow laws to horrific lynchings. Beneath those flagrant forms of violence simmered the symbolic violence of White memory, through which powerful public memories of slavery coalesced. As Black Americans articulated their memories of slavery during Reconstruction, White American groups redoubled their efforts to control public memories of slavery, the Civil War, and even the founding principles of the nation.[77] The United Daughters of the Confederacy, for instance, proved remarkably successful in funding and building Confederate monuments.[78] A contemporary report by the Southern Poverty Law Center shows that Confederate memorialization efforts were most intense between 1866 and 1945, peaking in 1911 with the dedication of more than forty named sites.[79] Memorials centering Lost Cause narratives and their whitewashed accounts of slavery severely constrained the ability of Black Americans to advance their own understandings of those events.

Starting during Reconstruction and continuing through the early decades of the twentieth century, Black women's public activism flourished.[80] Intersecting oppressions such as sexism and racism typically barred them from party politics, the polls, and many social movements. However, such discrimination did not stop their public rhetorical work of ascending lecture platforms, teaching students, writing poetry, stocking libraries, and forming associations. Through their collective action, Black women developed rhetorical and political strategies that enabled their communities to confront and survive oppression. As part of these public activities, Black women worked to preserve and promote memories that could destabilize dominant accounts. Embedded in this rhetorical work was a belief in the power of history to inspire pride in and deepen commitment to uplifting one's community. For instance, speaking about prominent African Americans of the past, author Jessie Redmon Fauset noted in a January 1922 essay in *The Crisis* that "their memory must be kept green, their tale be retold that we of a later day may take fresh heart."[81] Fauset argued that remembering past engagement could fuel present activism. Despite the limited contemporary reach of the memories Black women upheld, they shared stories that resisted and offered reprieve from White representations of Black women, advanced a critique of hegemonic White history, and preserved critical memories for the Black women of the future.

Although this book focuses primarily on memory work beginning during Reconstruction, it is important to acknowledge that Black women's activism preceded emancipation. Before the Thirteenth Amendment was ratified in December 1865, Black women, both enslaved and free, lived under the shadow of bondage. Much of their public discourse—both that oriented toward Black communities and that calling the White public to account—was focused on the horrors of slavery and the urgent need to eradicate it. Free Black women also invested their rhetorical efforts into developing support systems to enable their communities to survive in a society that ignored them or sought to destroy them. For instance, as Darlene Clark Hine and Kathleen Thompson have documented, women organized more than half of the one hundred nineteen Black mutual aid societies that were active in 1838 Philadelphia, home to a thriving free Black community.[82] Historians such as Hine and Thompson have noted the challenge of locating firsthand accounts from enslaved people, let alone stories that could be described as having risen to the level of "public discourse." However, we should not conclude that enslaved Black women were doing nothing to preserve or build a shared past. Rather, as Hine and Thompson explained, these women "often preserved African traditions and values, which reinforced their identity as people of worth and heritage."[83] Their invisible work yielded results that reverberated through subsequent generations.

Life changed for African Americans—enslaved and free—after emancipation, and with it changed Black women's memory work. Once the urgent demand of antislavery activism no longer dominated the lives of Black Americans, energies were invested in new forms of public activity. Most important, Black Americans faced the welcome challenges of supporting and educating those emancipated from slavery, strengthening their civic institutions, improving their economic status, and—in the case of Black men—becoming informed voters and skilled elected leaders. Carla L. Peterson has noted that Black women played a critical role in this transitional time: "[B]lack women in the Reconstruction period aspired to a comprehensive political vision that would encompass the place of African Americans within the nation as a whole. To construct a place for blacks within the nation, they needed to assess not only the strengths and weaknesses that lay within domestic and community spheres but also such questions as the commonality of interests between black and white women, the ballot as a tool of national Reconstruction, and the function of black labor within the nation."[84] Black women focused simultaneously on building Black communities and expanding Black access to the US public sphere. They also negotiated the tumultuous landscape of Reconstruction memory, in which groups of White Americans suppressed Black American remembrances by advancing White interpretations of the Civil War.[85]

For instance, Black women played important roles in the Emancipation Day celebrations that powerfully formed Black community memory during the Reconstruction period. Thavolia Glymph has explained that such celebrations "created spaces for black people to remember individually and collectively and to construct their own history."[86] These public celebrations, although attended and viewed by Whites, were largely orchestrated by and for Black communities. They featured a rich tapestry of activities, including original speeches, prayers, public readings, historical pageantry, musical performances, and dances. Although men dominated the speakers' podium, women actively contributed to emancipation commemorations in ways that were deemed suitable for respectable nineteenth-century women. Research by Amber Bailey, Mitch Kachun, Jeffrey Kerr-Ritchie, and Leslie Schwalm has shown that women prepared food, performed in historical pageants and tableaux, and read the Emancipation Proclamation or other texts.[87] Although African-American women's opportunities to write, speak, and publish remained limited during the nineteenth century, their participation in the diverse activities of Emancipation Day celebrations demonstrates that they played important roles in the creation and maintenance of community memory during this key period. Black women's memory work on behalf of Emancipation Day kept that commemoration in the public consciousness in ways that eventually enabled Juneteenth to become a federal holiday in 2021.

The end of Reconstruction brought a severe constriction of the rights and opportunities that Black Americans had briefly possessed. Paradoxically, the period after Reconstruction was considered both the nadir of American race relations and a time of great growth and activity for Black women.[88] Middle-class Black women, in particular, organized numerous associations to uplift their race by providing much needed social services to their communities. Frances Ellen Watkins Harper declared the late nineteenth century the "women's era" in 1893, and, starting in 1894, Josephine St. Pierre Ruffin broadcast that moniker in her newspaper, the *Women's Era*, the first produced by and for Black women. Tens of thousands of women participated in the Black women's club movement, which historian Glenda

Elizabeth Gilmore argued "kept civic activities and opportunities alive in the darkest days of Jim Crow."[89] Although not widely discussed, the preservation and promotion of Black American memories supplied persuasive fuel for this movement. For instance, Black women kept Phillis Wheatley's memory alive by creating dozens of clubs in her honor to house and support young Black working women.[90] In the early twentieth century, Black women's behind-the-scenes memory work advanced both community and critical goals. Mary E. Jones Parrish preserved Black memories of the 1921 Tulsa Massacre, writer Jessie Redmon Fauset promoted Black biographies for children, and librarian Augusta Baker prioritized Black history in children's library collections.[91] While the names of men such as Carter G. Woodson have become synonymous with the rise of Black history in the 1920s, Black women also actively advocated the teaching of Black history both to uplift Black communities and critique whitewashed versions of American history.[92] A handful of Black women, such as Ida B. Wells and Frances Ellen Watkins Harper, occupied more visible public positions as writers and activists, yet the vast majority performed their memory work in places invisible to White America and relevant primarily to Black communities.

Near the end of this time period and beyond, Black American women continued to expand their activist work from their communities to the Capitol. Black women performed memory work in a variety of roles during the 1930s and into the Black Freedom Movement, but perhaps no figures were more influential on community memory than Black teachers and librarians. Women such as Mary McLeod Bethune and Augusta Baker used their positions to advocate for Black narratives for Black children. As president of the Association for the Study of African American Life and History from 1936 until 1951, educator Bethune advocated the teaching of Black history to Black children. Significantly, Bethune also served as the Director of Negro Affairs for the National Youth Administration from 1936 to 1944, a position to which she was appointed by President Franklin Delano Roosevelt. Librarian Augusta Baker pushed for the New York Public Library system to include books for Black children that had more accurate and appropriate representations of Black people. In the 1940s, Baker helped bring a special collection of books to the 135th Street Branch Library in Harlem "in an effort to acquaint Negro boys and girls with their own heritage and racial achievements."[93] Baker deliberately called out the misrepresentation of Black people in public memory, insisting that "the complete picture of the Negro's part in American life should be represented, and not just the nostalgic old South with its plantations and loyal servants."[94] Baker understood the virulence of whitewashed memories and the power of children's books to inoculate Black children against those memories' damaging narratives. The work of women such as Bethune and Baker echoes into the twenty-first century, as demonstrated by the resurgence of debates about how racism is represented in books and curriculum for children in public institutions such as schools and libraries. These numerous examples illustrate that, from Reconstruction through the New Negro Movement, Black women have engaged consistently in both community-based and critically oriented memory work.

Contributions

Informed by deep engagement with this historical context and the theoretical context of Black feminist thought, the subsequent chapters undertake a rhetorical analysis of key instances of both community and critical memory work by Black American women. Chapter 2 examines how Black women speakers strategically invoked exemplary women from the past both to persuade in the present and to build a "storehouse" of memory to inspire future action. Chapter 3 focuses on the speeches of six Black women who addressed the 1893 World's Congress of Representative Women and argued for forms of commemoration centering the experiences of Black women. Chapter 4 analyzes Black women's rhetorical activism and commemorative stewardship in the 1923 debate over a proposed monument to "the faithful mammies of the South." Chapter 5 reads the 1926 book *Homespun Heroines and Other Women of Distinction*, a collection of biographical sketches by, about, and for Black women. These case studies enable me to examine instances of memory work that primarily address Black communities, those that primarily address White audiences, and those that engage in community and critical memory work simultaneously. These case studies offer worthwhile insights on their own, but they also illustrate the utility of the community and critical memory work framing.

Community and Critique demonstrates the critical power and value of Black feminist thought, through both the theorization of memory work and the analyses provided in the case studies. This is an important intervention in the field of rhetoric, which was historically dominated by "iconic" texts and "Great Men."[95] As Olga Idriss Davis explained, "To theorize the rhetoric of African American women from the perspective of our traditional and contemporary theories is what Lorde (1983) called 'using the Master's tools to dismantle the Master's house.'"[96] Using "the tools of a racist patriarchy" will not suffice when interpreting Black women's discourse: Critics must consult the body of knowledge that is invested "in black women's humanity, intellectual labor, and political visionary work."[97] This obligation is especially acute for non-Black scholars, like myself, who read Black women's discourse from outside of that experience. Although Black feminist thought begins with and is unequivocally centered in Black women's experience, scholars such as Collins and Nash have argued that it is a capacious knowledge project that can build coalitions for future action, both within historical moments and across time.[98] This rich and complex project can thus embrace both nineteenth-century "race women" and twenty-first-century activists.[99] My analysis of Black women's memory work as an expression of and contribution to Black feminist thought "places Black women across time and space in conversation with each other to theorize how Black women's truthtelling threatens white supremacy"—a critical move advocated by Ashley R. Hall in her essay on "Afrafuturist feminism."[100] This book also contributes to what Lisa Flores has described as "racial rhetorical criticism" by offering a historically grounded analysis that works to be "reflective about and engages the persistence of racial oppression, logics, voices, and bodies and that theorizes the very production of race as rhetorical."[101]

I examine Black American women's memory work to amplify Black women's voices and testify to the significant role that they played in shaping our national memory about our racial past and present, which has previously been underappreciated in scholarship on memory. In part, this is a recovery project, but it also shows how, in preserving and shaping memories for their own communities, Black women preserved the possibility for rehabilitating memories in their future, which is today. This goal was not always explicit in their words, but they were working to build a storehouse of memory from which future generations might draw once more Americans recognized the centrality of Black history and Black women's role within it. This goal is related to what Paul Ricoeur talks about in *Memory, History, Forgetting* as "forgetting in reserve": Basically, even though something might recede or be forced from the broader public memory, it can still be held "in reserve" for a time that is ripe for its re-emergence.[102] The story *Community and Critique* tells is intended to honor Black women today who continue to "go back and fetch" that past held in reserve for them by their ancestors and foremothers.[103]

TWO

"To Strive by Their Example"

Invoking Exemplary Women in Public Speech

In September 1833, Maria W. Stewart gave her last public speech to a mixed-gender audience in Boston. Stewart lamented having to fend off the many "fiery darts of the devil," let loose by those aiming to silence her Black female voice. Posing the rhetorical question, "What if I am a woman?" Stewart sharply defended her right to speak. She built her argument, in part, by identifying exemplary women from Israelite Queen Esther to Egyptian prophetesses, then declaring, "If such women as are here described have once existed, be no longer astonished, then, my brethren and friends, that God at this eventful period should raise up your own females to strive by their example, both in public and private, to assist those who are endeavoring to stop the strong current of prejudice that flows so profusely against us at present."[1] Stewart's invocation of female exemplars in this speech illustrates a powerful yet poorly understood rhetorical strategy of Black women speakers pursuing a place in public discourse and preserving space in public memory. Although Stewart used exemplars to criticize audience members who would limit Black women's agency, including these women in her speech also contributed to a public record of women's historical significance. Stewart performed community memory work by adding more women to a "storehouse of memory" from which future Black women could draw inspiration.

This chapter examines how Black American women speakers strategically deployed exemplary women in their public speeches and thereby engaged in memory work centering the needs and deeds of Black women. To showcase their rhetorical choices and their implications for memory, I take a contextually oriented thematic approach to highlight how the rhetorical choices of Black women speakers changed from the nineteenth to the early twentieth century. Specifically, I examine the different types of female exemplars invoked by those women, how the exemplars function rhetorically, and how changing audiences and circumstances constrained the women's choices. Black women's rhetorical strategies appear to have shifted gradually during this period in response to their degree of access to public discourse, the evolving and intersecting constraints of race and gender norms, and the insidious adaptations of White supremacy in the United States. In the antebellum period, when Black women's public words were beginning to be recorded, they invoked historical and biblical women of all racial identities to assert themselves within White- and male-dominated spaces. During Reconstruction and beyond, Black women drew from among their own ranks to provide evidence of their good character and accomplishments and to preserve memories of Black women for future generations. The strategy of publicly deploying Black women exemplars, in particular, constituted a significant form of community memory work, whereby Black women rhetors began to build a storehouse of Black women's memories. Black American women were able to make savvy use of exemplars, in part, because doing so was a familiar practice to US audiences. That familiarity also made exemplars effective vehicles for smuggling radical ideas into conservative spaces, thereby enhancing the potential for future activism.

Teachers and public figures have used exemplary individuals to instruct pupils and audiences for generations, yet the rhetorical implications of this commonplace practice have not been fully investigated. Furthermore, when it is theorized, exemplarity is typically approached as a pedagogical or religious practice rather than a rhetorical strategy, although it has both persuasive and publicly salient features. This chapter shows how Black American women have used exemplars as a deliberate rhetorical strategy to insert Black women insistently into public memory and offer evidence of past action and capacity for future action. As a rhetorical strategy, the use of exemplars also constitutes an important tool for both critical and community memory work. Stewart's 1833 speech illustrates how exemplars can be deployed critically, to challenge patriarchal memories that erase the contributions of women. In other instances, we can observe exemplars used in service to the Black community, especially when Black women are identified as virtuous models. Synthesizing scholarship on exemplarity and imitation with Black feminist perspectives, I examine public speeches by women such as Stewart, Mary V. Cook, Frances Ellen Watkins Harper, and Sojourner Truth that cite historical and contemporary women as examples. These speakers invoked exemplary women from Scripture, secular histories, and, later, from their own ranks of "race women" to gain a hearing from diverse audiences, bolster their ethos, defuse resistance to challenging ideas, and invite audiences to identify with others unlike themselves. I argue that, while their use of exemplars performed these rhetorical functions, it also performed community and critical memory work by reinforcing the relationships of Black women across time, adding Black women to a growing storehouse of memory, and inserting Black women into the public record. Such work equipped Black women of the present and future to negotiate intersecting oppressions, work toward racial uplift, critique White feminism, and enact advocacy and activism.

Exemplars as a Black Feminist Rhetorical Strategy

In this chapter, I read the specific discursive strategy of exemplars within the broader contextual fields of Black women's memory work and the Black feminist tradition, as well as scholarship on exemplars and imitation. The women whose words I discuss in this chapter lived before the wider uptake of the term "feminist" by Black women. Yet the ways in which these Black women speakers deployed exemplars resonate with the Black feminist tradition, as articulated by contemporary scholars such as Patricia Hill Collins, Brittney Cooper, and Jennifer Nash.[2] In the words of Regis Mann paraphrasing Ann DuCille, "nineteenth-century black women activists always reached up, anticipating contemporary black feminist concerns around the politics of intersectionality, understanding the experiential as epistemological, [and] building coalition across racial and gender lines."[3] These historical women, to various degrees, manifested commitments to Black feminist ideas, as described by Nash, by centering "analyses of racialized sexisms" and foregrounding "black women as intellectual producers, as creative agents, as political subjects, and as 'freedom dreamers' even as the content and contours of those dreams vary."[4] As Nash furthermore noted, Black feminists engage actively with accounts of the past. Black feminist theory is invested in "a rich and political counterhistory, one that draws on memory—personal, collective, or embodied—to demand an ethical reckoning with past and present."[5] Black women speakers' use of exemplars both centers Black women's actions and invites a critical engagement with the past.

Exemplars became a rich rhetorical resource for Black American women struggling to influence audiences, collect memories, and advocate for social change under the severe constraints of the late nineteenth and early twentieth centuries. Speaking as they were from precarious social positions, Black American women used exemplars to negotiate racist and sexist structures with creativity and moral clarity. They deployed female exemplars not only to teach virtue or right action but also to accomplish specific rhetorical goals, such as defending the right of women to speak publicly or gaining recognition for women's work in the Black church. These specific rhetorical goals dovetailed with Black women's memory work writ large, as the repeated citation of female agents—especially Black female agents, in the later speeches examined here—built a storehouse of memory from which future generations could draw inspiration. By drawing attention to Black female agents of the past, these rhetors themselves became the "agents of knowledge" that Patricia Hill Collins described.[6]

To gain purchase for their arguments in the face of intersecting racism and sexism, Black women often couched their claims within conservative discourses, such as the ideals of True Womanhood and the politics of respectability. Barbara Welter described how the nineteenth-century "Cult of True Womanhood" revered an ideal woman who exhibited the virtues of piety, purity, submissiveness, and domesticity.[7] Although Welter's analysis focuses on the mid-nineteenth century, Black feminist literary critics have shown that the ideology of True Womanhood affected Black women throughout that century and into the 1920s. Because the "true woman" was assumed to be White, Black women occupied a precarious, even impossible, position in relation to virtuous womanhood in the late nineteenth and early twentieth centuries. Predominant racist stereotypes of Black women rendered them as sexually deviant and therefore perpetually available for exploitation by White men.[8] To protect themselves and to counter these stereotypes, Black women developed specific strategies for self-representation. These strategies have been described by scholars as the "politics of silence"; the "culture of dissemblance"; and, most famously, the "politics of respectability."[9] Although the first two strategies were more directly concerned with preserving Black women's sexual virtue and autonomy, the politics of respectability came to apply to more publicly visible appearances and actions. Historian Evelyn Brooks Higginbotham developed the concept of a politics of respectability to explain Black women's activism in religious contexts. She argued that this politics "emphasized reform of individual behavior and attitudes as a goal in itself and as a strategy for reform of the entire structural system of American race relations."[10] Invoking praiseworthy exemplary women enabled Black women to negotiate constraining discourses and ideologies, but doing so often also meant relying on ideals of respectability and Christian virtue.

Although the use of exemplars and their connection with rhetoric stretches back millennia, the exemplar has not often been considered as a rhetorical strategy for doing memory work. Teachers of rhetoric in the ancient Western world, such as Isocrates, Aristotle, and Quintilian, primarily used exemplars as a pedagogical tool to train students of rhetoric to develop good character and good habits of mind. The exemplar took on a decidedly religious bent during the Renaissance and early modern period, where it was used by writers of diplomatic letters, literary texts, religious works, and historical treatises.[11] The idea of exemplarity fell out of favor during the modern period, as it came to be negatively associated with imitation and connotations of crude copying. However, it persevered in practice. As Jennifer A. Herdt explained, although "exemplarity did recede from theoretical consideration with the rise of modern moral philosophy," exemplars themselves "never ceased to play an important role in ordinary life."[12] One need only observe the persistent popularity of biography collections and series over the past two millennia—from Plutarch's *Lives of the Noble Greeks and Romans* to Christine de Pizan's *Book of the City of Ladies* to the Bobbs-Merrill Company's *Childhood of Famous Americans* series—to understand the enduring significance of exemplarity.

My understanding of exemplarity acknowledges its historical origins, especially the exemplar's connection with rhetoric, and reframes the concept to focus on its role in memory work. I approach exemplarity as a rhetorical strategy through which participants in public discourse remember, reconstruct, and often revise the stories of actual, historical persons to deploy them for particular persuasive purposes. My conceptualization relies on literary scholar Timothy Hampton's definition of the exemplar as "a kind of textual node or point of juncture, where a given author's interpretation of the past overlaps with the desire to form and fashion readers."[13] Hampton's case studies derive from Renaissance practices of exemplarity, yet his characterization highlights persistent features of the practice—specifically, its textuality, instrumentality, and interpretive nature—that are relevant for the analysis in this chapter. Most important, Hampton's definition describes exemplars as an "interpretation of the past" crafted with the goal of influencing people in the present. Although, historically, exemplars have been used primarily to shape people's character, I argue that they also function to "form and fashion" audiences' understanding of the past. Exemplars incorporated into public speeches thus perform public memory work by presenting certain individuals as worthy of remembrance and emulation.

My treatment of exemplars as a tool for memory work is further informed by interdisciplinary scholarship on exemplars, including rhetoric scholar Kirt Wilson's essay on the "racial politics of imitation," and Africana Studies scholar Christel N. Temple's concept of Black "hero dynamics."[14] Whereas scholarship on exemplarity from the fields of rhetoric, literature, philosophy, and education elucidates its form and function, Wilson's and Temple's works attend specifically to the racial dynamics of imitation and heroic narrative. Taken together, their scholarship illuminates how exemplars function and what makes them uniquely compelling for Black women speakers undertaking public memory work during this time period. First, exemplars possess an inherent ambiguity that can be used strategically by rhetors from marginalized groups to covertly advocate social transformation. Exemplars are, thus, an important rhetorical resource for rhetors seeking to persuade more powerful individuals while mitigating the risks of potential punishment. Second, exemplars invite imitation of particular, contingent virtues rather than abstract, general principles, which encourages thoughtful emulation rather than uncritical copying by listeners. Finally, exemplars possess a distinctive rhetorical power when deployed by African Americans, because of their role within a reclaimed Black practice of imitation and an African-centered philosophy of heroism.

In the first place, the rhetorical power of exemplars derives, in part, from their inherent ambiguity. Because they draw on the complex and ambiguous materials of human lives, exemplars contain the possibility for multiple—and sometimes conflicting—interpretations by listeners. As Samuel McCormick has argued, exemplars constitute a "linguistic device for introducing ambiguity into any given rhetorical situation, and in so doing open up possibilities for political judgment and social transformation."[15] McCormick's reading of exemplars as a "strategic resource of ambiguity" relies on Leah Ceccarelli's theorization of polysemy. According to Ceccarelli, strategic ambiguity is a type of *polysemy*—or multiple meanings—used deliberately by a rhetor to elicit a positive response from two different audiences whose interpretations might conflict.[16]

The strategic ambiguity of exemplars makes them especially valuable to rhetors speaking from severely constrained social locations. Exemplars offer two intertwined advantages to such rhetors: First, they shield those individuals from powerful figures by appearing to uphold hierarchy and social convention; and, second, they enable rhetors to covertly advocate for new or controversial ideas among those with ears to hear. In his analysis of Christine de Pizan's 1405 letter to the Queen of France, for instance, McCormick noted that exemplars have allowed women to speak despite the constraints of gendered decorum and social position. McCormick argued that Christine de Pizan's "rhetoric of exemplary figures enables her to confront the queen with potentially offensive advice, without in turn violating established codes of deference."[17] The exemplar's strategic ambiguity, McCormick explained, supplies its rhetorical power for marginalized speakers, "enabling its practitioners to contest, without directly challenging, established figures of authority."[18] Ceccarelli went even further in her conclusions about strategic ambiguity, saying that sometimes this rhetorical choice supplies "the only way for rhetors and audiences to critique an oppressive regime without inviting suppression, imprisonment, or death."[19] Carefully chosen exemplars can mean avoiding censure or worse, especially for rhetors in precarious positions.

Relatedly, the strategic ambiguity of exemplars enables rhetors to present new or controversial ideas while also appearing to maintain the status quo. When taken at face value, the exemplar exhibits a rather conservative rhetorical form that advocates accepted virtues and rejects recognized vices. Also, exemplars can certainly be one-dimensional and simplistic, as in the apocryphal story of George Washington and the cherry tree or a narrative about Martin Luther King Jr. that represents him as a colorblind sponsor of unity. However, invoking exemplary lives in their fullness and complexity, or other strategically ambiguous ways, has the potential to open interpretation to different meanings.[20] In many cases, rhetors use exemplars because they are committed to both reinforcing elements of the status quo and introducing more liberatory ideas. The letter of Christine de Pizan to the Queen of France, for instance, features discourse that is "undecidably split between the demands of duty and the urge to revolt, the legitimation of established authority and its unrelenting critique."[21] The ambiguous exemplar becomes an appealing rhetorical strategy for rhetors like Christine de Pizan who appear simultaneously obligated to the status quo and to social transformation. In other cases, exemplars operate more like a Trojan horse, a seemingly benign offering to the gods of convention that disguises the weapons of critique within. Opponents cannot necessarily discern whether rhetors are *actually* committed to the status quo or simply paying it lip service. In either case, exemplars are being used strategically to navigate restrictive social structures while creating space for new ideas and new memories.

This feature of exemplars is especially useful to individuals engaging in critical memory work, who seek to dislodge dominant memories protected by powerful people.

A second key feature of rhetorical exemplars concerns audience uptake: They invite audiences to reflect on and emulate contingent, particular virtues rather than universal ideals. Rhetoric scholars have noted that the form of reasoning required by exemplars—reasoning by example—fosters such reflection. The work of Aristotle has heavily influenced this line of thought and inspired a lively debate among rhetoric scholars about how reasoning from examples works.[22] This debate questions whether the "example" is a form of inductive reasoning and, if so, how it serves to mediate between universal ideas and particular circumstances. John Arthos has argued that the instability of the concept of the example stems from the gap between *phronesis* and *episteme* in ancient thought.[23] *Phronesis* refers to practical wisdom gained through action, whereas *episteme* refers to certain knowledge. Arthos noted that, because of the gap between these two concepts, scholars of argument have equivocated on the nature of the rhetorical example: Is it "a species of generalization . . . an illustration for clarity and forcefulness . . . the source of models or standards from which particular cases may be judged, or . . . a means to argue analogously"?[24] Arthos suggested that rhetorical example is, in fact, none of these. Rather, the example enables individuals to reason from particular to particular without the intervention of universal principles. As he put it, "When we argue from particular to particular we are not always working implicitly through a rule, but remain in the sideways movement from one example to the next. We use example precisely when the movement to and from the general is blocked, and deliberation must find a conclusion in the space of interruption."[25] Relying on the mental process of reasoning by example, then, exemplars can invite reflection on particular virtues rather than just universal values.

By encouraging engagement with the particularities of individual lives, exemplars can cultivate critical emulation rather than uncritical copying.[26] Moral exemplars—from a one-dimensional Joan of Arc to a sanitized Rosa Parks—have long been deployed to advance universal ideals, undergird absolutist moral structures, and secure allegiance to the status quo. Although ubiquitous, such an approach is not inevitable. Instead, exemplars can provide what McCormick has described as a "powerful resource for awakening the judging faculties of their audiences."[27] Some philosophers, such as Pieter Vos, consider this more complex approach to exemplars to be "modern," but cases such as the letter of Christine de Pizan suggest that the perspective predates modernity.[28] As Vos explained, "in this modern understanding moral exemplars are not seen as just ideals, i.e. as perfect examples of general truths they exemplify, but as real persons who embody virtues (and vices) and live out particular values in the midst of the moral complexity of their lives."[29] The ambiguity and complexity of exemplars can invite listeners to emulate their virtues or actions critically rather than carelessly. Philosophers interested in virtue ethics and character education, in particular, have emphasized how such a reflective response enables audiences to develop habits of judgment and thoughtful deliberation and, in some cases, tools for social transformation.[30] The audience is not conscripted into "mere imitation" or simple copying but urged to thoughtfully integrate certain virtues and actions into their own lives.[31] The function of critical engagement applies also to how audiences are invited to consider new interpretations of the past.

Although any rhetor can use exemplars as a rhetorical strategy, they possess particular power for Black women speakers of the late nineteenth and early twentieth centuries. Kirt Wilson has shown that nineteenth-century Black rhetors such as Frederick Douglass rejected racist stereotypes that represented Black imitation as derivative and morally sterile and instead reclaimed the practice as productive for Black Americans. Wilson observed that the very idea of imitation was deeply racialized in the postemancipation United States, as White intellectuals held that Black imitation was a "primitive" expression of their inferior abilities, whereas Black intellectuals such as Douglass claimed that imitation was a "constructive" practice.[32] Wilson argued that late nineteenth-century African Americans such as Douglass enacted a distinctive Black *mimesis* that constituted "a threat to white ideals" and an "engine" to "transform the U.S."[33] In other words, Black mimesis of this period could invite the kind of critical engagement and social transformation discussed earlier. Wilson's work demonstrates the power of imitation for Black Americans, which parallels the rhetorical power of exemplars for marginalized rhetors. Just as the exemplar's strategic ambiguity provides a means of covert resistance, the practice of Black imitation "provided some immediate protection from the hostile tendencies of European Americans" and "created a space from which blacks could resist oppression."[34] Christel N. Temple's concept of hero dynamics posits that both the invocation of exemplars (what she calls "heroes") and the imitation of exemplars are central to Black cultural mythology.[35] Temple explained that the "postenslavement, African-centered philosophy of heroism [is] defined organically from diasporic experiences with survivalist impact, achievement against the odds, and the extension of human capacity beyond the ordinary."[36] Temple traced what she characterizes as an "Ebonic use of heroes" back to figures such as Maria W. Stewart, who fashioned whatever exemplars were at her disposal into vehicles for inspiration and empowerment.[37] Neither Wilson nor Temple explicitly used the term "exemplar," but their arguments closely align with the way in which I have conceptualized it as a rhetorical tool for memory work. Their theories also underscore the significance of exemplars as an important historically and culturally situated strategy for Black women.

Exemplars in Black Women's Public Speech

Although Black American women used a variety of strategies to fill their storehouse of memory, public address became a particularly significant means during this period of increasing activism. Beginning with groundbreaking speakers such as Maria W. Stewart, Black women addressed audiences exhibiting a variety of racial, gender, and religious identities. Their own backgrounds, social positions, educational statuses, rhetorical styles, and purposes differed. Among the many public speeches given by Black women between the antebellum period and the New Negro Movement, I identified seventeen that intentionally engage female exemplars.[38] These speakers invoked exemplary women both in passing and through more sustained narratives. They listed groups of women and focused on individual lives. They cited familiar women such as Mary Magdalene, as well as more obscure figures such as Abigail Mathews. They mentioned women from ancient times such as the Hebrew judge Deborah and heroic Spartan mothers, and they cited their contemporaries. They identified women by name and described their lives but left them unnamed.

Four notable categories of exemplary women appeared in these speeches: biblical women, non-biblical historical women, White American female contemporaries, and Black American women. Organizing the analysis into these categories illuminates how these speakers strategically deployed certain exemplars to achieve their rhetorical goals within a particular context and for a particular audience. For instance, earlier in the period, speakers cited biblical women, both because doing so enhanced their credibility with religious audiences through the performance of Christian piety and because those exemplars were easily accessible to people with limited education. This memory work was primarily critical. Later in the period, as more Black American women were recognized as public figures, speakers turned their attention to praiseworthy peers. Many of these speeches advanced ideas radical in their time (and, in some cases, even for the twenty-first century), such as the right of Black women to speak publicly or to preach in churches. The increased attention to Black female exemplars reflects both critical memory work that sought to insert these women into the nation's history and community memory work that aimed to show Black women the contributions of their foremothers. Female exemplars provided distinct rhetorical advantages in these constrained contexts, as vehicles for generative ambiguity and contingent virtues. The following analysis illustrates how the speakers deployed these exemplars as worthy of imitation in ways that both upheld and challenged existing discourses about Black womanhood. By deploying female exemplars in this way, Black women speakers also argued—mostly implicitly but sometimes explicitly—that they and their Black sisters were worthy of remembrance.

Biblical Women

Women from the Hebrew scripture or Christian New Testament constituted a small but significant group of exemplars. Of the seventeen speeches surveyed, four of them cited such women.[39] Whereas Shadd (1858) mentioned sisters Mary and Martha of Bethany only in passing, Mary V. Cook's speech invokes twenty-seven exemplary religious women.[40] Mary Magdalene was mentioned by three of the four speakers—Stewart (1833), Truth (1867), and Cook (1887)—as a witness to the resurrection of Christ.[41] Although their speeches were given over a span of more than fifty years, all three women were deeply religious, addressed mixed-gender audiences, and made a case for women's right to speak and work on behalf of the Gospel.

Sojourner Truth, in her characteristically concise and clever manner, used Mary Magdalene as an example of women's devotion to Jesus. Drawing a bitingly humorous contrast between the men and the women healed by Jesus, Truth told the story of the man from whom Jesus cast out some especially awful demons. The demons were ultimately directed into a herd of pigs that promptly threw themselves off a cliff to their deaths. Truth reasoned:

> If a woman did have seven devils, see how lively she was when they were cast out, how much she loved Jesus, how she followed Him. When the devils were gone out of the man, he wanted to follow Jesus, too, but Jesus told him to go home, and didn't seem to want to have him round. And when the men went to look for Jesus at the sepulchre they didn't stop long enough to find out whether he was there or not; but Mary

> stood there and waited, and said to Him, thinking it was the gardener, "Tell me where they have laid Him and I will carry Him away." See what a spirit there is. Just so let women be true to this object, and the truth will reign triumphant.[42]

In this passage, Truth held up Mary Madgalene as an example of how enthusiastically women could follow Jesus. She praised the devoted, patient, and persistent "spirit" of Mary, exhibited in her willingness to wait at Jesus's tomb longer than the male disciples. The way in which Truth invoked Mary through narrative demonstrates the power of exemplars to illustrate contingent virtues. In this story, Truth used the word "spirit" to esoterically reference rather than explicitly name Mary's virtues: The audience was required to use their own judgment to infer the lesson. Furthermore, by noting that Jesus welcomed Mary's company but spurned that of the healed man, Truth implied that Jesus preferred the company of the more devoted female disciples. This interpretation of Jesus's disposition toward Mary Magdalene functions critically through strategic ambiguity to present her simultaneously as a model of feminine piety and devotion and an embodied critique of patriarchal Christianity. Truth's Mary both upholds traditional gender ideals and illustrates their subversion.[43]

In contrast to Truth's singular reference, speeches by Maria W. Stewart and Mary V. Cook invoke numerous biblical women, including Queen Esther, the judge Deborah, Mary Magdalene, and the unnamed woman of Samaria whom Jesus met at the well. Cook, in particular, was directly addressing the 1887 American Baptist Convention on the subject of "Women's Place in the Work of the Denomination." Stewart and Cook would have faced similar hostility from their audiences, although to different degrees. By enumerating lists of admirable biblical women, Stewart and Cook—especially Cook—engaged in a form of *accumulatio*, which Richard Lanham defined as "heaping up praise or accusation to emphasize or summarize points or inferences already made."[44] The numerous biblical exemplars collectively provide authoritative evidence that women had done pious and praiseworthy things, and they supply models for religious Black women who aspire to continue the work. In this sense, they uphold certain pillars of the Cult of True Womanhood, including piety, submissiveness, and domesticity.

However, Stewart and Cook did not simply uphold these pillars; they subtly shifted them to destabilize the patriarchal foundation on which their churches had been built. They refigured the memories of women of the past to create space for Black women of their present. Like Christine de Pizan, Stewart and Cook drew upon the lives of women whom their audiences already admired so that new ideas and virtues could be introduced through them. Stewart, for instance, cited biblical women as a means of demonstrating her own piety and purity when her very act of speaking in public to "promiscuous" audiences would have thrown both into question. Stewart began the speech by recalling an encounter with the divine. In this "spiritual interrogation," Stewart imagined herself sitting at the feet of Jesus, who asked her, "[A]re you able to drink of that cup that I have drank of?"[45] This opening passage bolsters Stewart's ethos as a messenger called by God. Undergirding the credibility argument here is Stewart's implicit claim that Jesus—the most revered *male* person in the Christian tradition—invited her to imitate him in his sacrifice and suffering. Stopping just short of comparing herself with Christ, Stewart then shifted to a more palatable set of exemplars for herself: Biblical women such as Deborah, Esther, and Mary Magdalene. Stewart clearly represented these women as actors in their own right, yet all were prompted by God to act. In this way, she contextualized their seemingly radical actions within a higher submissiveness to God, thereby adhering to that ideal of True Womanhood. Stewart's characterization of biblical women as accountable primarily to God also cleverly bypasses the human men—disciples, preachers, and lay leaders—who strove to maintain their role in a superfluous managerial class mediating women's relationships with the Divine.[46] The speech later applies this reasoning more broadly, to all women of the "sable race" whom God might "raise up" as messengers.[47] Black women, the address explicitly says, should follow the example of women such as Deborah and Esther in submitting to God's call to speak loudly and take on a leadership role. In Stewart's critical remembrance of biblical figures, women are called to submit to God, not to men.

Like Stewart before her, Cook listed biblical female exemplars to argue that women had a long tradition of doing—and being publicly recognized for—religious work. Whereas Stewart selected only a handful of familiar exemplars, Cook cited an impressive twenty-seven individuals, from the first woman, Eve, to lesser known supporters of the early church such as Phoebe and Joanna.[48] Cook began with a rhetorical question similar to Stewart's, inquiring, "Who is to wipe these iniquities from our land if it be not christian [*sic*] women?"[49] Keeping close to the domestic sphere, Cook rejected public solutions such as the ballot, political positions, and law, arguing that the best path to reform lay in "woman's unswerving devotion to a pure and undefiled christianity [*sic*]."[50] She explicitly noted that she would "establish this truth" by recounting "history as its light comes to us from the pages of the Bible."[51] Identifying this shared authoritative text as her source of evidence would have enhanced her credibility with her devout listeners. Cook then commenced her litany of the "wives, mothers and daughters of the Holy Scriptures" to demonstrate such devotion.[52] Cook cited these women in service of an overall critique of the male-dominated formal structures of her denomination. Yet, in accounting for their lives, she also selectively noted those qualities that aligned most closely with late nineteenth-century feminine ideals.

Cook's use of exemplars both to shore up traditional feminine virtues and to challenge assumptions about women's abilities results in complicated portraits. On the one hand, she reads the restrictive gender roles of the late nineteenth-century United States into the stories of biblical women. The same Sarah who laughed derisively at God's promise of a son in her old age was said to have possessed "reverence for her husband," "devotion to her son," and "faithfulness to duty." She was furthermore "beautiful, chaste, modest and industrious."[53] Other Old Testament women exhibited similar qualities: "We cannot forget the *maternal tenderness* of Hagar, the *well kept promise* of Hannah, the *filial devotion* of Jepthah's daughter, nor the *queenly patriotism* of Esther."[54] Each of these women was remembered for a virtue that she exhibited in a specific feminine role, such as mother (Hagar and Hannah), daughter (Jepthah's daughter), and wife (Esther). Women of the New Testament were praised for showing to Jesus "those personal kindnesses which our Lord ever appreciated," including the hospitality of sisters Mary and Martha and the loyalty of the Samaritan woman.[55]

On the other hand, Cook's address also proffers a critique of the many limitations placed on women, especially in religious communities. Although Cook's address elevates qualities firmly within the ideals of True Womanhood, the overall message of her address is more radical, as she calls for women to imagine themselves as leaders like Deborah.[56] Similar to Stewart, Cook needled biblical men, saying, for instance, that Deborah's husband apparently "took no part whatever in the work of God," whereas she led men and women alike. Furthermore, Deborah was called by God to show and tell her people that God would raise up whomever God pleased, regardless of sex: "He recognizes in His followers neither male nor female, heeding neither the 'weakness' of one, nor the strength of the other."[57] The transcription of the speech from the convention minutes denotes "weakness" in quotation marks, suggesting that Cook believed that such a description of women ought to be questioned. In another example of challenging women's roles, Huldah took on the traditionally masculine study of the law "to better prepare herself for the work of Him Who had called her."[58] Women of the New Testament are identified as "co-workers" with the apostle Paul. After providing these many examples of biblical women working as equals with men, Cook argued that it was "not [C]hristianity which disparages the intellect of woman and scorns her ability for doing good" but "custom" that limited them.[59] Citing dozens of female exemplars from the Christian scriptures enabled Cook to explicitly praise widely accepted "feminine" qualities as well as identify nonnormative virtues and forms of religious leadership. This strategy encourages her audience to envision specific, multidimensional women who embodied diverse virtues and abilities rather than one-dimensional saints to be placed on protective pedestals. By bringing them to her audience's consciousness in this way, she ensured that the women who were added to her community's storehouse of memory exhibited complex characteristics that could be adapted by future generations whose needs were yet unknown.

Historical Women

A second, smaller category of exemplary women were drawn not from the pages of the Bible but from history books.[60] These exemplars appeared in legends, the ancient world, and existing collections of "women worthies."[61] Most speakers seemed to have relied on such exemplars to demonstrate female achievements even in the face of restrictive social norms. Drawing on John Adams's 1790 collection of biographical sketches in her 1833 speech, for instance, Stewart cited an unnamed "a young lady of Bologne" who in the thirteenth century "joined the accomplishments of a woman to all the knowledge of a man" and whose eloquence was so powerful that "her beauty was only admired when her tongue was silent."[62] In 1887, Cook praised women who worked to educate girls and women, including Mademoiselle de Sainte-Beuve and Mary Lyons, as well as writers such as Sappho and Hannah More.[63] Described in some detail, the work of these women provided evidence for Cook's claims throughout this address about what women could accomplish and, therefore, should be empowered to do. Cook claimed that the "rare talents" of female authors afford "the strongest evidence that God created her for society."[64] Cook, notably, even reached beyond Western cultural traditions to draw an analogy between two reported virgins who bore key religious leaders: Mary, the mother of Christ; and Maha-Mahai, mother of the Buddha.[65] Cook's fellow Baptist Lucy Wilmot Smith admiringly named French thinker Germaine de Staël, "the philosopher whom all women delight to mention."[66] Speaking a year before Cook at the 1886 denominational convention, Smith used de Staël as "proof of [woman's] capabilities" and, in particular, her "right of having something to do."[67] Victoria Earle Matthews, in her 1897 speech "The Awakening of the Afro-American Woman," briefly invoked the brave "Spartan mothers" to help her audience understand the great heroism of African-American mothers.[68]

As in the case of biblical exemplars, historical women provide evidence of how women have successfully achieved traditionally masculine feats while exhibiting traditionally feminine characteristics. The lives of actual (and, in fewer cases, mythical) people supply rhetors with a persuasive means of strategically synthesizing seemingly divergent virtues such as beauty and bravery. Examples such as the Virgin Mary and the virgin mother of Buddha comfortably uphold the ideals of purity, and figures such as the "young lady of Bologne" emphasize feminine beauty. However, these same women also illustrate unconventional qualities such as "intelligence and skill," "eloquence," and "heroism."[69] These virtues subtly pull historical women from the domestic sphere into the public arena, thus marking them as worthy of remembrance and recognition. Exemplars enabled Black American women, whose social position was far from secure, to advance new ideas alongside old values. By naming specific, embodied historical women, these rhetors were able to harness the complexity of human life in service of their rhetorical goals. Although non-biblical historical exemplars appeared only sparingly, they served in those instances to illustrate the accomplishments of women across races and to enhance the rhetors' credibility by displaying their historical knowledge for skeptical audiences. Including these accomplished women in their speeches subtly criticized the gendered constraints that made their accomplishments noteworthy, and it also further augmented the storehouse of memory for women in their communities.

White Contemporaries

Just as biblical and historical exemplars enabled these rhetors to gain credibility with their male listeners of different races, citing White women contemporaries helped them to build connections with White listeners of different genders. This strategy was critically important for Black women when addressing White audiences, yet it was also used by speakers when addressing Black audiences. Many of the women speakers surveyed here addressed audiences diverse in race and gender, with several addressing audiences dominated by men or White women. Speakers including Mary Cook (1887), Mary Church Terrell (1898), Lucy Craft Laney (1899), and Beatrice Morrow Cannady (1928) specifically praised White women activists and suffragists. Notably, Cook, Laney, and Cannady all addressed primarily African-American audiences with both men and women in attendance. Terrell addressed primarily White women at the Fiftieth Anniversary Celebration of the National American Woman Suffrage Association.[70] As with other categories of exemplars, White women were briefly named as well as extensively described.

Cook's speech to fellow Black Baptists mentioned a handful of White contemporaries in her voluminous array of exemplary women. For instance, Cook included Harriet Beecher Stowe and Frances Willard in a list of female authors who used their talents on behalf of the abolitionist cause. Like Phillis Wheatley and Frances Ellen Watkins Harper, Stowe "gave vent to the fullness of [her soul] in beautiful lines of poetry and prose."[71] Willard was named alongside Harper as one of the "noble advocates" of temperance.[72] These examples function much as Cook's references to biblical and historical women do: as evidence of Cook's claims about women's capacities. Perhaps because of her Black audience, Cook could afford to mention only a few particularly significant White female contemporaries who would have been recognized by the male religious leaders in her audience. Furthermore, mentioning only White women tied to causes of which her audience would approve—abolitionism and temperance—rather than, say, the more radical cause of suffrage, enabled Cook to praise activists while remaining within women's traditional purview of art and home.

Laney, addressing the Hampton Negro Conference in 1899, an annual gathering of Southern Black leaders discussing a range of subjects, spoke alongside prominent figures such as Victoria Earle Matthews, the Reverend Francis Grimke, and George Washington Carver. Although the purpose of this convention would have been different from the denominational gathering at which Cook spoke, the two Southern Black audiences likely had overlapping ideological commitments. Laney, whose subject was "The Burden of the Educated Colored Woman," opened her speech by grounding her position in reference to the past—specifically, to "our first mission school—slavery."[73] After mentioning a few African-American exemplars in her introduction, she later turned to specific exemplars to convince her audience of "the good that can be done for humanity" by public lecturers. This list included White women Lucy Stone, Mary Livermore, Frances Willard, and Julia Ward Howe.[74] Notably, this list also included Harper, who was one of the best-known authors and lecturers of the late nineteenth century.

Beatrice Morrow Cannady's audience at the 1928 annual meeting of the National Association for the Advancement of Colored People (NAACP) in Los Angeles would have had similar demographics and concerns, although likely with a heavier concentration of northern and western Black elites. Cannady's audience included more White listeners, some of whom were NAACP officers and leaders. Most of Cannady's speech focuses on the role of Black women as leaders, teachers and "spiritual conservators of the race." However, the speech begins by praising Mary White Ovington, a White woman who helped to found the NAACP and who, in 1928, served as the organization's board chairperson.[75] Before introducing her by name, Cannady tied Ovington closely to the NAACP, calling her its "founder and mother" and the organization her "only child." Extending the maternal metaphor, the speech reasons, "[W]hile this woman is biologically white—yet her long years of laboring for and with the Negro entering so fully into the things that affect his life in America that she has become psychologically a Negro."[76] Cannady furthermore claimed that recognizing Ovington reflected well on their organization, saying, "we do ourselves and the Association honor when we honor our beautiful and beloved Mary White Ovington." Ovington is praised simultaneously for exhibiting the feminine ideals of motherhood and service and for being unusually aligned with the African-American experience. Most contemporary language and approaches to race would not describe someone as "biologically" raced or characterize a White woman as "psychologically" Black. Yet in 1928, when most White women throughout the United States—and especially in Southern locales where groups such as the United Daughters of the Confederacy held sway—would have rejected identification with Black Americans, this claim advances an ideal of racial solidarity long espoused by the NAACP. Cannady praised Ovington for her commitment to supporting Black people and communities. This idea is evident in the speech's conclusion, in which Cannady commended an "interracial program" through which "there will grow up a strong sisterhood between white and colored women which will be the safest protection of the ideals for which the NAACP stands."[77] Whereas earlier speakers tended primarily to invoke White woman suffrage activists, Cannady spoke after the passage of the Nineteenth Amendment, which afforded her the opportunity to focus on an individual more meaningful to the NAACP.[78]

In these addresses, Black women highlighted the activism of their White female contemporaries rather than specific virtues. Some of these exemplars are praised as noble or beautiful, yet the focus remains on their work on social reform causes such as abolition, temperance, and racial equality. As Christel N. Temple noted of Stewart's use of heroes, Black women rhetors transformed "European women into models for Black progress without featuring their European-ness as a condition to be emulated."[79] These activists were public figures, known for their work in areas that had recently become, for the most part, socially acceptable for women. For instance, Cook named Stowe not primarily for the political effects of her work but for the way she expressed her emotion through her art.[80] Rhetors harnessed the power of strategic ambiguity within exemplars when they named public women whose activism hewed close to women's sphere of hearth and home. Furthermore, by praising White women activists, Black women rhetors signaled to their White and/or male listeners that they all admired the same qualities, which created a foundation for identification and joint action. Such memory work enabled future activism.

Black Women

Black American women constituted the largest and most significant category of exemplars, cited in eleven of the seventeen speeches I surveyed.[81] References to Black women appear to have increased between the antebellum period and the interwar period, likely because of expanded educational opportunities for Black women and greater numbers of Black women in the public eye. However, the main rhetorical functions of these exemplars remain consistent. Examining this important category of exemplars reveals a variety of rhetorical functions, all apparently designed to address the expectations of a particular audience and moment. Speakers cited these women to praise diverse attributes, actions, and accomplishments rather than strictly to adhere to the ideals of True Womanhood. Publicly naming Black women enabled rhetors not only to achieve their immediate rhetorical goals but also, more significantly, to build a storehouse of memory on which future women in their communities could draw. Repeatedly praising exemplary figures in public address keeps them in the minds of listeners and produces a shared record that can, ideally, be accessed by future generations. This mission was especially vital to Black women of the nineteenth century, who had little access to Black histories, to the extent that even educated women of the time believed that they had *no* history.[82] It is in examining Black women exemplars that Black women's community memory work becomes most evident. Speeches to Black audiences—especially those dominated by Black women—tended to undertake the community memory work focused on self-improvement, pride, and uplift. Publicly remembering Black women also participates in what Christel N. Temple calls "ancestor acknowledgment," a feature of Black cultural mythology.[83] In contrast, appeals to biblical, historical, and/or White female exemplars served more of a critical function as Black women rhetors addressed audiences that included Black men and White people who needed to be both appeased and persuaded. Speeches to such audiences performed critical memory work that sought to supplant or at least dislodge White and/or male-oriented narratives about the past. Some addresses accomplished both forms of memory work simultaneously.

Speakers invoked Black female exemplars past and present, famous and obscure, with sustained examination and passing attention. Three speeches mention Frances Ellen Watkins Harper, a familiar public figure who was also then active on the lecture circuit.[84] Notably, Harper herself was the only speaker to mention contemporary Harriet Tubman, who, in the twenty-first century, is arguably the most widely recognized Black American woman of the nineteenth century.[85] Three speakers each mentioned poet Phillis Wheatley and activist Sojourner Truth, two of the few famous Black women of the past.[86] Other figures, such as Abigail Mathews, a Black cofounder of the Ladies' Literary Society of New York, would have been familiar only to the immediate audience.[87] Some women who were presented as exemplars are not even named, merely described. Some speeches simply name the individual women, whereas others, such as Rosetta Douglass Sprague's 1900 tribute to her mother Anna Murray Douglass, focus extensively on a single person. Black women speakers presented their fellow Black women as exemplars to exhort their fellow "race women" to self-improvement and action, to shore up community bonds and enhance community pride, and to preserve memories for future generations of their community. Addressing primarily other Black women—as Jennings, Davidson, Sprague, and Bethune did—freed some of these rhetors from the rhetorical constraints of Whiteness and maleness. Therefore, Black women's use of peer exemplars in such contexts centered on their own community's needs and priorities.

Although separated by half a century, speeches by Elizabeth Jennings and Olivia Davidson both cite Black women to urge their Black female audiences to "improvement." In 1837, Jennings addressed an audience of educated Black women assembled at the third anniversary meeting of the Ladies' Literary Society of New York, which was founded in 1834 by African-American women Henrietta R. Ray, Abigail A. Mathews, and Sarah Elston.[88] Jennings exhorted her listeners to "exert all our powers" to "improve" their minds. In doing so, she had to challenge assumptions that Black minds were "unsusceptible to improvement."[89] Echoing Stewart's rhetorical question strategy, Jennings invoked society founder Mathews to empower listeners to act. "My sisters, allow me to ask the question, shall we bring this reproach upon ourselves?" Jennings asked. "Doubtless you answer NO, we will strive to avoid it. But hark! methinks I hear the well-known voice of Abigail A. Matthews [*sic*], saying you can avoid it. Why sleep thus? Awake and slumber no more—arise, put on your armor, ye daughters of America, and start forth in the field of improvement."[90] Likewise addressing educated Black women, although fifty years later and in the South rather than the North, Olivia Davidson also invoked an exemplar to urge listeners to "improve" their condition and that of their communities. Davidson's 1886 speech to the Alabama State Teachers' Association in Selma espoused a philosophy of self-improvement guided by the politics of respectability and, significant to this analysis, good role models. Davidson reminded her listeners to use "every opportunity for inspiring" others to improvement, saying, "By your own example in dress and daily habits as well as by precepts show them how to clothe and care for themselves according to hygienic laws."[91] The speech concludes with an example of an unnamed teacher who "went into one of the worst communities" to befriend and help girls. Her "two years' earnest, patient work" resulted in a "spirit of improvement" in the community.[92] In keeping with her thinking about emulation, Davidson noted that this teacher also organized a reading club "among the more thoughtful and intelligent" of these girls "and read to them or told them about the lives of noble women and other things that would still further arouse their ambition to become good women."[93] Davidson not only cited an exemplar but also urged her "sister teachers" to build moral modeling into their educational efforts.[94]

Other speeches illustrate how invoking Black women of the past and present helped to cultivate community pride and strengthen community bonds. Mary McLeod Bethune's 1926 address to the Fifteenth Biennial Convention of the National Association of Colored Women (NACW) in Oakland, California, for instance, names two women who had led that organization: Mary B. Talbert and Hallie Quinn Brown. Speaking as the then-president of the NACW, Bethune recognized the two former presidents for their organizational leadership and legacy. Bethune pronounced that Talbert's "considerate soul . . . will ever be cherished in the amber of our memories for her part in leading the National Association of Colored Women to claim and preserve the Douglass Home."[95] Likewise, of Brown, Bethune said, "We can never forget Hallie Q. Brown for the constructive genius she displayed in proposing the Scholarship Fund to the National Association of Colored Women."[96] Bethune recognized both women as worthy of remembrance because of their leadership on specific projects that were near and dear to the hearts of NACW members. Both projects, notably, required foresight, stewardship, and activism on behalf of not just current NACW members but future Black women. Bethune's use of first-person plural pronouns emphasized the importance of collectively remembering women such as Talbert and Brown, as she asserted that "*we* can never forget them," and they would be "cherished in the amber of *our* memories."[97] Although Bethune here used fairly conventional epideictic language, she did so to remember women who were not typically the subjects of conventional epideictic discourse. Her community memory work strengthened the bonds among the Black women present in her audience and reminded them of their bonds with Black women past and future.

Simply recording the names of these Black women in public speeches has the potential to preserve them for future generations; offering detailed descriptions of their lives enriches the memories thus preserved. Rosetta Douglass Sprague provided such a detailed account in her spoken tribute to her mother, Anna Murray Douglass, at the eponymous Washington, DC, branch of the Women's Christian Temperance Union. More so than the other speeches to fellow Black women, Sprague's address elevates specific praiseworthy virtues by drawing on examples from her mother's life. Sprague began by linking her mother to her father, Frederick Douglass, calling them "two travelers . . . two lives that have indelibly impressed themselves upon my memory."[98] However, she quickly shifted her focus to her mother, noting that the story of her father "has been told—you all know it." Sprague claimed that Frederick Douglass's story was "made possible by the unswerving loyalty of Anna Murray, to whose memory this paper is written."[99] Throughout the address, Sprague portrayed her mother as the *sine qua non* of her father's success. This speech echoes the rhetoric of other middle-class Black American women of the period by praising certain domestic, feminine virtues both inside and outside the home. For instance, listeners heard of Anna Murray Douglass's reputation as "a thorough and competent housekeeper," a woman of "industrial and economical habits," a "faithful ally" to her husband, and a "self-sacrificing" and "untiring worker" in more public causes such as temperance.[100] Anna Murray Douglass exhibited traditional feminine virtues while also being a "recognized co-worker" in antislavery societies around Boston who was fit to be seated with the likes of White abolitionists Wendell Phillips and William Lloyd Garrison.[101] However, Sprague's multidimensional portrait also reveals her mother's complexity and resistance to convention, admitting that she was "strong in her likes and dislikes" and "not well versed in the polite etiquette of the drawing room."[102] Detailed descriptions of exemplars such as Sprague's of Anna Murray Douglass provide listeners access to contingent virtues embodied in complex individuals rather than inaccessible saints. Such detail also enriches the storehouse of memories of Black women by providing a rare sustained "glimpse" into one complicated life.[103]

In subtle contrast to the women who addressed their Black peers, rhetors who addressed other audiences struck a more critical posture when deploying exemplars. These speakers could not assume that their White and/or male audiences found them trustworthy or even cared about Black women's lives at all. Thus, some speakers used exemplary Black women to supply evidence of their capabilities and character, to establish such women as worthy of remembrance, and in some cases even to offer a critique of White perspectives. Frances Ellen Watkins Harper's 1866 address to the Eleventh National Women's Rights Convention illustrates all of these goals of critical memory work through its concluding reference to Harriet Tubman. At the time, Harper was one of very few Black women visible on woman suffrage convention platforms; her audience was predominantly White women. Her speech, commonly titled "We Are All Bound Up Together," attempts to forge what Shirley Wilson Logan described as a "community of interests" while also clearly articulating the divergent experiences of Black women and White women.[104] Harper concluded the speech with an extended reflection on her contemporary Harriet Tubman, whom she identified only as "Moses." Activating the Black Christian symbolism of the Exodus story, Harper explained that Tubman earned her moniker because she had "gone down into the Egypt of slavery and brought out hundreds of our people into liberty."[105] Harper continued by highlighting her own recent encounter with Tubman: "The last time I saw that woman, her hands were swollen. That woman who had led one of Montgomery's most successful expeditions, who was brave enough and secretive enough to act as a scout for the American army, had her hands all swollen from a conflict with a brutal conductor, who undertook to eject her from her place. That woman, whose courage and bravery won a recognition from our army and from every black man in the land, is excluded from every thoroughfare of travel."[106]

Harper's words present Tubman as an exemplar of bold action—brave, courageous, yet discreet. Her example provides evidence of Black women's capacity for such action and serves as a source of inspiration to all women. Yet this Tubman's heroism coexists with her experience as a survivor.[107] By juxtaposing Tubman's traditionally masculine virtues with her embodied experience as a Black woman subjected to abuse, Harper dramatized the racist hypocrisy of postbellum White Americans. Extending her denunciation of the mistreatment of Black Union soldiers after the Civil War, Harper's reference to Tubman serves as an example of how even exemplary Black women continue to be mistreated in everyday life. At the same time, Tubman remains an exemplar of heroic survival for Black listeners, present or future.[108]

Harper's critique of Whiteness, especially of White womanhood, emerges clearly in the subsequent conclusion. After the passage about Tubman, Harper continued, "Talk of giving women the ballot-box? Go on. It is a normal school, and the white women of this country need it. While there exists this brutal element in society which tramples upon the feeble and treads down the weak, I tell you that if there is any class of people who need to be lifted out of their airy nothings and selfishness, it is the white women of America. (Applause)"[109] Harper pointedly and deliberately placed this passage at the conclusion of her speech, making clear to her White female audience their need to confront the realities of non-White women. Ending as she did with this judgment of White women, Harper used Tubman not only as an exemplar for her Black listeners but for all listeners and, in fact, to draw a sharp contrast between Tubman's bravery and White women's "selfishness." Tubman is a woman of heroic substance; White women are surrounded by "airy nothings." This passage performs multiple functions of critical memory work: it establishes a Black woman in the White historical record, it presents a Black woman as worthy of remembrance, it provides evidence of Black women's praiseworthy qualities, and it advances a critique of Whiteness.

Likewise addressing primarily White female audiences, Hallie Quinn Brown, Anna Julia Cooper, and Mary Church Terrell cited Black women to achieve similar rhetorical purposes. Including Black women's examples of virtuous action in their speeches expanded White women's knowledge of this oft-ignored group and secured a place for their memory in White records that were more accessible to future generations. Brown and Cooper, two of only six Black speakers at the 1893 World's Congress of Representative Women in Chicago, cited both Black women past and present in their brief addresses, which I also discuss in chapter 3. Brown mentioned the skills and accomplishments of fellow lecturers Harper and Cooper, sculptor Edmonia Lewis, Phillis Wheatley, singer Amanda Smith, and Sojourner Truth. Using her characteristically mellifluous language, she attributed to them memorable monikers such as "authors of distinction" (Harper and Cooper), "genius" (Lewis), "the African poetess" (Wheatley), "the 'singing pilgrim' of the race" (Smith), and "black sybil" (Truth).[110] These monikers, combined with further description, do not praise one-dimensional "feminine" virtues but place these Black women alongside others worthy of remembrance, both male and female. Brown's reference to Harper is representative: "our own Frances Harper, who championed the cause of the oppressed in the early anti-slavery days, sang with lips and tongue touched by a live coal."[111] The last phrase alludes to biblical descriptions of Old Testament prophets, fashioning Harper as not only a skilled poet but also a prophet. By following that statement with a passage from one of Harper's poems, Brown provided further evidence of her claim. Most notably, Brown emphasized these women's exemplary contributions to the advancement of Black Americans generally and Black women, in particular. Like Harper before her, Brown concluded her speech with an admonition to White women, in Brown's case to "talk not of the negro woman's incapacity, of her inferiority," but rather to "clasp hands with the less fortunate black woman of America."[112]

Mary Church Terrell's 1898 speech "The Progress of Colored Women," which she delivered at the fiftieth anniversary of the National American Woman Suffrage Association in Washington, DC, identifies exemplars to challenge negative accounts of Black women and provide evidence of their progress. Terrell described the work of six Black women in some detail, but she identified only Phillis Wheatley by name, perhaps because she was speaking to a primarily White woman's suffrage organization that would be most familiar with Wheatley.[113] Terrell's speech begins with an intersectional analysis of Black women's achievements in the face of oppression. Her opening passage states: "Not only are colored women with ambition and aspiration handicapped on account of their sex, but they are almost everywhere baffled and mocked because of their race. Not only because they are women, but because they are colored women, are discouragement and disappointment meeting them at every turn." In Terrell's analysis, the present persecution emerged from past oppression, and it was exacerbated by "those who would maliciously misrepresent" Black women. Terrell claimed that such "foul aspersions upon the character of colored women" were cast "especially by the direct descendants of those who in years past were responsible for the moral degradation of their female slaves." By highlighting White hypocrisy, Terrell emphasized the significance of an accurate rendering of the past. She then provided this accurate rendering by referring to several Black women who had distinguished themselves despite the concerted efforts of some White people to malign their character and intelligence. Terrell cited two women who each served as "national superintendent" of a temperance organization, one woman who owned a cotton mill in Alabama, one woman who ran the largest ice plant in Nova Scotia, Phillis Wheatley, a sculptor (likely Edmonia Lewis), and a student of the French painter William-Adolphe Bouguereau. Terrell chose only to name Wheatley, whose name and work were more likely to be recognized. Terrell presented these women not as exemplars of True Womanhood but as evidence of—and potentially inspiration for—the distinctive potential of Black Womanhood. Her intersectional approach to exemplars performed critical memory work by confronting her White female audience with evidence that directly contradicted the predominant White accounts of Black women's past and present.

Rhetorical Strategy and Memory Storehouse

The rhetorical strategy of exemplarity stands at the intersection of past and future, citing lives lived to influence lives yet to be lived. This temporal orientation also makes the exemplar a generative starting point from which to explore rhetorical memory work. Like public memory, rhetorics of exemplarity are determined by present concerns, dependent on past accounts, and driven by a desire to build a different future. Although they have most often been understood as a conventional strategy for reproducing the status quo, they also have the capacity to do more complex work, especially when utilized by historically marginalized rhetors. Exemplars must draw from the life stories of actual persons and are therefore tethered to the material, historical record. Exemplars must engage with the raw materials of an individual human life and are therefore inherently complex, contingent, and ambiguous.

The first great power of the exemplar as a rhetorical strategy resides in its ambiguity. As Kenneth Burke reminded us, "Instead of considering it our task to 'dispose of' ambiguity, we rather consider it our task to study and clarify the *resources* of ambiguity."[114] Exemplars serve as resources of ambiguity because they can simultaneously appear to uphold and to question the status quo. Marginalized rhetors such as Black American women could activate the conventional function of exemplars to establish their credibility in the face of hostile or indifferent audiences while introducing subtle criticisms of those audiences and their ideologies and social structures. By citing biblical exemplars, for instance, pioneering rhetors like Maria W. Stewart could demonstrate their own piety and display their deep biblical knowledge while also advancing controversial claims about women's right to speak in public.

The second power of exemplars is their ability to make particular, contingent virtues accessible to audiences. Rather than simply exhorting audiences to adopt universal, abstract virtues, rhetors can deploy exemplary figures to ground virtues in lived, embodied experience. Regardless of whether the exemplars invoked actually possessed certain characteristics, rhetors can point to specific experiences or stories within a person's life to illustrate how they exhibited virtues that might be emulated by listeners. This feature is particularly important for marginalized rhetors speaking to audiences with relatively more power, such as Black women addressing Black men, White women, or White men. By presenting individuals through narratives that illustrate widely admired virtues, Black women could sidestep resistance that might come from audiences that would otherwise reject identification with Black female exemplars out of hand. Audiences of Black men or White women—let alone White men—suffering from a lack of imagination might be "blocked," to use Arthos's word, from identifying with Black women in a general sense. However, it might be possible for them to move "sideways . . . from one example to the next" and thereby indirectly create solidarity with others whose experiences they previously saw as completely foreign.[115]

Black women activated strategic ambiguity and particular virtues when they deployed exemplars to address dominant audiences. These rhetorical functions proved especially subversive when they cited Black female exemplars—or heroes, to use Temple's preferred language. Doing so enabled them to develop their own ethos by demonstrating their alignment with certain feminine ideals such as purity, piety, submissiveness, and domesticity. It provided evidence of Black women's past accomplishments and supplied materials for inspiring future action. When deployed before audiences with greater privilege, exemplars performed critical memory work. Although Black women used exemplars in complicated and sometimes conservative ways, this rhetorical strategy enabled them to gain traction for their more radical ideas—indeed, to argue for their very right to speak at all.

Beyond speaking to dominant audiences, collecting and naming or describing exemplary Black women enabled these rhetors to build a public archive of individuals worthy of remembrance. They contributed to a storehouse of memory that, as Pierre Nora said, might be "capable of lying dormant for long periods only to be suddenly reawakened," the "forgetting kept in reserve" described by Paul Ricoeur.[116] Or, to use a more elevated metaphor from Emma-Lee Amponsah's conceptualization of Black Cultural Memory, "an open-ended cloud that treasures memories of shared and interconnected histories."[117] They built this storehouse for their communities in the present; their communities in the future; and, eventually, for a future society prepared to appreciate the lives of Black women forebears.

THREE

"Self-Emancipating Women"

Commemorative Critique by Black Women Speakers at the 1893 World's Congress of Representative Women

On May 18, 1893, in Chicago, teacher Sarah J. (Woodson) Early argued that the "organized efforts" of Black women in the South had raised them "from a condition of helplessness and destitution to a state of self-dependence and prosperity." Early envisioned Black women as "a grand sisterhood, nearly one million strong, bound together by the strongest ties of which the human mind can conceive, being loyal to their race, loyal to the government, and loyal to their God."[1] Early was a part of this "grand sisterhood" of one million, as well as a much smaller sisterhood of six Black American women who were invited to speak at the World's Congress of Representative Women (WCRW): Hallie Q. Brown, Anna J. Cooper, Fanny J. Coppin, Early, Frances E. W. Harper, and Fannie B. Williams.[2] The remainder of the more than five hundred speakers hailed from twenty-seven different countries but were nonetheless overwhelmingly White women of European descent.[3] Convened in Chicago from May 15 until May 22, 1893, the WCRW attracted an estimated one hundred fifty thousand attendees and sought to present "the wonderful progress of women in all civilized lands in the great departments of intellectual activity."[4] Conducted in conjunction with the World's Columbian Exposition (also known as the Chicago World's Fair), the WCRW aimed both to commemorate the quadricentennial of Christopher Columbus's arrival in the Americas and to portray women's advances since that event.

The Black American women speakers at the Congress were invited to report on the progress of women of their race and to chart paths into the future. As Shirley Wilson Logan has noted, White female organizers framed these speakers as worthy "representatives" of other Black women and outlined their task in the titles assigned to their speeches.[5] The schedule published in the proceedings showed Williams, Cooper, and Coppin discussing "The Intellectual Progress of the Colored Women of the United States since the Emancipation Proclamation" on May 18, Early and Brown describing "The Organized Efforts of the Colored Women of the South to Improve Their Condition" on May 19, and Harper outlining "Woman's Political Future" on May 20.[6] The speeches by Williams, Cooper, and Coppin began by establishing a common interest among women across racial lines to secure a hearing from the audience and to remind them of the importance of understanding the experiences of Black women. A well-known Chicago socialite and educated Black woman, Williams engaged the crowd and urged them to be open to learning. Cooper issued a pragmatic call for unity among women, and Coppin exhorted White women to leverage their privilege into action. Speeches on the next day by Early and Brown reported on the abundant activities of Black American women. The lone Black woman on the platform on May 20, Harper addressed women more broadly, arguing that they possessed power that must be activated on behalf of the oppressed—especially Black victims of lynching—with or without the ballot.[7] These six speeches, although the products of individual speakers, worked collectively within the constraints of WCRW and World's Fair expectations to advance a Black feminist critique centered in more realistic memories of enslavement and emancipation, performing important critical memory work in an environment dominated by White narratives.

In this chapter, I demonstrate how Williams, Cooper, Coppin, Early, Brown, and Harper used their speeches to argue that a proper account of Black women's progress required truthful memories of enslavement and emancipation and recognition of Black women's agency. These six speakers collectively developed their arguments through three rhetorical moves. First, they reframed the commemorative situation by establishing emancipation rather than Columbus's landing as the "zero point." Second, they claimed that Black women's progress in the present could only be understood in relation to accurate memories of enslavement. Third, they consistently centered Black women as the agents of their own progress in the past, present, and future. I argue that their speeches thus engage in Black feminist critical memory work designed to insert Black women's histories into turn-of-the-century US public consciousness.

By addressing these six speeches as a group, this chapter contributes to a more substantive, complex understanding of how Black women both individually and collectively engaged rhetorical strategies to develop intellectual traditions at a critical historical moment. The 1890s was characterized by historian Rayford Logan as the "nadir" of African-American history because of its "oppressive climate of national racial hostility," including escalated lynchings and the rise of Jim Crow.[8] In the face of such trials, Black women were nonetheless engaged in "intense activity and productivity," developing rhetorical and political strategies that enabled their communities to confront and survive oppression.[9] The speeches at the WCRW exhibit many of these strategies. To highlight such rhetorical strategies, the analysis in this chapter intentionally attends to all six speeches as simultaneously individual and collective rhetorical acts.[10] Reading the speeches as a group illuminates the rhetorical agency that they enact both on behalf of individual speakers and on behalf of Black women collectively. As I noted in chapter 1, tacking back and forth between individual and collective rhetorical acts brings to bear Black feminist thought's emphasis on the communal features of Black women's resistance.[11] This approach also holds in tension women's singular lives and rhetorical choices alongside their common historical experiences as Black women.[12]

Examining these speeches also distills Black American women's strategic practices of commemoration and the theory of agency that interanimates those practices. Although they have not been considered as such, I argue that these speeches can be productively viewed as performing important public memory work. Following research by Roslyn Collings Eves and Patricia Davis, this chapter's analysis of the WCRW speeches demonstrates how Black women, individually and collectively, engaged in critical memory work by deploying the material reality of their own experience, combined with verifiable historical facts, to undermine hegemonic White fictions. As the work of Eves and Davis attests, the memory practices of Black American women build on a Black feminist conceptualization of agency, which Patricia Hill Collins defines as "an individual or social group's will to be self-defining and self-determining."[13]

Agency, in Black feminist thought, entails Black women defining their own identities and actions; resisting oppression, regardless of whether such efforts were widely recognized by White oppressors; and producing valuable knowledge from their experience.[14] Although scholars typically pinpoint the importance of agency in contemporary configurations of Black feminism, an analysis of the 1893 speeches suggests that these Black women of the late nineteenth century also viewed testifying to and creating space for agency as a key rhetorical goal.

To show how Black women speakers reframed the commemoration of progress and represented agency, I first describe the rhetorical positioning of African-American women at the World's Fair and the WCRW. I then examine their speeches, detailing, first, how they reframe the commemorative moment to focus on emancipation; second, how they remember enslavement as a time of deprivation; and, third, how they persistently center Black women's agency in their accounts of progress. I conclude by discussing how my analysis illuminates Black women's critical memory work in its immediate historical context and what that can tell us about critical memories of enslavement and emancipation more broadly.

African-American Women at the WCRW

The five-month-long World's Columbian Exposition of 1893 was a defining commemorative event for both White and Black Americans. It attracted between twenty million and twenty-seven million attendees to its "White City," which occupied prime real estate near the Chicago lakefront.[15] Chicago city leaders recognized the exhibition as a singular opportunity to prove the significance of their emerging metropolis. As historian Christopher Robert Reed noted, the Chicago World's Fair also provided an important opportunity for African Americans to prove themselves as a race. Most African Americans—particularly leaders and the elite—were keen to demonstrate their achievements since emancipation.[16] The Fair presented the chance to commemorate "a generation of freedom" and to invite White Americans into "an important ritual of national redemption" for the sin of slavery.[17] These hopes and expectations led to enthusiastic involvement and effort among Black Americans, despite their being systematically excluded from top-level Fair planning. In fact, Black Americans attended the Fair, worked at the Fair, organized state exhibits, displayed the work of Black universities, gathered in the Haitian Pavilion, showed up for "Colored American Day," participated in auxiliary events and congresses, and even publicly criticized the event. The most notorious critique came from journalist Ida B. Wells and the coauthors of her pamphlet, *The Reason Why the Colored American Is Not in the World's Columbian Exposition.*[18] Although the hoped-for redemption did not materialize, it was certainly not due to Black Americans' absence or their failure to call White Americans to repentance.

Recognizing the significance of the event, Black women worked strenuously—and ultimately, unsuccessfully—for representation in Fair planning. Black women, both collectively and individually, appealed to the Fair's Board of Lady Managers (BLM) to appoint a Black woman to its ranks.[19] Several groups were formed to advance this purpose, each reflecting a different "procedural" strategy for seeking Black representation.[20] White BLM chairwoman Mrs. Parker Palmer, however, excluded these groups by reducing their differences of opinion to mere "quarreling."[21] Individual Black women such as Hallie Quinn Brown also lobbied for inclusion. After she turned down the small clerical position that the Board offered her in 1892, Brown wrote to the BLM, arguing that if their goal was "to present to the world the industrial and educational progress of the bread winners—the wage women—how immeasurably incomplete will that work be without the exhibit of the thousands of the colored women of this country."[22] Unfortunately, Brown's argument exposing the Board's hypocrisy did not effect change: Only two Black women—Fannie Barrier Williams and A. M. Curtis—were employed at the national level, and each only temporarily.[23] The dearth of Black female leadership in the WCRW meant that the Black women speakers were one of very few visible groups of women of their race sanctioned by the Fair.[24] Their position offered the opportunity to remedy White ignorance about the lives of Black women and to critique assumptions about White superiority, yet they had to temper the views in their speeches sufficiently to garner the support of sympathetic White women.[25]

These six "true race women" were among what Brittney Cooper has identified as the "first Black women intellectuals."[26] As Jacqueline Jones Royster explained, "This generation of African-American women recognized the burdens they carried in the interest of the race," and "used their rhetorical abilities" to advance those interests in public spaces.[27] Before the Congress, the Black women who were WCRW speakers had established themselves as leaders, thinkers, and teachers. The sixty-eight-year-old writer and speaker Frances E. W. Harper would likely have been the best known to the international WCRW audience. Born to free parents in Maryland in 1825, Harper was orphaned very young and subsequently raised and educated by relatives. She participated in the abolition, woman suffrage, and temperance movements and published poetry and fiction.[28] The lesser-known Early was born in 1825 to free parents in Ohio and spent her life as a teacher and temperance lecturer. Born into slavery in 1837, Fanny Jackson Coppin became free when an aunt purchased her freedom. She graduated from Oberlin College in 1865 and spent her career as a teacher, African Methodist Episcopal church leader, clubwoman, and missionary.[29] The three youngest women—Williams, Cooper, and Brown—were all born around midcentury. Williams was raised in a well-to-do free family in upstate New York, and she later married prominent Chicago journalist S. Laing Williams. Reed explained that her status in Chicago's community of "refined" African Americans made her "one of the most prominent African Americans, regardless of gender, to represent the race" at the Fair.[30] Williams, therefore, would have been most familiar to the Congress attendees who hailed from Chicago and the Midwest. Cooper, on the other hand, was born to an enslaved mother in North Carolina around 1858. After earning a degree from Oberlin College, she pursued a career in education. Her essay collection, *A Voice from the South*, appeared the year before the Fair.[31] Born in the late 1840s to free parents in Pittsburgh, Brown was a "charismatic public speaker, teacher, and civil and women's rights advocate."[32] She graduated from Wilberforce University in 1873, where she later served on the faculty. In May of 1893, she had recently concluded a year as Lady Principal at the Tuskegee Institute in Alabama. Together, these women, as Brittney Cooper put it, endeavored to "shift public perception and ideas about African-American women through their work on the public stage."[33] As individuals, their views differed in subtle ways that affected each one's unique approach to the rhetorical challenges of the Fair and their enactment of Black feminist ideals.

Commemorating Emancipation as the "Zero Point" for Black Women's Progress

Convened to "celebrate progress in the New World" by commemorating the arrival of Columbus, the Chicago World's Fair and its attendant congresses advanced stories of progress marked by the timeline of White colonialism.[34] Kristy Maddux has explained how those stories were racialized: "As [the Fair's narrative] demonstrated the progress of humanity from savagery and barbarity to civilization, it used people of color to demonstrate the first two categories and white men to demonstrate the third."[35] Theories of evolutionary progress drove those narratives and imbued them with scientific authority. Perhaps for this reason, these theories made "measuring racial progress," as David Blight explained, into "a major preoccupation in black America around the turn of the century."[36] African Americans' accounts of their progress most commonly began with the "zero point" of emancipation.[37] These six speakers reframed the commemorative moment of the Congress by identifying emancipation as the starting point for their accounts of progress. Marking emancipation as the zero point enabled these speakers both to distinguish the present from a past characterized by enslavement and to commemorate emancipation as a moment of possibility. Furthermore, as Maddux pointed out, such rhetorical work "manipulated the chronology of evolutionary progress" and "gave African American women's progress a compressed timeline" so that their achievements were being assessed according to their own self-defined temporality.[38] Although their individual yardsticks differed slightly, the Black WCRW speakers together insisted on commemorating emancipation as the appropriate starting point for their work.

Delivering the first of the six speeches, Williams tried to correct Whites' misguided views on Black women's progress by informing them of the changes wrought by emancipation. Williams was uniquely equipped both to diagnose and remedy White misconceptions, because of her prominence among the Black elite and recognition in White society. As one writer for the *Plaindealer*, the Detroit newspaper, noted in a March 1893 piece about the World's Fair, "All who know Mrs. Williams's ability to think clearly and write forcibly will feel confident that the Colored Woman's [*sic*] cause will be worthily represented."[39] Williams indeed argued clearly and forcibly throughout her speech that Black women's progress should be assessed using the temporal marker of emancipation. She began by asserting that the system of slavery had rendered it impossible even to apply the term "progress" to Black women; before emancipation, such progress "would have been an anomaly."[40] Although emancipation, in her view, had since made progress possible, many White Americans remained oblivious to its impact. Williams exclaimed, "How few of the happy, prosperous, and eager living Americans can appreciate what it all means to be suddenly changed from irresponsible bondage to the responsibility of freedom and citizenship!"[41] While noting their ignorance about emancipation and its effect on Black women, Williams softened her criticism of White listeners by referring to them as "happy, prosperous, and eager." Williams developed that idea later in the speech by observing how the contrasting realities of Blacks and Whites yielded divergent experiences of the moment of emancipation. Black Americans entering the "new life of freedom" had launched "a distinctly new era in their career," whereas White Americans struggled to accept the new reality.[42] Williams simultaneously emphasized how

FIGURE 1. *A photograph of Fannie Barrier Williams taken in 1885 by Paul Tralles. Library of Congress, Prints & Photographs Division, Robert H. McNeill Family Collection, LC-DIG-ppmsca-50312.*

swiftly Black people had improved their condition after emancipation and provided cover for her White audience by saying that such improvement had occurred "so quickly that the American mind has scarcely had time to recognize the fact, and adjust itself."[43] The moment of emancipation had inaugurated a "new life" and "new era" for Black Americans, yet it remained unacknowledged by White people. To improve the chance that this message would be received, Williams portrayed White listeners as well-intentioned observers simply in need of information.

Having diagnosed White American ignorance about Black women, Williams posited the moment of emancipation as a temporal break that demanded new definitions and judgments of progress. For instance, Williams argued that Black women should be judged "not by the standards of slavery, but by the higher standards of freedom and of twenty-five years of education, culture, and moral contact."[44] Williams insisted that Black women be measured by metrics of their own choosing rather than by the outdated assumptions of White Americans. That new metric was built on a temporal shift between slavery and freedom marked by emancipation. Williams then used the starting point of emancipation to reframe Black women's progress in relation to White women. She observed, "The path of progress in the picture [of enslaved women] is enlarged so as to bring to view these trustful and zealous students of freedom and civilization striving to overtake and keep pace with women whose emancipation has been a slow and painful process for a thousand years."[45] This subtle comparison with White women implies that Black women would emerge favorably as they strove not only to "keep pace with" but also to possibly overtake White women who had had more time to improve their condition. By describing Black women as "striving to overtake," Williams projected their progress onto a future horizon. In contrast, Williams bound White women to the past by describing the "slow and painful process" that had already trudged on for a millennium. When marked by the zero point of emancipation, Black women's progress could be said to have outstripped that of White women, according to Williams.[46] This comparison furthermore distinguishes the histories of Black women and White women, performing a restrained form of intersectional critical memory work.

Cooper's response to Williams likewise established emancipation as a turning point to reframe the White audience's understanding of Black women's progress. Roundly rejecting any definition of progress that judged Black women solely by their trajectory since emancipation, Cooper declared that a "brief space of thirty years" would be insufficient for any group to spontaneously attain the "higher fruits of civilization." Such work, instead, demands "the long and painful growth of generations."[47] Her portrayal here more forcefully echoes Williams's comparison with White women's thousand-year labor for rights. Unlike Williams, Cooper characterized emancipation as the first step on a crucial yet uncertain path rather than as an instant of revelatory clarity. She eschewed a linear progress narrative, saying, "Since emancipation the movement has been at times confused and stormy, so that we could not always tell whether we were going forward or groping in a circle."[48] Cooper thus challenged White assumptions that progress followed a linear course marked by certain signs of "improvement." Cooper remarked that, despite uncertainty about their future, Black Americans maintained a "simple faith" that God "would in his own good time make all right that seemed most wrong."[49] Although the outcome of any "progress" since emancipation would be revealed only in the divinely appointed future, Cooper drew attention to the ways Black people had filled the time since emancipation with the activity of growth. Cooper then grounded her argument by using the familiar biblical metaphor of yeast from a New Testament parable, describing the work of Black schools as "the little leaven hid in the measure of meal, permeating life throughout the length and breadth

FIGURE 2. *Anna Julia Cooper, seated, with a book on her lap, 1901–1903. Library of Congress, Prints & Photographs Division, C. M. Bell Studio Collection, LC-B5-50626.*

of the Southland."[50] Cooper perceived the potential of the enslaved during the time of their bondage, represented by the "little leaven" that was "hid" in the meal until the moment of emancipation. This metaphor represented education as a power that expanded and filled the new era for a people who had previously endured restriction and emptiness. Although "leaven" and "meal" may seem like innocuous domestic references, using this language subtly invokes the parable's subversive context: Jesus deployed it to confront and confound the Pharisees, powerful religious leaders who sought to suppress his radical actions. In this context, the allusion to the leaven suggests that Black education would expand geographically, throughout the South, and also temporally, into the future wherever Black communities could access it.

Coppin's speech dwells less on the moment of emancipation, yet it also characterizes that moment as pivotal for understanding Black women's progress. Near her conclusion, Coppin noted that both women and Black people who pursued schooling were often asked: "What are you going to do with an education?" She traced this question to emancipation, recognizing that African Americans encountered this question only "when the days of slavery were over, and we wanted an education."[51] Like Williams, Coppin noted that perspectives on emancipation diverged sharply along racial lines. Those who "classed [African Americans] among the working people"—that is, White Americans—viewed emancipation as the uneventful continuation of Black manual labor in service of White capital, whereas African Americans viewed it as a dramatic turning point toward Black agency. Coppin thus portrayed emancipation as a break with the past, as a moment of transformation. Within this framework, Coppin assumed rather than argued that Black women had made progress. This assumption enabled her to present an *a fortiori* argument that challenged White women's understanding of their own progress: If Black women have advanced in spite of their oppression, Coppin argued, then White women should be expected to advance so much more when faced with fewer obstacles.[52] For instance, Coppin began by asserting, "For if we have been able to accomplish anything whatever in what are considered the higher studies, or if we have been able to achieve anything by heroic living and thinking, all the more can you achieve it."[53] This *a fortiori* structure inverted the claim that Black women ought to be measured against White women (as Williams sometimes implied), instead urging White women to measure their own ignorance and inertia against the rapid and improbable progress of Black women.[54] Although Coppin did not dwell on emancipation as an event, her argument about progress is predicated on its function as a transformative moment. Coppin thus continued the critical memory work begun by Williams and Cooper before her: She argued that Black women's progress should be remembered not as deficient but as different from White women's progress.

Early and Brown, focusing on Black women in the South, likewise established emancipation as a definitive moment for understanding progress. Instead of comparing Black women with White women, Early and Brown compared Black women of 1893 with those of 1865. Early deployed statistical evidence and serial examples to demonstrate how Black women had organized themselves. She then proceeded to "compare the present condition of the colored people of the South with their condition twenty-eight years ago" to show "how the organized efforts of their women have contributed to the elevation of the race and their marvelous advancement in so short a time."[55] Like Cooper, Early contrasted the abundance of these twenty-eight years with the impoverished centuries of slavery, and she dramatized this contrast through a series of antitheses between Black women past and present.[56] Recognizing the prejudices of her audience, she noted

FIGURE 3. *A photograph of Fanny Jackson Coppin from the frontispiece of her 1913 book* Reminiscences of School Life, and Hints on Teaching. *Philadelphia: A.M.E. Book Concern, 1913. Documenting the American South, University of North Carolina Library. https://docsouth.unc.edu/neh/jacksonc/jackson.html.*

that "these feeble efforts" might "seem insignificant to the world" but that they foreshadowed even better things to come.[57]

Brown's response likewise testifies to Black women's progress since emancipation, but her argument insists even more forcefully that Black women be judged only according to their own timeline. Marking time appears to be particularly important to Brown, who made numerous temporal references throughout her brief address.[58] Portraying the last days of enslavement as a period of prophetic anticipation, Brown quoted Harper's poem "Ethiopia" to portray emancipation as the result of the humble supplication of Black people and God's righteous redemption. Emancipation instantly revived Black women to consciousness: "With freedom's first sweet draught came the thirst for knowledge," and "the drowsy intellect awoke" to its own powers.[59] Brown urged the audience to weigh two hundred fifty years of enslavement against the brief span of freedom so that they, too, might be in awe of Black women's achievements since their moment of liberation. For Brown, as for many Black Americans since, a fair assessment of the progress of Black Americans in the present depended on an accurate understanding of their past. Rather than plead for acknowledgment, Brown boldly

FIGURE 4. *A photograph of Sarah Jane Woodson Early, taken between 1885 and 1889 by Thuss Photographers. Women's Christian Temperance Union Archives.*

declared, "Twenty-five years of progress find the Afro-American woman advanced beyond the most sanguine expectations" to become "one of the marvels of the age."[60] Brown concluded her address by characterizing this short span of time as "but a day" in the "history of a nation."[61] By measuring Black women's few years of freedom against the epic history of nations, Brown simultaneously magnified their marvelous achievements and challenged White temporalities of progress. She concluded by rebuking those who would judge Black women's progress by improper standards, exhorting the audience to "talk not of the negro woman's incapacity, of her inferiority, until the centuries of her hideous servitude have been succeeded by centuries of education, culture, and refinement."[62] Brown refused to measure the Black woman's progress against the White woman's; she pointed instead back to the zero point of emancipation and forward into Black women's future. Black women's progress would only truly be made manifest, Brown argued, in a yet-unrealized future.

FIGURE 5. *A photograph of Hallie Quinn Brown taken between 1875 and 1888 by Fred S. Biddle for Brown's cabinet card. Library of Congress, Prints & Photographs Division, Robert H. McNeill Family Collection, LC-DIG-ppmsca-50302.*

Harper's speech focuses least on commemorating emancipation as the zero point for progress. Although Harper also cast a future-oriented vision for progress, her temporal framework applied deliberately to all women. Harper spoke of a new time not only punctuated by the point of emancipation but also characterized by the emerging views of empowered women of all races throughout the United States. In her single reference to emancipation, Harper used strategic ambiguity to gesture toward Black freedom without mentioning it directly. Here, she claimed that woman's advancement up to that point "bears the promise of the rising of the full-orbed sun of emancipation."[63] Her reference to the light of emancipation could have been interpreted generally to apply to all women or specifically by Black women listeners to mean the end of enslavement. Either way, emancipation is represented as a time marking the promise of future progress.

Together, these speakers argued that an accurate understanding of Black women's "progress" required a temporal framing that accounted for the history-altering moment of emancipation. Each woman's position—both in life and in the Congress—influenced her specific claims about time.

FIGURE 6. *Frances Ellen Watkins Harper, pictured in the frontispiece of her 1898 collection of poetry. Library of Congress, Prints & Photographs Division, LC-USZ62-118946.*

Yet all of these speakers argued that, regardless of their own relationships to slavery, the progress of Black women could only be meaningfully measured from the point at which they *all* became free under the law, and it could only be understood as unfolding along a horizon of radical possibility. Almost ignoring Christopher Columbus altogether, the Black female speakers instead commemorated emancipation, thereby rejecting White Americans' colonizing historical narratives. Each of the speakers thus became what Mitch Kachun described as an "advocate of a positive historical interpretation" of emancipation.[64] Marking the moment of emancipation, however, also entailed certain memories of enslavement, to which I now turn.

Remembering Enslavement

The Black women speakers at the WCRW addressed their White audiences at a watershed moment in the development of American memories of slavery. Much of the "Civil War nostalgia" of the twenty-first century is "rooted in the fateful memory choices made in the latter two decades of the nineteenth century," according to Blight.[65] By that time, narratives of sectional reconciliation had produced the popular White memory of slavery as "an inoffensive institution," in which Black Americans were imagined as "faithful, devoted slaves [. . .] who were content with white supremacy."[66] African Americans, meanwhile, deliberated about whether to forget what was considered by some to be a shameful history of enslavement or to advocate for more and more accurate memories of the institution to combat harmful White accounts.[67] Thus, addressing a primarily White immediate audience at the Congress afforded the Black women speakers an opportunity both to counter White narratives and to represent Black memories of enslavement as a preferable alternative. Although none of the women had been asked to speak directly about the institution of slavery, all of them referred to it explicitly and thereby destabilized whitewashed memories of benevolent masters and happy slaves. These Black women denounced the system of slavery—and, in some cases, its White participants—and remembered enslavement as a time of absence and lack.[68] The Black WCRW speakers could only speak of "progress" once they had properly remembered that from which enslaved Black Americans had been emancipated.

First speaker Williams framed subsequent speeches by arguing that enslavement left both Black and White Americans wanting: White people lacked knowledge about Black people, and enslaved Black Americans had lacked opportunities for moral action. Utilizing her prominent social position, Williams cultivated trust with her White audience by acknowledging their discomfort with memories of slavery. "While I duly appreciate the offensiveness of all references to American slavery," she explained, "it is unavoidable" when addressing the question of African American "progress."[69] Williams recognized White feelings while not allowing them to dictate her effort to privilege Black memories of slavery. By yielding both to Victorian social norms and to White sensitivities—what today we might call "White fragility"—Williams bolstered her credibility with her White audience. Listeners who imagined themselves open-minded may also have viewed her candor as a sign of reliability.

Williams remembered enslavement as a system that victimized Black women by depriving them of the context for virtuous and moral action. Inhibited by "two centuries of ill-treatment" and the "long-enforced degradation" of slavery, Black women suffering enslavement became "children of darkness."[70] The institution of slavery, in Williams's view, systematically denied enslaved women the rightful human experience of intimate relationships that could cultivate virtue and morality. She claimed that "the mean vocabulary of slavery" supplied "no definition of any of the virtues of life."[71] Plainly assigning blame, Williams declared that it was "unavoidable to charge to that system every moral imperfection that mars the character of the colored American" because "the whole life and power of slavery depended upon an enforced degradation of everything human in the slaves."[72] Williams argued that any deficiency on the part of Black women resulted from slavery as a system of deprivation rather than from their innate character or biology, as the White audience may have assumed. According to Kristy Maddux, racial uplift discourses like Williams's often reframed Black people's supposed inferiority from biological—a common White view—to environmental.[73] Blaming the institution of slavery enabled Williams to vindicate Black women themselves, to some extent, without explicitly accusing White listeners of being complicit in that system.[74] As the first of the Black women speakers, Williams may have risked alienating most of her White audience had she blamed White people rather than the institution of slavery for its degradations.

Cooper's response both reinforced and complicated Williams's memory of enslavement and her representation of enslaved Black women. Although Cooper likewise characterized slavery as a time of absence for Black women, she pushed beyond victimhood to praise Black women's dignity as survivors. Cooper argued that the system of slavery had left Black women "utterly destitute,"[75] which allowed Whites to dismiss them as "no more than a chattel, an irresponsible thing, a dull block, to be drawn hither or thither at the volition of an owner."[76] Although admitting, like Williams, that emancipation revealed disadvantages attributable to the circumstances of enslavement, Cooper countered Whites' extreme belittling of Black women by detailing their plight. She explained that emancipation found newly freed people with "no homes nor the knowledge of how to make them, no money nor the habit of acquiring it, no education, no political status, no influence."[77] Despite being deprived of these basic rights, Cooper argued, most enslaved Black women—especially mothers—maintained their dignity by engaging in a "heroic struggle" to survive.[78] Cooper, who had been born into slavery, subtly amended Williams's more privileged views by imbuing memories of enslavement with a more intimate account of the struggles faced by enslaved women. Although Cooper did not directly address the differences in social status between her and Williams, it is plausible that she used her speech to offer a more sympathetic account than what the elite Williams could provide.

The speeches by Early and Brown also portrayed enslavement as a time of oppression characterized by lack. Early used fraught yet familiar light–dark metaphors to convey this absence. To Early, enslavement was "the long night of oppression, which shrouded their minds in darkness, crushed the energies of their soul, robbed them of every inheritance save their trust in God."[79] Enslavement thus became an oppressive absence of light that "shrouded," "crushed," and "robbed." Like Cooper, Early emphasized that slavery actively stole material and immaterial resources from the enslaved, who, when emancipated, "found themselves penniless, homeless, destitute . . . poverty and inexperience prevailing everywhere."[80] This profound privation had left enslaved people in what Early characterized as a "condition of helplessness and destitution."[81] By symbolizing slavery as a thief, Cooper and Early denied the notion, popular among Whites, that enslaved people benefited from their bondage. Coppin's and Harper's speeches made similar use of the "thief" metaphor by noting how slavery had robbed enslaved people of an education.[82] These speeches remember slavery as a time of lack not primarily to elicit pity for Black women but to contextualize Black women's progress within a long history of oppression.

Brown's address amplifies such memories of enslavement by vividly describing Black women's experiences, rejecting slanderous misrepresentations of those women, and condemning slavery's White perpetrators. She opened by quantifying the time of enslavement and exposing its crass economics, stating, "For two hundred and fifty years the negro woman of America was bought and sold as chattel."[83] Unusually plain for the dramatic elocutionist, this sentence bluntly confronted the audience with the stark historical reality of a system that regarded people as property. Brown then detailed how slavery deprived women of relationships, resources, and reputation. Their "sacred ties" with others were "broken and disdained," they were "said to possess neither a brain nor a soul," they suffered "every privation," and ultimately experienced "a helplessness born of despair."[84] Brown represented White perpetrators of slavery—the "so-called master" and the "slave-driver"—as working actively to dispossess enslaved women of their labor and their dignity.[85] Brown thus attributed responsibility for Black women's oppression to individual White figures exercising unrightful authority ("so-called"). She also directly correlated the enslaved woman's deprivation and the White man's enrichment. Active verb choices dramatize the ways in which labor stolen from Black women generated bounteous gain for White enslavers. The Black woman "toiled," and "tilled," "enlarged . . . estates," "heaped . . . coffers," and "filled" the slaveholder's home with "the splendors of the world."[86] Brown's descriptive language strikingly recalls enslavement as an inequitable time of absence for Black women and conspicuous abundance for White enslavers. Elsewhere, Brown compared slavery with sleep, a time during which the powers of the enslaved were not altogether absent but simply dormant.[87]

Williams, Cooper, Coppin, Early, Brown, and Harper collectively argued that audiences hoping to understand Black women's "progress" must remember slavery as a system that, for hundreds of years, deprived Black women of material possessions, intellectual opportunities, and—in some characterizations—moral guidance. Although the speeches shared this central theme, the women's views were by no means monolithic. For instance, northern socialite Williams viewed enslavement as a time of moral stasis, whereas formerly enslaved Southerner Cooper represented slavery as a time of painful but courageous struggle. However, working together in sequence, these speakers insisted that any assessment of Black women's efforts, achievements, and progress must accurately account for the legacy of slavery. These women's critical memory work also roundly rejected white-washed public memories that recalled benevolent masters and happy slaves, along with the inherent racism of those memories. Furthermore, by remembering enslavement as lack, absence, and negation, they also implied that it was a time of suppressed possibility, of pent-up potential poised to act.

Enacting and Projecting Black Women's Agency

By commemorating emancipation and remembering enslavement, the Black WCRW speakers both enacted agency and recentered the agency of Black women in accounts of their progress. The speakers built on their accounts of the past to develop future-oriented temporalities of progress that hinged on Black women's actions. These speakers argued both that Black women possessed an innate desire to improve their situation and that Black women consistently and successfully acted on their own behalf in ways that would continue into the future. The six WCRW speeches anticipated twentieth- and twenty-first-century Black feminist thought by arguing that Black women's agency is embodied, self-determined, and future-oriented, features that I discussed in chapter 1. Additional commentary from contemporary Black feminist scholars illuminates how these features are expressed in the WCRW speeches. First, as Brittney Cooper explained in her work on "race women" of the same era, "the black female body takes center stage in much of the thought work produced by Black women, as they discuss the material effects of poor social conditions on African American life chances."[88] Shardé Davis has noted that Black feminist thought builds on the knowledge produced by those embodied experiences to portray "Black women as self-defined individuals whose conscious understanding of their own standpoint serves as a tool of resistance against the dehumanizing definitions of Black womanhood."[89] Finally, Black feminist thought, as Jennifer Nash has argued, is strongly oriented toward future action. What Nash calls "Black feminist love politics" has "long been invested in the 'open end,' in radical possibility, orienting itself toward a yet-unknown future."[90] The WCRW speakers both enacted and elucidated these features of agency to show how Black women's action produced past progress and pointed toward future progress.

First, these women enacted embodied agency by simply appearing in their Black female bodies on stage at the Congress. Their verbal arguments supported the visual arguments of their bodies; they drew attention to their own bodies as sites of agency and told stories of how other Black women actively resisted attacks on their bodies. Although her elite status and light skin shielded Williams from some discrimination, Williams nonetheless recognized the effects of embodied experience on (relatively) privileged Black women. For instance, Williams testified to racial discrimination by telling about "a bright young woman" whom she recommended for employment at a bank in Chicago. Although the applicant had been initially judged by the bank president as "exceptionally qualified," she was ultimately passed over by the board of directors because they "scented the African taint" of her "blood."[91] Williams thus attributed this injustice to the board members' racial prejudice, declaring that "no other question but that of color determined the actions of these men."[92] Her use of vivid sensory language bolsters her claim that Black women faced embodied forms of discrimination. However, Williams also implied that, although Black women's bodies had often been sites for enforcing White male supremacy, their bodies were also sources of knowledge and potential action.

Anna Julia Cooper's speech turns from the embodied experiences and agency of middle-class Black women to those of enslaved women. Cooper argued that such women engaged in a "heroic struggle" for control over their own bodies and those of their children despite "fearful and overwhelming odds." Although she described the struggle as "heroic," Cooper refused to romanticize it by admitting that "the majority of our women are not heroines." Then Cooper visualized this struggle as "the painful, patient, and silent toil of mothers to gain a free simple title to the bodies of their daughters, the despairing fight, as of an entrapped tigress, to keep hallowed their own persons."[93] Cooper acknowledged the difficulty that Black mothers faced in protecting their bodies and those of their children while sidestepping a direct discussion of rape. Using words such as "painful," "toil" and "fight" also emphasized the exhausting effort to guard against such violations. If undertaken by a less credible rhetor, comparing an enslaved mother with an animal may risk further dehumanizing her. However, Cooper's sympathetic image of the noble tigress evokes dignity and physical strength not often ascribed to Black women.

Brown's speech makes perhaps the most compelling case for the embodied agency of Black women. A noted teacher of elocution and physical culture, Brown deliberately drew attention both to her own body as a visual representation of her young Black students and to her attire as evidence of their skilled physical labor. In the second half of the speech, Brown identified her relationship to those women, saying, "I have come to this Congress to represent the women of the black belt of Alabama."[94] She outlined her role as the present, embodied emissary of a group of absent Southern Black women—her charges in her position as Tuskegee's Lady Principal. She then presented her body and its clothing as evidence of the women's agency, saying, "And if you would have a slight idea of the work they [the students] can do, they instructed me to say that you should look at the gown their representative wears, made by girls who six months ago could handle only the hoe and the plow."[95] By mentioning the dress, Brown emphasized her presence while also praising the physical labor and technical expertise of the Tuskegee students. Brown's comment amplifies the abilities of Black women by noting that these students had mastered their craft in a mere six months. The dress thus demonstrates both the young women's desire and talent for self-improvement.

The speeches also demonstrate the significance of self-definition or self-determination to Black women's agency. Specifically, they argue that Black women—both as individuals and as groups—determined and drove their own actions. Insisting on the Black woman as a vector of agency enabled these speakers to refute the popular notion that she was, as Anna Julia Cooper put it, merely "an irresponsible thing, a dull block, to be drawn hither or thither at the volition" of a White agent.[96] The speeches represent Black women as agents in part by frequently appending the prefix "self" to certain actions or qualities. For instance, Williams characterized Black women as "self-emancipating"[97] and praised their abilities to demonstrate "the power of self-help."[98] Cooper also cited Black women's "organized efforts for self-help."[99] Coppin emphasized self-determination by debunking the racist myth that any intellectual achievements of Black Americans resulted from their "natural" penchant for mimicry.[100] Blacks' educational aspirations "did not come out of wanting to imitate anyone whatever" but rather "grew out of the uneasiness and the restlessness of the desires we felt within us; the desire to know."[101] According to Coppin, African Americans—including women—possessed a natural desire for knowledge that led them to pursue education. Black women were neither dependent on the charity of White women nor desiring to emulate them. Rather, the engines of Black women's progress resided within *themselves*.

Early's speech, "The Organized Efforts of the Colored Women of the South to Improve Their Condition," provides the most sustained attention to self-determined agency. Marking emancipation as the point of departure, Early explained that "the first impulse" of the newly-free was "to improve their social condition," which led them "immediately to organize themselves" to improve their communities.[102] She then focused specifically on Black women, who had organized with "wonderful wisdom and forethought." After describing the fruits of this organizing, Early concluded that "our people have shown a self-dependence scarcely equaled by any other people."[103] Early not only rejected the paternalistic myth that Blacks depended on Whites for survival, but she also asserted that Black people were more self-sufficient than other groups. More than any other speaker, Early supported her claims about self-determination with statistical evidence, pointing out that women's associations numbered "at least five thousand" and that their membership included "at least a half-million women."[104] This widespread self-organization of Black women, Early argued, "has taught them the art of self-government."[105] Like Brown, Early strongly implied that Black women were especially adept at acquiring new skills and knowledge—clear signs of self-determined agency.

These speeches also point repeatedly to Black women's future action as a promise of future progress. Having remembered emancipation and enslavement, the speakers practiced what Nash described as "educated hope" by projecting their agential vision into the future.[106] For instance, Williams argued that, if Black women were granted "the same opportunity" as other women, they would quickly rise to influential positions and achievements.[107] Williams's speech also clearly illustrates how the women tied future progress to their accounts of the past, as when she reasoned, "If this hope seems too extravagant to those of you who know these women only in their humbler capacities, I would remind you that all that we hope for and will certainly achieve [. . .] is more than prophesied by what has already been done, and more that can be done, by hundreds of Afro-American women."[108] This passage implies that White listeners who were skeptical of Black women's "extravagant" hopes simply lacked accurate information.

Black women leaders such as Williams, however, had witnessed the continued progress of their sisters and were, therefore, confident that they "will certainly achieve" even "more than prophesied." Early concluded her speech with a similar refrain, claiming that Black women's progress since emancipation provided ample evidence to predict future progress. Similarly addressing the audience's disbelief, she explained, "These feeble efforts at organization to improve our condition seem insignificant to the world, but this beginning, insignificant as it may seem, portends a brighter and nobler future."[109] This orientation continues to the final line of the address, when Early described thousands of Black female students as the "first fruits" of their race. These girls and women augured abundant harvests of progress into the future.

Although she spoke about women of all races, Harper nonetheless also exhibited an orientation toward future action in the coming "woman's era."[110] She likewise based her visions of future agency on past action, declaring, "To-day women hold in their hands influence and opportunity, and with these they have already opened doors that have been closed to others."[111] Her conclusion reiterates the theme of futurity by exhorting the "women of America" to take advantage of "one of the sublimest opportunities that ever came into the hands of the women of any race or people"—specifically, to improve public sentiment and seek justice.[112] While admonishing women broadly to build the "national conscience," Harper embedded within her argument a mandate that women do so to eliminate the scourge of lynching. Harper's language in this speech echoes that of radical antilynching activist Ida B. Wells (who, as noted, did not speak at but protested the Fair) in her February 13 speech "Lynch Law in All Its Phases." Both women exhorted Americans to build "public sentiment" against the "lawless" act of lynching.[113] Harper argued that women—Black and White—were uniquely positioned to undertake such persuasive work. Her forward-looking speech urges women of all races to prepare for increasing power and agency.

These six speeches thus enacted, demonstrated, and anticipated the agency of Black women. Although each speaker's distinct position influenced her vision of agency, the themes of embodiment, self-determination, and futurity permeated their entwined messages. Their views of agency meaningfully foreshadowed the approaches to agency later developed by twentieth- and twenty-first-century Black feminist thought. Furthermore, in all cases, they built their testimonies to Black women's agency and progress on their accounts of emancipation and enslavement, illustrating in the process how understanding of the future is predicated on honest remembrances of the past. Agency thus served as the cornerstone for the critical memory work performed in these speeches.

Commemorative Critique Past and Present

In a 2015 essay on intersectionality, Patricia Hill Collins claimed that "Black feminism's immediate concern in the United States was to empower African American women through critical analyses of how mutually constructing systems of oppression of race, class, gender, and sexuality framed the social issues and social inequalities that Black women faced."[114] Although the term "Black feminist" did not yet exist in 1893, the group of six Black female speakers at the WCRW nonetheless deployed their understanding of history to advance "critical analyses" of "systems of oppression" that affected Black women. In a basic sense, their analyses simply reminded audiences about the millions of Black women who had been excluded from narratives of both Black male progress and White female progress. However, they also provided a critique of the contemporaneous discourses of history and progress that pervaded the Fair. Because the World's Columbian Exposition had been designed to showcase national advances in the years since Columbus's landing, the Fair articulated a vision of American "progress" that was coterminous with Whiteness, which was evident in the paucity of Black Americans in official Fair planning and performance and in the infamous exhibitions of Black "otherness." Furthermore, these speakers argued that only Black women could meaningfully characterize their own progress—an argument that resonates strongly with Collins's emphasis on Black women as "agents of knowledge."[115] Thus, the WCRW speakers offered a critique of White visions of "progress" by exploiting the ambiguity of the term and shaping it to their own purposes. Rather than assenting to the White colonial origin of progress in the Americas as 1492, they posited 1863 (or 1865). Rather than accepting a rosy yet racist account of enslavement, they demonstrated its deprivations. Rather than dismissing Black women as passive objects, they attested to their ongoing agency.

Considering the contextual constraints of the WCRW brings the risk and radicalism of their critical memory work into striking relief. As Jeanne Madeline Weimann pointed out, White organizers consistently made choices that depoliticized the event, rendering any remotely controversial topic "political" by contrast.[116] This dynamic will be familiar to anyone who has tried to offer an account of the past that flies in the face of hegemonic memory: The alternative perspective is always deemed "political," whereas the dominant account is portrayed as transcending politics. Against such a backdrop, these women's allusions to slavery, rape, and lynching in fact appear quite bold. Furthermore, as Black women, they had to contend with the audience's ignorance about and indifference—if not outright hostility —toward their lives and the lives of the millions of women they were asked to represent. This ignorance and indifference apparently emerged in reports on their speeches in the White press, as the Reverend D. A. Graham noted in his June 22 account in *The Christian Recorder*. Graham praised the Black women speakers but lamented, "Oh! How shamefully the white papers of this city garbled the reports of these colored ladies' addresses in some instances they were not reported at all, while in others they were made to appear in a most ridiculous light."[117] Part of the task of overcoming that indifference required them to perform a "respectable" Black womanhood without completely capitulating to White definitions of womanhood. Finally, as "representative women," they were expected to act simultaneously as exceptional exemplars and as ordinary instances of their race. Each individual speaker met these and other rhetorical constraints with imperfect ingenuity, crafting her speech with the unique resources of her own experience. At the same time, their shared position as educated Black women at an overwhelmingly White national event yielded similarities across the speeches. Examining them thus provides critical information about how the few Black American women permitted to be visible and vocal in the Fair's predominantly White spaces navigated rhetorical challenges in order to advance their own narratives of commemoration and progress.

Reading these speeches within their historical moment and in conversation with contemporary Black feminist thought illustrates how Black women have long been building their own memories of enslavement and emancipation. Twenty-first-century American publics are still grappling with how the memories of emancipation and enslavement shape the nation and its racial structures. Evidence of this fact abounds, whether in the manufactured controversy about the *New York Times Magazine*'s "1619 Project," the Southern Poverty Law Center's report on the abysmal state of education around slavery in the United States, or continued controversies over Confederate monuments and memorials.[118] Similar to how the 1619 Project sought to "reframe American history" and "place the consequences of slavery and the contributions of black Americans at the very center of the story," the six Black WCRW speakers reframed history to place Black women at its center.[119] Showing how the speakers used rhetoric to shape audience perspectives on the past both exposes the dogged persistence of

White supremacist memories and illustrates how Black Americans have often advocated more accurate critical memories.

This chapter's analysis of the WCRW speeches follows Ashley R. Hall's outline for Afrafuturist feminism, which "places Black women across time and space in conversation with each other to theorize how Black women's truth-telling threatens white supremacy."[120] By reading the WCRW speeches in conversation with twentieth- and twenty-first-century Black feminism, it becomes clear how the Black women speakers did exactly that. Working with the rhetorical resources at hand, they challenged White accounts of the origins of progress, reframed the experience of enslavement and emancipation, and insisted on centering Black women's agency in narratives of progress. All these strategies contributed to their ongoing critical memory work. One can imagine how they might have even recognized that their "grand sisterhood" extended well past their historical moment to a "future-oriented community"[121] of women who would someday manifest their visions of progress and benefit from the memories they advocated. In the next chapter, I turn to those future Black women to explore how they organized to oppose the problematic memories and stereotypes represented in the "Black Mammy" monument proposed by the United Daughters of the Confederacy in 1923.

FOUR

"The Shadows of the Past"

Black Women's Commemorative Stewardship and the Demise of the "Black Mammy" Monument

More than a century ago, on February 28, 1923, the US Senate authorized a proposal from the Jefferson Davis Chapter #1650 of the Washington, DC, division of the United Daughters of the Confederacy (UDC) to build in Washington, DC, a monument to "the faithful mammies of the South." This effort was two decades in the making, according to historian Micki McElya.[1] The UDC had long cherished a desire to memorialize the enslaved women who had raised them, their mothers, and their grandmothers. Those who proposed the memorial sought not merely to preserve a particular version of the past but to shape action in the future. McElya noted, "As the UDC sought to build a memorial to the faithful mammies of the past, they hoped that the public representation of white benevolence and mutual affection might shape the behavior of contemporary black people. It would make clear their place, and keep them there."[2] The Jefferson Davis Chapter of the UDC raised funds and selected a sculptor but ultimately met defeat when their proposal died in the House of Representatives. Black opposition, especially from organized women, appears to have hastened the project's demise. In this chapter, I show how Black women publicly opposed this "Black Mammy" monument by challenging how White Southern women had performed as "commemorative stewards" for memories of enslaved Black women. The critical memory work of these Black women critics made it much more rhetorically and politically difficult for White women to construct the memorial, ultimately resulting in its defeat.

In early 1923, Black women leaders and clubs issued several written protests that outlined the perils of the proposed monument. These include Charlotte Hawkins Brown's telegram to North Carolina Representative Charles Stedman, which was reported in the *New York Age* on February 3; a formal protest presented to Congress on February 6 by the women of the Phyllis Wheatley Young Women's Christian Association (PWYWCA), which was reported in the *Washington Evening Star* on February 7; an editorial written by Mary Church Terrell and published in the *Washington Evening Star* on February 10; a fictional short story penned by Maude Nooks Howard and republished in the *Baltimore Afro-American* on February 23; and an essay written by Hallie Quinn Brown in the April 1923 issue of *National Notes*, the organ of the National Association of Colored Women (NACW).[3] Mary Church Terrell and Hallie Quinn Brown occupied key roles in the NACW at the time, with Brown as president and Terrell as one of the honorary presidents. Through their roles and their rhetoric, they fashioned themselves as representatives of Black women across the country, who they claimed were opposed to the building of the monument. Charlotte Hawkins Brown was a prominent educator and founder of North Carolina's Palmer Memorial Institute. The PWYWCA is a prominent Black women's club founded in 1905 in Washington, DC.[4] Howard was a writer and composer from Circleville, Ohio.[5] The core texts of this chapter's analysis were produced primarily by Black women of relatively high social status, educational attainment, and institutional power. Although Black clubwomen and educators may have driven rhetorical advocacy against the monument, there were likely other women who participated in this resistance behind the scenes through letters to the editor, private correspondence, and word of mouth.

Examining these public texts shows how Black women of the late nineteenth and early twentieth century engaged in critical memory work that sought to correct harmful stories about the past and to propose more productive forms of commemoration. Although Black enclave publics engaged in their own lively debates about memories of "Mammy," and of enslavement more generally, an examination of the public responses of Black women to the UDC proposal illustrates the rhetorical power of a coherent, consistent critique, even if that critique issued from different individuals.[6] This case reveals when harmful hegemonic memories must be publicly and repeatedly countered and which rhetorical strategies have been used to advance such a critique. Significantly, the case of the "Black Mammy" memorial provides insight into a rare failed commemorative campaign by White Southern women and a successful oppositional campaign by Black women.[7] Black women's critical memory work proved rhetorically effective, because it helped to create a public environment in which it could no longer be assumed that the UDC had either noble intentions toward or accurate memories of "Mammy." It demonstrated that the very people who were assumed to be most "honored" by this memorialization were, in fact, insulted. According to Black women, the true stewards of "Mammy's" memory would honor her actual experiences, acknowledge her exploitation as a form of property, and seek justice for her descendants—in short, they would memorialize her humanity rather than that of her oppressors.

"Mammy's" Memorial Moment

Renewed sectional divisions and racial tensions during the 1920s created a fraught atmosphere for the birth and death of the "Mammy" monument. Micki McElya has argued that the Senate's 1923 approval of the UDC monument ought to be understood against the backdrop of several key events in the previous decade.[8] In 1912, Woodrow Wilson was elected as the first Southern president since the Civil War; in 1913, Alice Paul and Lucy Burns organized the Woman Suffrage Parade; in 1919, attacks on Black communities tore across the United States in what James Weldon Johnson dubbed the "Red Summer"; and in 1920, the Nineteenth Amendment was ratified. These events simultaneously elevated the status of some women and revealed persistent racist undercurrents in the United States, as White suffragists excluded Black clubwomen from public activism and White supremacists attacked Black male veterans returning from the First World War.[9]

As a son of the South, Woodrow Wilson brought a Southern sensibility and sympathy to the presidency that created a more welcoming environment for the UDC's memorial aspirations. Wilson was born in 1858 in Virginia and lived with his clergyman father and mother in a series of Southern cities and towns, including Augusta, Georgia; Columbia, South Carolina; and Wilmington, North Carolina. Wilson lived through the Civil War, yet, as biographer Charles E. Neu notes, "the Civil War seemed to have made little impact on him" as a privileged White child protected from the privations of war.[10] Although he had initially studied the law, he eventually earned a bachelor's degree at the College of New Jersey (now known as Princeton University) and a doctorate at Johns Hopkins University. He rose quickly through various faculty appointments until he was appointed president of his alma mater, Princeton University, in 1902, at the relatively young age of forty-five. Wilson honed his already strong oratorical skills (although not his diplomacy) in this role, and he became one of the most famous university presidents of the era. His notoriety as Princeton president helped him get elected governor of New Jersey in 1910 and, only two years later, president of the United States.[11] Wilson was the first Democrat elected president in twenty years and the first Southern-born person since the Civil War.[12] During the 1912 presidential campaign, Black leaders such as W. E. B. Du Bois and William Monroe Trotter endorsed Wilson as a suitable alternative to Teddy Roosevelt, whose Bull Moose party had rejected their civil rights proposals out of hand.[13] However, after Wilson entered office in March 1913, he set out to resegregate not only the White House staff but also the federal government, and "the hopes of Du Bois and the talented tenth crashed."[14] Once in the White House, Wilson hosted a 1914 screening of *The Birth of a Nation* and was widely known to tell "darky stories" in dialect. Kenneth O'Reilly has argued that Wilson's public comments during this time "helped create the climate for the first major wartime riot by accusing the Republicans of 'colonizing' black voters in East St. Louis, Illinois, and other cities."[15] Although Wilson met with Black leaders such as Trotter and James Weldon Johnson during his eight years in office, the president never backed away from his commitment to segregation as the best policy solution to the race "problem."

As the specter of segregation again haunted the White House, it also plagued the woman suffrage movement during the decade before the UDC's "Mammy" monument proposal was passed in 1923. White supremacy had numerous opportunities to divide women of different racial backgrounds. In the late 1860s, White woman suffrage leaders such as Elizabeth Cady Stanton and Susan B. Anthony reacted to the proposed Fourteenth and Fifteenth Amendments by initiating a split in their movement to prioritize securing the vote for White women over Black men.[16] Black women's clubs founded in the 1890s increased their opportunities to organize and give voice to their collective priorities, which did not always emphasize the franchise to the same extent as many White women. Many Black clubwomen strategically advocated for Black male suffrage while not sacrificing their commitment to universal suffrage and thereby found themselves subjected to misrepresentation by White female activists.[17] The exclusion of Black women from the women's rights movement became increasingly visible during what Roslyn Terborg-Penn has called the "woman suffrage blitz" of 1910–1920.[18] During that time, the movement engaged in what Belinda Stillion Southard described as "a militant campaign against Democratic members of Congress between 1913 and 1916 in a national effort to pressure Democrats to support a federal woman suffrage amendment."[19] For instance, in the Suffrage Parade of 1913, Black women were separated from White women to placate Southern suffragists.[20] The exclusion of Black women was further evident in the 1919 Prison Special, "a cross-country train tour of 26 white women who had been jailed as a result of their protest activity for woman suffrage" sponsored by the National Woman's Party.[21] Both of these events, and other actions, put great pressure on President Wilson and Congress to act on the federal level. The Nineteenth Amendment was passed in 1918, ratified in 1920, and protected by two critical Supreme Court decisions in 1922.[22] The goal of a Constitutional amendment was finally achieved, but it came to some degree at the expense of the cross-racial coalitions that Black women (and some White women) had cultivated. Moreover, as Terborg-Penn has rightly noted, many Black women lost the vote just as soon as they won it through "state constitutional loopholes" designed to exclude African Americans.[23] Nonetheless, this decades-long struggle on multiple fronts had helped African-American women build the organizational and political skills to undertake other battles, "battles where they refused to separate their identification by both race and gender," such as the proposed "Mammy" monument.[24]

By the time Congress approved the UDC proposal in early 1923, the United States had been through an intense period of racial strife. A confluence of several factors contributed to this situation, including the rise of xenophobia and revival of the Ku Klux Klan, the increased migration of African Americans to northern cities, the exploitation of Black workers as strikebreakers amid labor disputes, and animosity toward Black veterans returning from World War I. Racial terror lynchings continued during this period. As the Equal Justice Initiative has painstakingly documented, between 1915 and 1940, lynchings increasingly focused on Black community leaders who resisted mistreatment and even targeted whole communities.[25] The height of this racial strife was the "Red Summer" of 1919, during which at least twenty-five US cities erupted in violence, as White residents terrorized Black communities from Baltimore, Maryland, to Bisbee, Arizona. Even after this summer had ended, the violence continued into the early 1920s, with events such as the 1921 massacre of "Black Wall Street" in Tulsa, Oklahoma, resulting in anywhere from thirty-six to three hundred deaths and $1.8 million in property losses.[26]

FIGURE 7. *Sculptor Ulric Stonewall Jackson Dunbar with his model for a possible monument to the "Black Mammies of the South," June 27, 1923. A different model, which was created by sculptor Julian George Zolnay, was identified as the design for the proposed statue in a photograph in the* Washington Post *on June 24, 1923. Dunbar claimed that Zolnay had copied his earlier design. Library of Congress, Prints & Photographs Division, LC-F81-25106.*

Amid these changes of the early twentieth century, various groups vied for control over public memories of slavery. The formerly enslaved stood at the center of this struggle, although their voices were often silenced. Historian Thavolia Glymph has observed that "former slaves stepped forward to articulate and remember the violence at the heart of slavery" and thereby became the "foremost narrators" of interpretations that viewed emancipation as the key outcome of the Civil War.[27] White Southerners sought to discredit these individuals and suppress their accounts of slavery. By the early twentieth century, memorials centering Lost Cause tropes—such as the proposed monument's "faithful mammy"—proliferated "as an explicit rejoinder to the memory-work of black southerners," who had been commemorating emancipation for decades.[28] It is no coincidence that this same period witnessed the highest rate of Confederate memorialization in US history; both the symbolic violence and the material violence of this era served to reinforce racial hierarchies.[29] The pervasive nature of these whitewashed accounts of slavery and the powerful positions of their proponents severely limited the persuasive potential of Black Americans' memories outside of their own communities.

Within their communities, however, Black women had already been developing stories that could resist and offer reprieve from White representations of Black women, advancing a critique of hegemonic White history, and preserving memories for the Black women of the future. As we saw in chapter 2, Black women named their ancestors and foremothers on public platforms. They took leadership roles in celebrating Emancipation Day and educating African-American children. They sustained Phillis Wheatley's memory by creating dozens of clubs in her honor to house and support young Black working women.[30] They worked individually, as well: Mary E. Jones Parrish preserved Black memories of the 1921 Tulsa Massacre, writer Jessie Redmon Fauset promoted Black biographies for children, and librarian Augusta Baker prioritized Black history in children's library collections. As Joan Marie Johnson explained, by engaging in these forms of community memory work, "African Americans did not simply react against the actions of whites; they had already established a tradition of creating their own history and monuments without which they would not have been able to fight the Mammy monument effectively."[31] Black women drew sustenance from their stores of community memories to advance critical memories of the enslavement period. The case of the "Mammy" monument highlights the important role of Black American women in shaping memories of slavery and, in particular, enslaved women, during this critical period.

African Americans protested the monument even before the Senate voted to approve the UDC proposal in February of 1923. The proposal quickly rocketed into public consciousness after Representative Stedman's impassioned January 9 "plea" to Congress on behalf of the authorizing bill.[32] A lively debate subsequently unfolded across Black and White communities about the monument—its purposes and pitfalls, the motivations of its proponents. Several national newspapers reported on Stedman's speech, including Black outlets such as the *Richmond Planet* and the Omaha *Monitor*.[33] Both Stedman's speech and the "Mammy" monument were frequent topics in the Black press during those months. Although some individual writers and (male) community groups approved of the monument, most Black voices vehemently opposed it.[34] In a January 19 editorial in the *Monitor*, for instance, B. B. Cowan declared, "I believe that I speak for our entire group when I say that we are astounded and bewildered . . . that such a sedate old house of representatives, republicans and democrats alike, should cast aside their masks and openly cheer such a proposition and its sponsor."[35] By February, numerous Black papers had reprinted or responded to criticisms written by Neval H. Thomas and Mary Church Terrell in the

White *Washington Evening Star* on February 6 and 10, respectively.[36] Writers argued that it was the wrong time to commemorate "Mammy," that such a monument would fix Black Americans in a subservient role, and that it was a publicity stunt by the UDC.[37] But the most prominent argument advanced on the pages of Black newspapers focused on the monument's troubling irony. Numerous writers opined about the hypocrisy of White people who would move mountains to memorialize "Mammy" but refused to educate Black children, employ Black workers, or protect Black bodies from lynching. A cartoonist for the *Baltimore Afro-American* represented it in a clear image: A "Mammy" statue against a backdrop of well-known Washington landmarks holding out her left hand in a plea and displaying in her right hand a standard that reads, "Use that monument fund to pass a law that will STOP lynching of my children!!"[38] These words imply that the intentions of the monument's sponsors are misguided and nostalgic: The sponsors invest time and energy in commemorating the "Mammy" of a bygone era but pay no mind to her suffering descendants in the present. A reading of the Black newspapers during this time period suggests that many other African Americans felt the same.

Black Women and the Rhetoric of Commemorative Stewardship

Although the debate over the proposed "Mammy" monument ranged across many topics, the question of who was doing the commemorating and how they were doing it remained central. This theme aligns with scholarship on public memory that emphasizes the significance of the sponsor of a particular account of the past.[39] Who is behind the memory, and what do they hope to achieve by it? The White Southern women of the UDC who promoted the commemoration had numerous goals. Whereas some members of the UDC, like Mary Solari, represented their project as a means of convincing "southern children" of the capacity of Black people for love and self-sacrifice, others, like Rassie Hoskins White, recognized it as way of making visible the women's behind-the-scenes work on behalf of the Confederate (lost) cause.[40] African Americans then and scholars today have argued that the purpose of the monument was, in fact, to reinforce racial hierarchies through the "Black Mammy," the symbol of subservient and self-sacrificing Blackness. Johnson has explained: "Recognizing the power of public image to shape race relations, many African Americans found it crucial to take control over their public representations, a charge particularly enhanced by the surging popularity of the Lost Cause, a movement to honor the Confederacy. The UDC, an organization dedicated to the

Lost Cause, dotted the Southern landscape, and even the nation's capital, with monuments to the Confederacy. Imbedded in the meaning of these monuments was a particular telling of Southern history in which African Americans had been content as slaves and reverted to savagery without the mitigating influence of their master."[41]

Such arguments about who has the authority to shape public memories are arguments about what I call "commemorative stewardship." This concept applies the idea of stewardship—common in discourses about material matters such as finances, historic preservation, and the environment—to the more symbolic realm of public memory. Commemorative stewardship, as I have argued elsewhere, enables individuals and groups to "secure the credibility to speak on, make decisions about, and ultimately control interpretations of public memories."[42] Rhetors who are involved in controversies over public memory often rely on appeals to ethos, drawing attention to the good character, good sense, and goodwill that they have exhibited in previous efforts to interpret memory.[43] Such efforts are made in an attempt to "cultivate trust among members of the public by representing themselves as committed stewards" of the past.[44] The rhetoric of commemorative stewardship exhibits four central themes: It acknowledges a sense of public responsibility for specific things or people, such as enslaved Black women; it reinforces the sacredness and value of that for which the steward is responsible; it signals a commitment to shared responsibility and accountability to other stakeholders, such as White Southerners or Black women; and it asserts the steward's significance by emphasizing their work on behalf of future generations. These themes—public responsibility, sacred value, accountability, and futurity—are present both in the UDC's discourse in defense of the monument and in Black women's criticism of it.[45]

Black women who entered the debate over the proposed monument used the rhetoric of commemorative stewardship to perform critical memory work. That is, they challenged the memory of the "faithful mammy" in part by calling into question the UDC's credibility and intentions. Black women's critical memory work has often confronted "disremembering," which Glymph has described as "a conscious act of community betrayal, a deliberate act of false consciousness."[46] Beyond simply naming the content of the memory as inaccurate, identifying disremembering requires attention to the rememberer's motives. Are they acting in good faith on behalf of the whole community? Or are they preserving false memories that only serve one group or even reinforce hierarchy and division? Although not often posed explicitly, such questions appeared to animate Black women's rhetoric as they crafted public statements in opposition to the "Mammy" monument. Given their own vulnerable position when addressing a White public, Black women could not just assert that the "faithful mammy" image was false; they had to develop a more comprehensive argument that undermined the commemorative discourses on which the UDC proposed to build their monument. The rhetoric of commemorative stewardship offered a powerful rhetorical resource for doing so. My analysis of Black women's engagement in the debate over the proposed monument traces how they criticized the UDC and reconstructed their own ethos as commemorative stewards.

As McElya, Johnson, and others have pointed out, the UDC had spent decades behind the scenes cultivating their commemorative ethos. Black women had likewise been acting as commemorative stewards, although White supremacy limited their influence primarily to Black publics and domestic and educational spaces. In this case, the proposed "commemoration" of enslaved Black women brought these two groups of stewards into direct rhetorical conflict in a way that was not often visible in public discourse at the time. Whereas the White Southern women of the UDC sought to commemorate the "faithful slaves" of Lost Cause mythology, Black clubwomen demanded an honest accounting of the exploitation of so-called "mammies." Black women rightly pointed out that the proposed monument commemorated not what UDC member Solari called the "self-sacrifice and devotion" of individual enslaved women but the institution of slavery itself.[47] These arguments relied on a critique of Southern White women's motives: Their disremembering was a symptom of corrupt commemorative stewardship.

Public Responsibility as Goodwill

Good commemorative stewards attempt to build goodwill with their audiences by acknowledging a sense of public responsibility for a specific memory. As David Lowenthal has explained, "the traditional steward is not an owner but an agent, a keeper for another" who "cares intensely about what is in his [*sic*] custody."[48] Working as a "keeper for another" or a custodian requires good intentions, so that the public can trust that a memory is being stewarded for the benefit of the community. Many White Americans assumed that members of the UDC were operating from virtuous motives and thus acting as good stewards. Representative Stedman's January 9 speech on the floor of the US House expresses this sentiment memorably. After noting that humans had long been building monuments out of "exalted sentiment and high ideals," Stedman reasoned that the UDC's proposal was even rarer and nobler: "[Y]ou will search the history of all ages in vain for the record of any people who have erected a monument to another race or to any class of that race dwelling among them to perpetuate the memory of qualities which entitle them to remembrance and gratitude." This monument "in memory of the faithful colored mammies of the South," Stedman argued, would become a singular and unprecedented example of memorialization that transcended racial lines. His argument worked enthymematically so listeners might conclude that any group that would seek to commemorate someone of another race or class is more virtuous than any commemorative steward in human history. In this case, the UDC was represented as such a group. According to Stedman, the righteous women of the UDC proposed to erect the monument as "a gift to the people of the United States," deliberately siting it on "public grounds" in Washington, DC.[49] Should any listener doubt the intentions of the UDC, Stedman gushed about the organization's history, which was "resplendent with great deeds," including caring for Confederate soldiers in life and in death.[50] Stedman's speech drew on common White views to argue that the women of the UDC were committed commemorative stewards with unimpeachable motives.

Many Black women, on the other hand, found the UDC's motives misguided, at best, or malicious, at worst. Their arguments questioned the sense of public responsibility exhibited by the UDC by interrogating their intentions. Although some Black women gave Southern White women the benefit of the doubt when interpreting their motives, others implied that White women's professed "care" for enslaved Black women was patronizing and possessive. In her telegram to Representative Stedman in response to his House speech, Charlotte Hawkins Brown acknowledged the presumably good motives of the UDC while condemning the memory that they promoted. She stated, "The intelligent Negro women of the South appreciate your motive in advocating some kind of a memorial to the faithful services of Negro women during slavery, but deplore the fact that it should take the form of a 'mammy monument.'"[51] The intention was good; the memory was not. Mary Church Terrell likewise carefully reframed the UDC proposal in the more flattering light of forgetting rather than blatant racism. She opined, "Surely in their zeal to pay tribute to the faithful services rendered by the ["Black Mammy"] the descendants of slaveholding ancestors have forgotten the atrocities and cruelties incident to the institution of slavery itself." She generously reframed their negligence as a result of their "zeal" for the memory of "Black Mammies," thereby attributing a more positive commemorative motive. In their eagerness to become good stewards, Terrell supposed, White Southern women ignored the reality of the memories they were supposedly stewarding. Yet the fact that Terrell chose to begin that sentence with the word "surely" suggests more than a hint of sarcasm.

The women of the PWYWCA likewise raised questions about the memorial motives of White people. They began their petition by clearly stating their opposition to the monument, testifying to the great progress of African Americans, and noting how little White Americans knew about middle-class Black people. Then, they observed that White people were selective in their memorialization: "The white Americans do not speak of their earlier decent [*sic*] except with sympathy and sadness. They do not raise monuments to accenturate [*sic*] their humble origin."[52] This petition implies that attempts to commemorate enslaved Black women are, at least, misguided, if not outright malevolent. If the desire to commemorate a group at their most afflicted moment stems from such pure motives, why hadn't White people yet built a monument to their own less distinguished past?

Other rhetors engaged a slight variation on this theme, using a conditional argument to identify what commemorative stewards with virtuous motives should do. Conditional arguments follow from an "if" statement—the antecedent—to a "then" conclusion—the consequent. Black women reasoned, "If the members of the UDC indeed have admirable motives and a decent sense of public responsibility, then they will do these things." This logical structure implies that a right remembrance depends not on the intention of the rememberer but on its material manifestation. Mere goodwill is not enough. By using this argument form, Black women could question the UDC's motives without explicitly accusing White women of malicious intent.

Hallie Quinn Brown repeatedly deployed conditional argument in her statement in the NACW's *National Notes*. She contended that "if the Daughters of the Confederacy are actuated by any deep reverence and gratitude for the former slave," then they would build a monument to enslaved men who defended White homes during the Civil War against their own interests. Read in the context of Brown's whole statement, her argument functions to expose Southern White women's hypocrisy rather than to generously interpret their motives. The rhetorical question immediately preceding the conditional antecedent makes Brown's message clear: "Why erect a dumb statue to the ["Black Mammy"], while thousands of living monuments attest the strength, the virility, they drew from the mammy's milk—the milk of human kindness?" She used this argument structure in other parts of the statement, prompting "if they wish to salve their conscience and make amends" and "if the Daughters of the Confederacy wish to make restitution." She followed both of these conditional antecedents with consequents recommending action. Addressing her audience of Black clubwomen, Hallie Quinn Brown could more directly interrogate the UDC's professed public responsibility, although she still avoided explicit accusation.[53]

Charlotte Hawkins Brown used a similar, if less biting, strategy in her telegram to Representative Stedman. She argued, "If the fine spirited women, Daughters of the Confederacy, are desirous of perpetuating their gratitude, we implore them to make their memorial in the form of a foundation for the education and advancement of the Negro Children descendants of those faithful souls they seem anxious to honor."[54] Unlike Hallie Quinn Brown's manifesto, Charlotte Hawkins Brown's telegram begins with the generous assumption that Southern women are "fine spirited." Hawkins Brown's comment identifies a positive motive—wanting to express "gratitude"—and recommends a better means of accomplishing that goal than building a monument.

In an even less direct form of argument, Maude Nooks Howard of Columbus, Ohio explored the motives for the monument by imagining an answer to the question, "Just what would the Black Mammy say?" Howard began her fictional narrative by saying that she had been hearing about a monument to the enslaved caretaker which was to serve as "a 'reward' (they are calling it) for her faithfulness." Her story paints a picture of a young girl traveling to heaven to find her departed nanny: "Angel Gabriel, swing wide dem pearly gates and page Mammy Lou for Missy Nellie Lee of Georgia." The entire purpose of this visit is to tell the Black woman Mammy Lou about the "beautiful and costly monument" being built by Missy Nellie Lee and other White women because their enslaved caretakers were "good and faithful and true." Like many White women before and after her, Missy Nellie Lee exhibits concern not primarily for the Black woman to whom she is indebted but for how she is perceived by that woman. Nellie draws attention to her supposedly noble intentions by traveling all the way to the afterlife to make sure Mammy Lou knows about this grand tribute. After confirming that the monument will be made of marble, Mammy Lou replies, in exaggerated "slave" dialect, "Chile, doan you'll go'n spen' all dat money 'cause we wuz good 'n faithful 'n true. Dat wa'nt nuthin'. Jesus jes' teached us to lak dat, da's all, honey. But Missy, ef yo'all wunt de 'pinion of yo' Mammy 'bout yo'all shownin' 'preciation, tell all dem Missys back dah to je' treat dem we lef' behin' fa'r; quit bu'nin' 'em quit hu'tin' dah feelin's; gin 'em a suar' deal, honey, dey's folks lak you alls; spell ma race's name lak yo' do eberbody's."[55] First of all, Mammy Lou's response subtly reminds her former charge that none of Mammy's behavior was actually about her; being "good 'n faithful 'n true" was a natural expression of enslaved Black women's faith. Mammy Lou's conditional argument begins by acknowledging that what Missy Nellie Lee is actually after is her Mammy's approval of her motives—her "shownin' 'preciation." In effect, the argument is: "If you want me to acknowledge that you are showing appreciation to me, then you will tell other White women to treat Black people with care and respect." Howard here uses Mammy Lou as a mouthpiece for the same logic presented by Charlotte Hawkins Brown and Hallie Quinn Brown. All three use the "if–then" or conditional argument to obliquely question the motives of the UDC. They acknowledge a potentially virtuous intent while also pointing out more meaningful possibilities for enacting a sense of responsibility to remember their "Black Mammies."[56]

Memories as Sacred and Valuable

Commemorative stewards also claim to care deeply for and thereby reinforce the sacredness and value of that for which they are responsible. Whereas the first aspect of commemorative stewardship pertains to the commemorative intention, the second aspect pertains to the content of the memory itself. The women of the UDC claimed to care for the enslaved Black women of yesteryear. They advocated for an image of the "mammy" that would enshrine Lost Cause mythology and reinforce hierarchical relationships by emphasizing the sacrifice of Black women on behalf of their charges. As McElya has pointed out, the UDC campaign reinforced the sacredness and value not of Black women but of the paternalistic relationships between enslaver and enslaved that kept each "in their place." The UDC wanted to literally place enslaved Black women on a pedestal to preserve racial hierarchies. Black women responding to the proposed commemoration criticized this version of Black "mammies," sometimes by identifying aspects of their experience that had been omitted and other times by rejecting the image as shameful or unrepresentative of middle-class Black women. Both groups of critics pointed out that the "Mammy" monument would not tell the whole story.

According to Black women critics such as Terrell, Howard, and Hallie Quinn Brown, valuing the memories and lives of Black "mammies" would require an honest and holistic representation of their experience. A nostalgic image of the happy slave certainly did not meet this requirement. Terrell reminded readers of the true plight of enslaved women throughout her letter in the *Evening Star*. She noted the "pitiably, hopelessly helpless" position of the "Black Mammy," and she described how enslaved Black women were often deprived of home and marriage and, instead, subjected to the sexual whims of "any . . . white man on the place who might desire her." Terrell saved the most vivid description, however, for one of the enslaved Black woman's greatest sorrows: The loss of her own Black children while being forced to care for the White children of her enslavers. The passage is worth quoting in full: "No colored woman could look upon a statue of a ['Black Mammy'] with a dry eye when she remembered how often the slave woman's heart was torn with anguish, because the children, either of her master or their slave father, were ruthlessly torn from her in infancy or in youth to be sold 'down the country,' where, in all human probability, she would never see them again." By invoking imagined Black women visitors to the hypothetical monument, Terrell subtly reminded White readers that Black women's perspectives on this supposed tribute were very different from their own. Furthermore, in this passage, Terrell emphasized the role of Black women as mothers, thereby reminding her White audience of their virtuous commitment to their own children and activating sympathy among readers who would also have valued the mother's role. After describing in detail the common suffering of enslaved women, Terrell wondered "how any women, whether white or black, could take any pleasure in a marble statue to perpetuate her [the 'Black Mammy's'] memory." She continued with this emotional appeal to female readers, saying, "One cannot help but marvel at the desire to perpetuate in bronze or marble a figure which represents so much that really is and should be abhorrent to the womanhood of the whole civilized world."[57] Although declining to specify which particular features of the figure she found abhorrent, Terrell suggested that they were numerous and should be obvious to women of different races and nations. She drew on a shared experience of womanhood to urge female readers to recognize their misunderstanding of the meaning of the monument. Rather than serving as a paean to Black women's mothering of White children, the monument would have become a constant reminder that Black women were forced to forfeit their mothering responsibilities to their own children. Terrell argued that White Southern women's deeply misguided attempt to commemorate Black "mammies" in their state of enslavement transgressed the sacredness of their memory by ignoring reality and by valorizing a relationship that was based on exploitation and cruelty.[58]

Maude Nooks Howard's fictional narrative likewise suggests that the proposed monument's account of the "Black Mammy" is inaccurate. The Mammy Lou character testifies about her own difficult experiences to correct Nelle's incomplete memory. Although Mammy Lou does not deny that she loved and cared for her charges, she also reminds Nellie that her life included hardship and pain similar to that described by Terrell. She says, "Dey tuk ma ol' man 'n sol' 'im f'um me: I cried in de lonely hou's of de night, honey, but I wuz good to yo' wa'nt I? Ma purty li'l Jane, yo'all 'members huh? Purty as a picher, wa'nt she? Ma ol' hea't broke w'en Mas' sol' huh honey, da's why I'se heah; hom, safe 'n happy, wid ma sweet Jesus."[59] In the fictional story reflecting many women's real experiences, Mammy Lou's testimony about her daughter being sold away from her convinces Nelle that Black women's sacrifices were for their own descendants, not for their White charges or as a ploy to be memorialized in marble. By centering Mammy Lou's own painful memory, Howard reminded readers what ought to be valued and held sacred.

In keeping with her reputation as a speaker, Hallie Quinn Brown's rhetoric proves most dramatic and direct. Like Terrell and Howard, Brown centered the distressing experiences of enslaved Black women. Brown's middle-class Black female audience would likely have afforded her more space for candor, and she used her signature theatrical style to fill that space. She began with biblical allusion and antithesis to highlight the hypocrisy of the would-be memorializers: "One generation stones the prophets and the next builds monuments to their memory. One generation held the ['Black Mammy'] in abject slavery; the next would erect a monument to her fidelity." Throughout the statement, Brown confronted the violence of slavery by declaring that it left Black women "brutalized," "tortured in mind and body," and ultimately "polluted through two hundred and fifty years of slavery by scions of a supposed superior people." The system did not only affect those who were enslaved but produced "generations of oppression and suppression."[60] Brown's statement on the monument left no doubt about what she believed would have been a more accurate account of the "Black Mammy's" experience. Although she did not say it outright, the whole statement argues that what ought to be treated as sacred is the humanity of Black people both past and present.

Not all of the Black women critics of the monument believed that the enslaved woman's experience should be remembered and honored in the way Brown advocated. Women such as the signatories of the PWYWCA petition, rather, argued that a commemoration of the "mammy" should be avoided, because it would simply represent Black women at their worst and thereby overshadow contemporary Black women who were aspiring to be their best. As middle-class Black Americans had been doing for decades before the 1920s, the PWYWCA petition emphasizes the "rapid advance" of this group and notes the relative ignorance of White Americans to this progress. Echoing the claims of Fannie Barrier Williams in her 1893 speech at the World's Congress of Representative Women, the petition reads, "Many of the refined and the intelligent whites of America are utter strangers to the better class of our people." Animated by the politics of respectability, this familiar argument divides both White and Black Americans along class lines, relegating racism and its effects to the uncouth and unintelligent of each racial group. The petition concludes by stating that "the Old Mammy as a slave, however well she may have performed her part as a foster mother to many of the progeny of the South, represents the Shadows of the Past." The women of the PWYWCA objected to the representation of the "Old Mammy as a slave" because it would besmirch the reputation of those like them who had worked to separate themselves from what they perceived as a shameful history.[61] Such images, the petition argues, are unpleasant reminders of the "unfortunate condition" of oppressed ancestors that can become festering "irritants" in Black women's attempts to join in the "harmony of citizenship." The women of the PWYWCA specifically objected to the memory of Black women as enslaved. Calling such memory an "irritant" seems dismissive, as if the recollection of the "Old Mammy" were a buzzing fly to be swatted away. This attitude aligns with early twentieth-century Black ambivalence toward memories of slavery and reveals the effects of class prejudice. Yet the petition's argument does more than dismiss "Mammy": It also notes the hypocrisy of White Americans who were eager to memorialize a servile role for Black women while failing to commemorate their own "humble origins" likewise as "serfs" or other unfree social positions. The women of the PWYWCA may have been ashamed of "Mammy," yet their argument also suggests that they sought to protect her and her vulnerable offspring from unnecessary exposure by

White Americans. They believed that doing so would help Black women of the present access the rights of citizenship.

Although more sympathetic toward the "mammy's" experience, Charlotte Hawkins Brown relied on similar views about how certain memories of enslaved women might influence perceptions of her middle-class contemporaries. Claiming to represent "the intelligent Negro women of the South," Brown declared that they "deplore the fact that it [a memorial] should take the form of a 'mammy monument.'"[62] By using the descriptor "intelligent," Brown subtly invoked the same class associations as the PWYWCA while also drawing attention to her role as an educator and a representative of educated Black women. Despite their ambivalence about class dynamics, these arguments nonetheless foreground their care for Black women, albeit more of the present than the past. Both types of arguments dispute the content of the proposed monument's memory by questioning why the UDC's nostalgic version of the "Black Mammy," specifically, must be its focus. By identifying parts of enslaved women's experience that had been omitted from the memorial representation or rejecting the "mammy" entirely, these Black women implied that the UDC valued not Black "mammies" themselves but the exploitative relationships they signified.

Loyalty to Stakeholders

The third feature of rhetorics of commemorative stewardship is expressing a commitment to shared responsibility and accountability to other stakeholders. Although we might assume that the UDC saw themselves as accountable to those whom they were commemorating (i.e., Black women), UDC commentary on the project demonstrates that they were more committed to serving the supposed interests of White children and future White Southerners. Black women critics of the monument highlighted this reality and gave voice to the stakeholders to whom would-be stewards of Black women's memory instead ought to be accountable. These speakers did not directly claim that Black women had not been consulted, nor did they advocate a specific means by which Black women should be consulted regarding such a monument. Rather, they repeatedly asserted what they represented as the views of contemporary Black American women throughout the country. The critics argued that memorializers should be accountable to Black women contemporaries because the monument purported to represent their historical experiences.

Several of the Black women critics challenged the commemorative stewardship of the UDC by implying their lack of accountability to Black women. They did so indirectly, by beginning their statements with a declaration that they were speaking on behalf of other Black women, whom they perceived as the true stakeholders in this commemoration. Charlotte Hawkins Brown, for example, began her telegram to Congressman Stedman by situating herself as a representative of "the intelligent Negro women of the South." She underscored her roles as part of that key group by using first-person plural pronouns. Brown concluded the telegram with a plea on behalf of her fellow Southern Black women, saying "we implore" the UDC to support education for Black children rather than funding the monument.[63] A few days later, the Washington, DC, clubwomen who penned the Congressional petition identified the specific community on whose behalf they were writing and detailed the process whereby their representation had been established: "The Board of Directors of the Phyllis Wheatley Y.W.C.A., representing 2000 women in the District of Columbia, met last night and after discussion voted to protest against the granting of a site for the erection of a statue to the 'Black Mammy of the South'; as also against the erection of such a statue anywhere."[64] The names of the board members were also inscribed on the second page of the petition, boldly declaring to the leaders of the nation their identities and leadership roles in an esteemed African-American women's club. Although the number of women represented is much smaller than that in Charlotte Hawkins Brown's large yet nebulous group, an organization of two thousand middle-class Black women in geographical proximity to the proposed monument would have had more focused rhetorical impact. Like Brown, the signatories used first-person plural pronouns near the end of their statement to remind readers of the key stakeholders in this business. They announced, "We, the colored women of the city of Washington, do not like to be vividly reminded of the unfortunate condition of some of our ancestors. . . ."[65] They clearly identified themselves as Black women and residents of the District, and they furthermore tied themselves to those represented by the proposed monument—"our ancestors." Although they evidently wished to distance themselves from that past, they nonetheless claimed it as their own and thereby positioned themselves as key stakeholders in the debate.

Whereas Charlotte Hawkins Brown and the PWYWCA represented more limited regional groups of Black women, Mary Church Terrell and Hallie Quinn Brown claimed to speak for hundreds of thousands of middle-class Black women across the United States. Both women were national leaders of the NACW, and they opened their statements by establishing a united front for the group of stakeholders whom they believed had been overlooked. They left no question about those for whom they spoke, nor about what those people thought about the proposed monument. Terrell affirmed that "colored women all over the United States stand aghast at the idea of erecting a ['Black Mammy'] monument in the capital of the United States."[66] Brown more explicitly identified herself as both the spokeswoman for and a member of this group, proclaiming, "In the name of 500,000 intelligent, educated colored women, citizens of this country, we register our strongest protest against the erection of a statue in the Capitol of this Republic, by the Daughters of the Confederacy, which is to be dedicated to the 'Black Mammy' of the South." These opening salvos center Black women as key stakeholders and unequivocally assert their disapproval of the proposed monument. Whether speaking on behalf of regional, local, or national groups of Black women, these rhetors used their position to expose the failure of the UDC to be responsible and accountable to—or even acknowledge—the people whom they were supposedly memorializing. Displaying their loyalty to their community as stakeholders further cemented Black women's credibility as commemorative stewards.

Commemoration for Future Generations

In the fourth and final rhetorical move of commemorative stewardship, commemorative stewards assert their own significance by emphasizing their work on behalf of future generations. As the previous section illustrates, the UDC's lack of attention to Black stakeholders reveals that their central concern was not for African Americans at all—past, present, or future. The UDC viewed its main stakeholders as future generations of White Southerners. As UDC leader Mary Solari put it, the story of the devoted "Black Mammy" had to be preserved for "coming generations," to "hand down to posterity" this narrative of Black sacrifice within a relationship of beneficent bondage.[67] In contrast, Black women critics argued that true commemorative stewards should be concerned not only with preserving memories of Black women of the past but with the welfare of Black people of the present and future. Critics affirmed their own care and concern for fellow Black Americans by repeatedly reframing the conversation around the plight of those individuals. Rhetorically, they accomplished this by insisting on temporal continuity from past to present to future through the figure of "Mammy's descendants." Critics used the language of "Mammy's descendants" or "Mammy's children/sons/daughters" to refer both to the people who were the literal children and grandchildren of enslaved women and to future generations of Black American heirs to these historical experiences. Whether intentional or not, the ambiguity of these references operates rhetorically to blur temporal boundaries and project the implications of this monument controversy into the future. Black female critics used this argument about future generations in ways that sharply contrasted with the rhetorical work of the UDC. Black women strengthened connections among Black people across time in the hopes that they might effect change in the future. This aspect of their critical memory work also served important community functions by claiming space for memories that centered Black experiences and lives. The UDC, on the other hand, aimed to enshrine enslavement as a timeless emblem of the ideal relationships between Black and White Americans. The UDC looked to the past to prevent change in the future.

The PWYWCA, Terrell, and Hallie Quinn Brown invoked lineage across time to underscore their arguments about the symbolic impact of the monument. Although at first glance the Black clubwomen of the PWYWCA appeared to be advocating a break in lineage, closer attention reveals that their argument depends on the idea that Black Americans past and present are connected. For instance, they specifically pointed out that representing "our ancestors" in the "unfortunate condition" of slavery would interfere with their efforts to act as citizens.[68] Terrell concluded her editorial with an evocative statement about how, if the monument were built, thousands of Black men and women would "fervently pray that on some stormy night the lightning will strike it and the heavenly elements will send it crashing to the ground." According to Terrell, their prayers would rise up specifically to prevent future generations—the "descendants of Black mammies"—from being forever "reminded of the anguish of heart and the physical suffering which the mothers and grandmothers of the race endured for nearly 300 years."[69] Whereas the PWYWCA and Terrell emphasized the seeming permanence of such a monument, Hallie Quinn Brown noted its insignificance in the grand sweep of history, relative to other, more practical forms of commemoration such as education for Black children. Her statement offers numerous alternatives for commemorating enslaved women, saying that these other "memorials" would endure "not only for time but for eternity when stone statues erected to ['Black Mammy'] shall have perished from the face of the earth," reaching well beyond the current generation into the future.[70]

With the exception of the PWYWCA petition, all of the texts use the language of kinship to question the UDC's decision to commemorate the "Black Mammy" with a sentimental stone monument rather than practical investment in the welfare of future generations of Black Americans.[71]

Notably, in many instances, critics used this language in combination with the conditional argument discussed earlier: If you want to make an appropriate commemoration, they argued, then you will address the needs of the descendants of the enslaved. The argument strongly implies, although it rarely explicitly states, that those who commemorate without addressing contemporary material needs are hypocrites. For instance, Charlotte Hawkins Brown argued that if the UDC wanted to express their gratitude toward enslaved women, they should do so "in the form of a foundation for the education and advancement of the Negro children descendants of those faithful souls they seem anxious to honor."[72] Maude Nooks Howard also invited readers to consider the kinship that joins future generations with the "Black Mammy" of the past. Having been to heaven to visit Mammy Lou, Missy Nelle returns convinced of the "indelible truth" that these enslaved women cared for their White charges "in faith that her kith and kin would be rewarded by a 'square deal' and a 'happy life,' unspoiled by little n's and prejudices." This passage implies that any proper commemoration of the "Black Mammy" would prioritize fair treatment of her descendants, and it furthermore suggests that Mammy Lou herself had focused on future generations to endure the hardships of enslavement.

Although Charlotte Hawkins Brown and Maude Nooks Howard gestured toward enslaved women's descendants only in passing, Hallie Quinn Brown made them the center of her critique. She argued repeatedly that "mammy's descendants"—or those to whom Brown also refers as "mammy's children" and her "sons and daughters"—ought to be the proper focus of any "monument" intended to honor enslaved women. A true monument to present and future generations, according to Brown, would denounce and eradicate the lynching, discrimination, poverty, and poor education that afflicted these descendants. After several paragraphs vividly enumerating the many actions that White women could take to "salve their conscience and make amends," Brown concluded her statement by contrasting the proposed monument to "a class of dead saints" with their "living descendants [who] cry for succor, for a fair chance in life."[73]

By drawing attention to the living descendants of enslaved women and future generations of Black children, these Black women again suggested—or outright stated—that the women of the UDC were acting only as stewards of their own interest and the continued supremacy of their White children. Furthermore, the language of lineage deliberately emphasizes continuity through time to connect contemporary and future generations of Black Americans to the experiences of their enslaved ancestors. Some middle-class Black women might have preferred to remember the "Black Mammy" in the privacy of their own thoughts and homes rather than on a public pedestal. However, none of these critics failed to claim the enslaved Black woman as their forebear. None of the critics denied the inheritance of slavery, even if their own ancestors were not enslaved.[74]

Viewing Black Women's Anti-"Mammy" Discourse as Critical Memory Work

My analysis illustrates how Black women of the early twentieth century deployed their rhetorical skills to engage in critical memory work that challenged the UDC's memorial plans. The debate over the so-called monument to the "faithful slave mammies of the South" illustrates their pointed and deliberate protests against White efforts to control memories of slavery —especially memories of enslaved women. The debate over the monument centered around the question of who has the authority and credibility to control commemoration and how. A key component of their rhetorical work in this particular case is the critique of the commemorative stewardship of White Southern women, which emphasizes the question of who has the right to control and circulate the memories that affect Americans for generations to come. This chapter thus demonstrates how appeals to commemorative stewardship can function as critical memory work.

Harvey Young offered a description of critical memory that is especially relevant to the "Mammy" monument case: "Critical memory invites consideration of past practices that have affected the lives and shaped the experiences of black folk. It looks back in time, from a present-day perspective, and not only accounts for the evolution in culture but also enables an imagining of what life would be like had things been different. The appeal of critical memory is that it grants access to past experiences of select individuals. At the same time, it does not blind us to their (or our) present reality."[75] The Black women engaged in public critique were, in a sense, "imagining what would have been," as they argued for alternative commemorations that would take into account the needs of "Mammy's descendants." Looking back from their present to the past of the enslaved woman, Black women of 1923 were "not blind [. . .] to their (or our) present reality." Their critical memory was clear-eyed about what happened in the past, as well as what that meant for their present. Regardless of whether they wanted to publicly remember "Mammy" (e.g., the PWYWCA), they still insisted on recognizing the enslaved woman's experience as it was, not how the UDC wished it was or how White supremacy had taught them it was.

This case also offers insight into how critical memory work exhibits rhetorical sensitivity to the audience. To be sure, the Black women critics directed their commentary at White folks, whether it was Representative Stedman, or Congress, or the UDC, or White women in general. However, their strategies differed slightly depending on the context and outlet of their rhetorical activity. For instance, Charlotte Hawkins Brown wrote to Stedman as the proponent of the monument in Congress, the PWYWCA addressed Congress as a whole, Terrell published in a major White daily newspaper, Howard published in Black newspapers, and Hallie Quinn Brown wrote to Black women in the *National Notes* (perhaps hoping to be picked up by the White press). These women clearly recognized that a campaign to challenge the UDC's proposal required critique on multiple fronts and in multiple forms. It is possible that this varied approach contributed to the overall rhetorical effect of their critical memory work in this case: the death of the UDC proposal in Congress. Although direct influence cannot be demonstrated, the case nonetheless provides an example of a rare, failed commemorative campaign by White Southern women and a successful rejoinder from Black Americans. Placing themselves on the record in this way again contributed to building the storehouse of memory from which future Black women could draw, whether to combat White supremacy or, as I describe in the next chapter, to cultivate positive community feelings.

FIVE

"Planting Good and Joy Instead"

Cultivating Community Feelings in *Homespun Heroines and Other Women of Distinction*

In 1926—just a few short years after the "Mammy" monument plans were thwarted—twenty-eight Black women worked together to write, edit, and publish one of the earliest biography collections by and about Black American women. *Homespun Heroines and Other Women of Distinction* featured fifty-five biographical sketches of recognized African-American women such as Phillis Wheatley, Harriet Tubman, and Sojourner Truth and personal acquaintances such as "Aunt Mac." This multibiography was distinctive because of its collected subjects and because of its collected creators: Black female teachers and leaders wrote the sketches; and noted educator and elocutionist Hallie Quinn Brown contributed sketches and edited the volume. As Brown outlined in the introduction, the book's contributors collectively labored "to preserve for future reference an account of these women, their life and character and what they accomplished under the most trying and adverse circumstances."[1] They did so with the understanding that their accounts of the past were not often recognized, let alone valued, by White US society. For instance, writing about Tubman, Brown declared that "when America writes her history without hatred and prejudice she will place high in the galaxy of fame the name of a woman as remarkable as the French heroine, Joan of Arc, a woman who had not even the poor advantages of the peasant maid of Domremy, but was born under the galling yoke of slavery with a long score of cruelty."[2] The creators of

Homespun Heroines—and many others like them—strove to preserve and promote memories of other Black women not only for the young people in their present but also for a future in which their history would be valued.

This chapter examines the community memory work of *Homespun Heroines*, through which Brown and her coauthors strove to preserve and present memories of Black women by and for other Black women. I consider this text as both an exemplary and a representative instance illustrating how Black women deployed collective biography as a rhetorical tool for memory work. The collection provides a rare glimpse into middle-class African-American women's collective textual memory work during the 1920s. One of this collection's distinctive features is the way that it instructs readers on the appropriate feelings one should have in relation to those who have gone before. This chapter shows how Black women used these biographical sketches to articulate a Black feminist memory that was not limited by the framework of trauma and grief by cultivating memories of gratitude and celebration centered in Black womanhood. I argue that the biographies and the feelings that they invite constitute a distinctive communal resource for Black women during the time and, especially, in the future.[3] Like the speakers discussed in chapter 2, the writers of *Homespun Heroines* contributed Black women exemplars to a community storehouse of memory that could inspire future activism. Reading these sketches illustrates that Black women's memory work does not only articulate itself *against* White memories but also simply *for* Black memories.

The analysis in this chapter examines how the sketches in *Homespun Heroines* cultivate gratitude and celebration through the development of three key themes, each of which connects to Black women's memory work of the period. First, the sketches highlight memories of struggle, of which some are framed as collective challenges and others are presented as individual hardships. By relating these narratives alongside expressions of gratitude and celebration, the sketches communicate the coexistence of joy and pain in Black women's lives. Second, the collection intentionally blurs the line between "extraordinary" and "ordinary" women by emphasizing the ordinary qualities of the exceptional and recasting the ordinary as the great. This blurring suggests to readers that they ought to respond with gratitude for the lives of *all* Black women, regardless of whether White US society has deemed them "exceptional." Third, the biographies display varied manifestations of excellence in the lives and work of Black women both to challenge the restrictive roles assigned to Black women in the early twentieth century and to provide as many types of exemplars as possible for readers. The celebration of remembered Black female excellence is marked by expressions of gratitude and joy. Before examining each of these themes in turn, I describe the collection and its relationship to Black biographies and multi-biographies in more detail, and I describe how gratitude and joy function as crucial communal feelings in Black women's community memory work.

Homespun Heroines and Black Biography at the Turn of the Twentieth Century

Homespun Heroines reflects both the individual influence of Hallie Quinn Brown, editor and author of numerous sketches, and the collective influence of the other twenty-seven women who contributed sketches.[4] In this way, the book is similar to other collective biographies of women of the period, which in literary scholar Alison Booth's observation "value collaboration and imitation rather than originality."[5] Throughout her active century of life, Brown deployed rhetoric to inspire and equip other African Americans—especially women—to become leaders and advocates in their communities. Brown was herself a student and teacher of elocution, lecturer, and author of a textbook on the subject called *Bits and Odds: A Choice Selection of Recitations for School, Lyceum, and Parlor Entertainments.* As such, she was familiar with the exemplar tradition in both the teaching and practice of rhetoric.[6] According to her contemporary Mary McLeod Bethune, Brown was "a leader of great talents and many interests [. . .] an educator in the broadest sense of the word."[7] The collection's index notes Brown as the author of twenty-one sketches, Maritcha R. Lyons as the author of eight, Anna H. Jones and Ora B. Stokes as the authors of three sketches each, Sarah L. Fleming as the author of two, and twenty-two other women each the author of one.[8]

All of the sketches focus on Black women, including both well-known figures such as Harriet Tubman and unfamiliar local characters such as "Aunt Mac." As Randall K. Burkett explained, "Many of the writers knew their subjects personally, as mothers, grandmothers, or aunts; as teachers or mentors; or as friends; hence, the sketches are written with the special insight and appreciation that such familiarity can bring."[9] Although the vast majority of the sketches were composed specifically for this volume, Brown incorporated some previously published material, such as an obituary of Tubman from the *American Review* and a collection of short sketches about Black women pioneers in California. The sketches range widely in detail and length, anywhere from a short paragraph to fourteen pages. The sketches are accompanied by forty-five images, primarily photograph portraits of the subjects, some etchings, images of homes and, in one case, a photo of a historical marker.

The collection appeared alongside a small group of biographical texts by and about Black Americans during the late nineteenth and early twentieth centuries. Rising literacy rates among African Americans since emancipation created new opportunities for disseminating Black histories in textual form.[10] Accessible to a growing number of Black readers, biography collections served the critical rhetorical purpose of preserving and promoting accounts about African Americans to counter racist White accounts of the Black past.[11] Whitewashed histories were not simply a matter of words: They fed the White supremacist culture that led to intensified racial terror and violence across the United States. As Black Americans left behind the white-robed racism of the South for the covert discrimination of the North, Black arts and culture flourished in cities such as Chicago and New York. The Harlem Renaissance—or New Negro Movement, as that cultural period has been called more recently—also fostered attention to the historical experiences and creative contributions of Black Americans from the end of World War I into the 1930s. According to rhetoric scholar Eric King Watts, this movement "required a population of black folk who saw themselves (more or less) as public agents 'free' to form clubs, newspapers, and magazines" and thereby do "public work on behalf of African America." Participants in this movement debated the meaning of art, history, music, literature and political activism to Black Americans. They acted and spoke publicly in ways that enacted their views that Black Americans deserved stories and images that built up their communities. Thus, as Watts has noted, "The New Negro Movement was, in part, a product of a special kairos."[12] It was a time ripe for rhetorical and artistic work in Black communities—and for community memory work.

Biographical and historical texts by, about, and for Black Americans began to emerge in the 1890s and appeared steadily into the New Negro Movement. Although the number about women remained particularly small, Black authors and compilers produced a handful of biographical texts, beginning in 1891 with Susie I. Lankford Shorter's *The Heroines of African Methodism*. Booth has suggested that the collections published in the 1890s appeared in direct response to the exclusion of African Americans from the planning and execution of the 1893 World's Fair, discussed in chapter 3. Biographical collections about Black women—Shorter's volume; Monroe A. Majors's *Noted Negro Women: Their Triumphs and Activities* (1893); Lawson A. Scruggs's *Women of Distinction: Remarkable of Works and*

Invincible of Character (1893); and Mrs. N. F. [Gertrude E. H. Bustill] Mossell's *The Work of the Afro-American Woman* (1894)—proffered a critique of the unrepresentative White vision of womanhood being advanced by the World's Fair and the World's Congress of Representative Women by praising Black women who exemplified more expansive expressions of feminine virtue.[13] In doing so, these collections also extended the work done by the public speakers to present exemplary women for emulation, described in chapter 2.

A fleet of important biographical texts also appeared in the 1920s, arriving in both the terrifying wake of the Red Summer of 1919 and the heady waves of the New Negro Movement. From rural Elaine, Arkansas, to Tulsa's "Black Wall Street," to Rosewood, Florida, Black men returned from the First World War to find their communities under attack by White assailants. Yet in 1926—the same year when *Homespun Heroines* was published—Zora Neale Hurston wrote one of her first plays; Langston Hughes published his first collection of poetry, *The Weary Blues*; and historian Carter G. Woodson inaugurated "Negro History Week." Other key texts published during the 1920s included Elizabeth Ross Haynes's *Unsung Heroes* (1921), a collection of biographical sketches about Black men and women, and *The Brownies' Book* (1920–1921), the monthly children's periodical published by the National Association for the Advancement of Colored People and edited by W. E. B. Du Bois and Jessie Redmon Fauset, which featured life sketches of individuals of African descent.[14] Brown's compilation appears to be the only one of these early texts collaboratively constructed and exclusively produced by and about Black women. This distinction makes Brown's text a rich and unique instance of multibiography and Black women's community memory work during the period.

Black Women's Multibiography as Memory in Reserve

Brown's volume participates in the rhetorical tradition of collective biographies of women, which Booth detailed in her extensive study *How to Make It as a Woman*. According to Booth, "Group biohistoriography or prosopography has been instrumental in constructing modern subjectivities and social differences."[15] Differences in racial and gender identity figure particularly prominently in texts of the late nineteenth and early twentieth centuries, when Americans were actively renegotiating the social and legal meaning of such differences.[16] Biographical collections (or "multibiographies," as Booth also called them) shape not only identities but also the communities in which those identities exist, from the neighborhood to the nation. Multibiographies may exercise more persuasive power over their readers than individual biographies, because the former outline explicit criteria for selecting their subjects. Identifying such criteria entails isolating specific characteristics and values for consideration by readers. Booth explained that collective biographies require "an additional rhetorical frame besides that of any biography: the definition of the category or principle of selection," which "prevents the illusion of a transparent, objective account of a person's life."[17] In this sense, collective biographies are more plainly rhetorical than individual biographies.

A unique multibiography, *Homespun Heroines* rewards close attention because it is a collaborative, collective project of community memory work about Black women. Furthermore, it was produced by "self-confident and historically self-conscious" Black women who not only were committed to Black women's flourishing but also exhibited sophisticated rhetorical sensibilities.[18] Although editor Hallie Quinn Brown did not reflect at length on the principle that guided her selection of subjects, she and her coauthors clearly had rhetorical designs to deploy these Black women's stories to uplift, as they might have said, Black readers and communities. Brown's introduction to *Homespun Heroines* implies a principle of selection by succinctly describing the collection's subjects as "history-making women of our race" and "our pioneer women."[19] By using "our," Brown both claimed these women as part of her community and identified them as fellow African Americans, although no specific racial category is used in either Brown's introduction or Josephine Turpin Washington's foreword. Brown also redefined what "history-making" might mean for "women of [her] race," simply by claiming that such women were historically significant. Focusing on Black women during this time period thus constitutes a departure from—and, implicitly, a critique of—previous multibiographies' historical focus on White women.[20]

The *Homespun Heroines* collection provides a rare glimpse into middle-class African-American women's community memory work and theories during the early twentieth century. This volume is particularly notable because it signifies a *collective* rhetorical effort by Black women to preserve and pass on memories, and it utilizes traditional rhetorical modes to advance alternative memories. Although minimal research in rhetorical studies has explicitly examined Black women's community memory work, studies by Rosalyn Collings Eves and Patricia Davis have begun to theorize Black women's memory practices by exploring the cases of cookbooks and historical reenactment, respectively.[21] Both Eves and Davis have shown how

African-American women of the recent past worked cooperatively, using traditional means such as cooking and dress, to resist mainstream memories of Black women. Eves's analysis of three cookbooks produced by the National Council of Negro Women in the 1990s, in particular, highlights the collective rhetorical work of such texts. Eves argued that the "cookbooks offer a forum for multiple voices to be heard, and they represent a subtle refusal to accept the memories of African-American women dictated by voices other than their own."[22] Davis's study of contemporary Black women who were engaged in the embodied practice of historical reenactment of the antebellum and Civil War periods illustrates the importance of traditional values as a starting point for critique. Davis examined specifically how reenactors "combine an embodied performance of respectability with a narrative performance of black women's historical agency."[23] Rather than being only a simplistic accommodation to dominant White, patriarchal culture, the performance of respectability enabled Black women to gain rhetorical traction. As Davis argued, the "traditionalism" performed by these historical reenactors became for them a "site of resistance to both dominant structures of representation and mainstream feminist discourse."[24] In a similar fashion, the authors of the *Homespun Heroines* sketches used the traditional genre of biography to offer their own arguments about what constituted historical significance, virtuous character, meaningful lives, and even physical beauty. Even merely by presenting Black women as exhibiting such admirable features, these authors resisted White mainstream memories and actively theorized what better memories should look like for their communities. However, as I describe in this chapter's analysis, the volume is not primarily a reaction or response to histories dominated by Whiteness but a positive exhortation to gratitude for and joy in the richness of remembered Black womanhood.

Cultivating Community Feelings of Gratitude and Joy

As Matthew Houdek and Kendell R. Phillips noted, "our memories are not solely constituted by how we envision the past, but also by how those visions make us feel."[25] Studies of public memory share a widespread assumption that public memory is "animated by affect," as Carole Blair, Greg Dickinson, and Brian Ott put it. They continued, "Public memory embraces events, people, objects, and places that it deems worthy of preservation, based on some kind of emotional attachment."[26] Public memory can emerge from emotional attachments; it can also invite emotional attachments. *Homespun Heroines*, as an artifact of public memory, deliberately aims to cultivate certain kinds of feelings in its readers through meditation on the lives of Black women. Such feelings, I argue, are meant not to be kept as individual and private but shared by members of a community. Therefore, this chapter draws inspiration from work that explores a constellation of concepts related to "public feelings."[27] According to Ann Cvetkovich, focusing on public feelings shows how "political identities are implicit within structures of feeling, sensibilities, everyday forms of cultural expression and affiliation that may not take the form of recognizable organizations or institutions."[28] Lisa M. Corrigan draws this approach into the orbit of rhetoric in *Black Feelings*. Corrigan emphasizes what Agnes Heller described as "cognitive feelings," which "function as pedagogical tools in building identification with and against objects of affection and derision."[29] As these passages indicate, public feelings connect human beings in politically salient ways, although those connections are not always expressed in traditional political forms.

Homespun Heroines is an "everyday form of cultural expression and affiliation," as well as a repository of "objects of affection"—the biographical subjects—that invites affiliation through the sharing of certain community feelings. The volume fosters a variety of connections among Black women: connections among their creators (e.g., Brown and her coauthors), between the authors and their audience, and between the biographical subjects and likely readers. The affiliations created are both contemporaneous (among women of the same moment) and transhistorical (between women of different historical periods). Brown and her coauthors craft life stories that establish and maintain connections among Black women by emphasizing feelings of gratitude and joy. The feelings of gratitude and joy serve, in turn, as a resource for Black women oriented toward organizing and activism.[30]

As communal feelings, joy and gratitude are expressed and produced, in part, through rhetorical texts. The American Psychological Association's *Dictionary of Psychology* defines joy as "a feeling of extreme gladness, delight, or exultation of the spirit arising from a sense of well-being or satisfaction," which can be experienced as passive or active. Active joy involves a "desire to share one's feelings with others" and is "associated with more engagement in the environment than is passive joy."[31] The concept of active joy aligns with the more pointedly political practice of Black joy. Damaris Dunn and Bettina L. Love define Black joy as "the radical imagination of collective memories of resistance, trauma, survival, love, and cultural modes of expression."[32] Although Black joy in itself is by no means news, amplifying

Black joy has become a critical political and social task in the 2010s and 2020s for Black people around the world who have been inundated with media representations of Black suffering and death. Numerous Black scholars, thinkers, and creatives have theorized Black joy as a mode of resistance to and expression of liberation from White supremacy.[33] For instance, considering Black joy in the context of Michael Brown's murder in Ferguson, Missouri, Javon Johnson viewed it as "a real and imagined site of utopian possibility." Johnson continued, "More than a method to endure, Black joy allows us the space to stretch our imaginations beyond what we previously thought possible and allows us to theorize a world in which white supremacy does not dictate our everyday lives."[34] Philosopher Lindsey Stewart theorizes a "politics of Black joy," reframing it as a form of productive refusal. Like Johnson, she views Black joy as a communal practice for Black people outside of the constraints of Whiteness: "While resistance foregrounds an oppositional relation between oppressed and oppressors, joy foregrounds a flourishing relation of the self to the self (or, in the case of Black joy, how Black folks relate to each other)."[35] Rather than covering over or negating pain, Black joy asserts Black life *in the presence of* suffering. Black joy also connects Black people to one another through shared public feeling. As such, the purposes and functions of Black joy parallel the purposes and functions of community memory work.

Whereas twenty-first-century conceptualizations of Black joy are closely tied to contemporary public movements such as Black Lives Matter, practices of Black joy in the late nineteenth and early twentieth centuries would have been more limited to Black community spaces such as churches and dance halls. Yet the expressions of feeling in these varied Black spaces were also fraught by the status anxieties plaguing African-American communities during this time period. For instance, Tera W. Hunter documented how, in the early twentieth century, debates over certain kinds of dancing in Southern Black churches and "jook joints" revealed tensions among Black Americans of different class backgrounds.[36] Hunter noted that "it was not dancing per se that the black elites rejected" but the public nature and "social atmosphere" of dance halls and "Holy Roller" churches.[37] Lindsey Stewart's analysis of Zora Neale Hurston's essays argues that intense and important discussions about Black joy occurred during the time of the New Negro Movement, when *Homespun Heroines* was published.[38] Unbridled public expressions of joy such as vivacious dancing would likely have been frowned upon by the middle-class Black women creators of *Homespun*

Heroines. However, more cloistered expressions of joy and celebration—especially of kind, virtuous, and accomplished Black women—would have operated within the bounds of propriety while still creating opportunities for cultivating bonds of public feeling.[39]

Whereas Black joy is deeply communal and political, gratitude is typically framed as individual and personal. For instance, the field of positive psychology and popular discourse in the late twentieth century and early twenty-first century has touted the role of gratitude in personal happiness.[40] Psychology researchers Robert A. Emmons and Michael E. McCullough identify gratitude as both an emotion and a virtue.[41] As an emotion, gratitude comprises "pleasant feelings" about receiving a benefit "freely bestowed."[42] As a virtue, gratitude has been viewed as a "necessary ingredient for the moral personality" and essential to live a good life. It is something that a moral person should feel toward another person (or entity) who has conferred a benefit.[43] The person toward whom one feels gratitude can be present (such as a parent or partner) or absent (such as in the practice of expressing gratitude to one's ancestors). Thus, gratitude has the capacity to solidify social relationships both in the same moment and across different historical periods. Gratitude is important to the study of memory, because it has the capacity to connect individuals and communities across time.[44] As Georg Simmel put it, "Gratitude, as it were, is the moral memory of [hu]mankind."[45] Christel N. Temple emphasized the special significance of Black gratitude through her concept of "ancestor acknowledgment," one of the features of Black cultural mythology. This concept both "normalizes the layered consciousness that the living, the deceased, and the unborn are active and interrelated modes of existence" and "affirms that any life lived well deserves gratitude and appreciation."[46] Although gratitude has been valorized as a praiseworthy feeling, it also has the potential to operate unethically in situations of marked social inequity.[47] For Black women who were expected to perform gratitude toward White benefactors and even their Black male counterparts in unjust contexts, cultivating gratitude toward Black women past and present serves a similar function to contemporary Black joy: It expresses freedom from White supremacy and patriarchy by solidifying affiliative bonds among Black women.

Attending to positive feelings produced through memory, such as joy and gratitude, deepens scholarship on Black memory that has emphasized trauma. Following scholars such as André Brock Jr., Badia Ahad-Legardy, Catherine Knight-Steele and Jessica Lu, Lindsey Stewart, and Christel N.

Temple, I recognize the traumatic inheritance of slavery and racism while also seeking to understand the rhetorical power of other Black feelings.[48] Brock argues that Blackness is, in part, defined by its ability to encompass both the positive and negative aspects of Black experiences. Defending this view, he notes that "while racism is an inexhaustible fountain of energy for whiteness, it is only part of how Blackness navigates the world."[49] Ahad-Legardy develops a similar argument through the cultural analysis of Black memory and nostalgia. She argues that relying on trauma as the "largely uncontested and seemingly natural framework for interpreting black memory" affords "little space to apprehend other modalities of memory operative in African American culture."[50] Ahad-Legardy's development of the theory and practice of "Afro-nostalgia" illustrates the need for work about Black American memory to attend to the coexistence of pain *and* joy in Black life.[51] Although Brock and Ahad-Legardy examine contemporary examples such as Black cyberculture, cuisine, music, and social media, analyzing a historical example such as *Homespun Heroines* illustrates how for generations Black American communities have cultivated positive shared feelings such as joy and gratitude as a mechanism of survival and reservoir of political agency. Examining this collection of biographies also shows how memory work—and especially community memory work—operates affectively.

Brown's introduction to *Homespun Heroines* foregrounds such feelings as it outlines the volume's four main purposes: to express gratitude to the collection's subjects, to present accurate historical accounts, to preserve the stories of notable women, and to bring joy to authors and audiences alike. Emotional terminology predominates, especially in the descriptions of the first, third, and fourth purposes. Brown described her "appreciation" and "regard" for her subjects, her "anxious desire" to safeguard their memory, and her "pleasure" in producing the volume as well as the pleasure she anticipates for readers. The feeling of gratitude is foregrounded in the introduction, which opens by stating, "This book is presented as an evidence of appreciation and as a token of regard to the history-making women of our race." This statement frames the volume as material proof of the "appreciation" and "regard" in which its authors hold the profiled subjects. The second clause of the sentence positions the biographees as the ones toward whom its authors express gratitude. In a possible gesture toward eavesdropping audiences,[52] Brown used passive construction so that the sentence might be read by those outside the community as evidence of

Black women's gratitude and, by extension, moral rectitude. However, her focus remained on the primary audience of Black women readers. Brown concluded the introduction by emphasizing the positive feelings that derive from learning about Black women's lives. Intertwining her authorial perspective with readerly experience, Brown conveyed her hope that the audience "may find as much pleasure in its perusal as the writer had in its making."[53] Brown here identified pleasure—closely related, though not identical, to joy—as a goal and thereby implicitly endorsed it as an appropriate response to reading the volume. Although the word "pleasure" in this passage functions conventionally and does not evoke the erotic undertones of the word as used by contemporary Black feminist scholars, it nonetheless names positive public feelings produced in the context of community memory work. The focus here is not on the feeling of pleasure itself but on the bonds that enjoyment creates. By naming a common source of pleasure, Brown dissolved barriers between author and audience and invited readers to identify with her and her co-creators.

Facing Memories of Struggle

Difficulties are ubiquitous in the stories of *Homespun Heroines*. In detailing the women's lives, the sketches identify both personal hardship, such as being orphaned at a young age, and shared oppression, such as being an enslaved woman. Struggle is present both as a historical fact and as a rhetorical feature of the narratives. Although individual histories vary, almost all Black women who lived before the mid-twentieth century faced significant obstacles, whether they were enslaved, orphaned, widowed, bereaved by the death of their children, laid low by illness, or some unhappy combination thereof. Struggle, in the lives of these women, is a fact. Struggle, in the narratives recounting their lives, is also used rhetorically to frame and amplify the women's contributions. For instance, Brown's introduction points out that the women profiled in the book accomplished great things "under the most trying and adverse circumstances."[54] Brown connected this emphasis to a central purpose of the collection—specifically, to provide for young people an "instructive light on the struggles endured and the obstacles overcome by our pioneer women."[55] Here Brown argued that remembering women who endured struggle and overcame obstacles serves as a source of encouragement for those who remember them. As Brown's introduction implies, viewing these women's lives in light of their struggles emphasizes both the contrast and the connection between the two.

Enslavement constitutes an enduring source of struggle in the biographies. Although many of the women profiled were born to parents who had been enslaved, Randall Burkett has noted that only thirteen were enslaved themselves.[56] These thirteen include well-known figures such as Phillis Wheatley, Sojourner Truth, and Harriet Tubman, as well as more obscure women such as Dinah Cox, Caroline Sherman Andrews-Hill, and Frances Jane Brown (Hallie Quinn Brown's mother). The sketches sensitively portray the range of experiences of slavery. For instance, the sketch of Andrews-Hill notes that her parents occupied relatively powerful positions in the hierarchy of enslavement on their plantation—the father was the foreman, and the mother was a "favored and highly esteemed member of her owner's household."[57] Their daughter was similarly positioned and thereby able to marry an educated enslaved man. The narrator explains that "this noble-spirited couple did not allow the strenuous task of their own family life to render them narrow and selfish, but both united in striving to brighten the lives of their fellows in bondage."[58] This passage acknowledges the "strenuous" nature of their lives while also noting their commitment to bringing joy to their enslaved community. The sketch of Dinah Cox highlights a different but not uncommon experience of recently freed people: being defrauded of rightfully inherited or earned property by Whites.[59] In cases of famous women who had been enslaved, the sketches emphasize that severely marginalized status to underscore the subject's later social mobility. The story of Fanny Jackson Coppin, for instance, begins with such a framing, stating that this woman "rose from the depth of slavery and became one of the most eminent educators of this country."[60] The narrative about Harriet Tubman describes her rise in even more vivid language. Comparing Tubman with Joan of Arc, the sketch claims that both women's names should be placed "high in the galaxy of fame," Tubman even more so because of her origin "under the galling yoke of slavery."[61] The stories about Coppin and Tubman both foreground their early enslavement to dramatize their later achievements and to argue that, because of their hardships, the accomplishments of Black women ought to be considered even more remarkable than those of the most lowly White women.[62]

Although slavery was a hardship shared by all of the enslaved (and even some of the free, for those living in the wake of the 1850 Fugitive Slave Act, as some of the sketches argue[63]), these women also experienced more personal struggles. The sketches note that several of them, such as Phillis Wheatley and Frances Ellen Watkins Harper, lost their parents when they were young. Of the fifty-three married women profiled, eleven of these were noted to have been widowed—and two women were widowed twice.[64] Sketches name many women who were thwarted in their pursuit of an education. For example, in the story of Coppin, Brown wrote that "the hardships of her childhood, the struggles for an education are sad to contemplate."[65] As in the stories of enslavement, the sketches often document early difficulties to amplify later achievements. Coppin, for instance, graduated from Oberlin College as one of a few women allowed to take the "gentleman's course."[66]

The sketches occasionally expand their view to consider the struggle of Black people more generally, thereby connecting the individual hardships of the women with the challenges of the race as whole. For example, in the story of Harriet Tubman, Brown compared the "struggles of the [White] pioneer mothers" to the "equally unique tales of the self-abnegation of the black woman of the South," which were no less common.[67] Maritcha Lyons noted the racial terror faced by all Black Americans after the Fugitive Slave Law was passed in 1850. Lyons introduced the profile of Sarah Harris Fayerweather by explaining that free Blacks during this part of the antebellum period maintained "race loyalty" in the midst of enduring "a thralldom none the less vicious because invisible."[68] Lyons's sketches often draw connections between the individual subjects and the shared experiences of Black women. This rhetorical choice is illustrated in the narrative of Henrietta Cordelia Ray, which is introduced with a lengthy meditation on the importance of "the lives of even the obscure." Lyons explained that "many, many, of 'our women'" lived "under most untoward conditions."[69] The sketch continues by noting that their experiences of life likely had "seasons of unrequited toil, undue anxiety, and devastating pain."[70] The sketch as a whole argues that learning about the lives of these little-known women remains essential because their hardships were common and, therefore, more relatable. Lyons's sketches also reveal the rhetorical implications of mixing the famous and the obscure in this collection, as discussed later.

Throughout the collection, the authors name and confront their subjects' struggles, both shared hardships produced directly by the racialized caste system and personal challenges resulting from other causes. Struggle thus becomes a consistent framework for interpreting the lives of these women. However, the sketches do not only narrate stories of pain but also describe the pursuit of joy in the midst of struggle. This combination resonates with what Temple has characterized as an "African-centered *philosophy of heroism*," through which stories of Black heroes emphasize "unusual endurance, perseverance, physical strength, grit, and emotional resilience."[71] The figures presented in this collection provide exemplars, to use the language of chapter 2, for navigating and overcoming life's inevitable struggles. As I discuss in the next two sections, weaving together joy and pain emerges as a key strategy for authors aiming to supply their readers with resources for resistance.

Remembering the Ordinary and the Extraordinary through Inclusive Gratitude

One of the distinctive features of this collection is its intentional undermining of the "great [wo]man" approach to biographies. Instead of praising only women who would be deemed historically significant by traditional standards, the volume argues that both extraordinary and ordinary women deserve gratitude.[72] The title, *Homespun Heroines and Other Women of Distinction*, implies that the volume prioritizes lesser known "homespun heroines"; those "other women of distinction" become almost secondary. Many of the sketches strongly suggest that these categories at least overlap and, possibly, completely coincide. A few sketches remark on their subjects' exceptional qualities, as when they attribute "uncommon intelligence" to poet Phillis Wheatley or describe Sojourner Truth as a "singular and impressive" figure and "orator of a superior type."[73] Although the authors represented some women's lives as exceptional, they also diminished the distance between everyday readers and extraordinary figures. Many authors thus argued that any reader could aspire to the extraordinary and that "ordinary" women, in fact, exhibit a quiet, overlooked greatness. The everyday eminence of these women is, in several cases, illustrated by citing the gratitude that others have expressed to them. Readers learn, for instance, of young mothers who were grateful for the generosity of "Aunt Mac," successful students who were grateful for the influence of Miss Patterson, and parents who were grateful for the "devoted service" of teacher Miss Baldwin.[74]

Brown's sketch of Harriet Tubman presents an extraordinary woman who possessed remarkably ordinary qualities. On the opening page, Brown asserted that Tubman could be "justly styled a Homespun Heroine" and immediately followed that statement by claiming that Tubman is "in a class to herself."[75] Brown juxtaposed Tubman's exceptional achievements with her humbler characteristics throughout the sketch, subtly arguing that even ordinary women can achieve renown. A notable example appears in the beginning of the sketch, as the narrator explains that Tubman, also called "General Moses," was "an Amazon in strength and endurance" who appeared to be "a most ordinary specimen of humanity" and "yet in point of courage, shrewdness, and disinterested exertions to rescue her fellow men she had no equal."[76] In this passage, Brown shifted back and forth between the exceptional ("an Amazon") to ordinary and back again to exceptional ("she had no equal"), weaving these qualities together so that they became inseparable in her subject. Maritcha Lyons's sketch of Tubman likewise dramatically juxtaposes such features, asserting that "in personal appearance, Harriet was ordinary to the point of repulsiveness."[77] This interweaving seems geared toward engaging the audience, who might otherwise tune out endless hymns praising godlike figures. Instead, the rhetorical tacking between extraordinary and ordinary invites readers to recognize themselves in even the most exceptional lives.

In an inverse rhetorical move, other sketches select obscure women to argue that an ordinary life can be viewed as extraordinary. Several of Maritcha Lyons's profiles take up this theme. For instance, Lyons begins her sketch of New England abolitionist Sarah Harris Fayerweather by describing the nineteenth century's "great political activity," which swept up the famous and the unknown alike.[78] The narrator explains that she chose Fayerweather "to exemplify a group of unhonored heroes" who were often considered "too commonplace to merit record or comment."[79] Connecting this sketch to others on this theme, Lyons stated that Fayerweather was "representative," and, in fact, that such women "were to be found everywhere."[80] Fayerweather's virtuous life and actions were typical, not exceptional, thus making her all the more meaningful as an exemplar to contemporary Black women. Sarah Fayerweather and "her noble band of sisters," declared Lyons, are "a precious legacy to our women of today."[81]

Lyons's introduction to her profile of poet Henrietta Cordelia Ray articulates a similar view through the use of natural metaphors. This eloquent passage exemplifies that language: "A tiny rill has its mission as well as a majestic river. Aggregated rain drops unite to form mighty billows. The faint flush of dawn though lacking the resplendence of cloudless noon, is none the less a direct emanation from the primal source of light."[82] By fashioning Ray's poetic contributions as the "tiny rill," "rain drop," or "faint flush of dawn," Lyons both established Ray as part of a larger artistic force and associated her with more illustrious Black female writers such as Phillis Wheatley and Frances Ellen Watkins Harper.[83] The sketch argues emphatically that it is worthwhile to know about women like Ray, because even a "minor bard" can "give and receive joy in proportion to [her] ability and [. . .] opportunity."[84] Lyons explained that most of her biographical subjects likewise "had during their existence reputations that were limited and local" yet influenced many in their families and communities.[85] Although Lyons did not represent unfamiliar individuals as identical to figures such as Harriet Tubman, she argued that reading about lesser known women was especially edifying because they were nearer to the experiences of readers. "Any record of good repute attached to the lives of even the obscure," Lyons opined, "embraces much that is illuminating . . . [to] every day folk."[86] She later further elevated these obscure individuals by remarking that "all consistently good women are truly great women."[87] This statement—seemingly an aside—argues that the greatness of Black women derives not from their exceptional notoriety but from their everyday piety. Lyons introduced this idea in other sketches as well, including that of Agnes Adams. The narrator notes that "good women" like Adams are "in daily evidence," to be found "among us [in] countless numbers."[88] Lyons thus suggested that, among Black women, virtue is common, typical, expected.

By blurring the lines between the exceptional and the everyday, these sketches challenge assumptions about which lives deserve to be remembered and celebrated. The collection also implicitly argues for expanding the group of Black women to whom subsequent generations should be grateful. This argument appears both in Brown's introductory framing of the volume as a "token of appreciation" and in individual sketches including expressions of gratitude.[89] The collection instructs audiences in a capacious practice of gratitude for *all* Black women's lives. In so doing, the authors of the sketches actively theorized both historical significance and exemplarity for Black American women.

Remembering and Rejoicing in Black Female Excellence

A third theme that shapes this collection is the idea that Black women exhibited excellence in their work and that this excellence is represented as a source of joy for them, for those they encountered, and for Black readers. In reflecting on all varieties of Black women's excellence, the sketches invite shared expressions of joy and gratitude. The lives of these Black women were undoubtedly marked by "the toils, vigils and prayers of the many whose lives have been lived in shade," yet this collection also recognizes the joyful aspects of their work.[90] The idea of work—especially on behalf of one's beloved community—as joyful is evident in two verses included in the collection: one by Sarah G. Jones as an epigraph and the other by Susie Lankford Shorter. Both poems were used by the Ohio Federation of Women's Clubs. As Jones wrote in her "Ode to Women," "The 'Joy of Service,' her fond heart endures / From infancy, through many years / Of development; mingled with faith, hope and trust, / She builds to the great, the good and the just, / That the Future may fairly decide."[91] Such service may include difficult work to be "endured," but Jones suggested that the "joy" came from the way in which one's work was oriented toward the "great, the good and the just." In similar fashion, Shorter's poem—which, when sung to the tune of "Glory, Glory, Hallelujah," became the Ohio Federation Song—presents Black women's obligation to uplift as a source of deep joy: "We must give our time and talent— / and the hungry must be fed, / We must root up sin and sadness, / planting good and joy instead, / Our motto, 'Deeds not words.'"[92] These poets issued a call to Black women not to lives of subservient drudgery and toil but toward the self-conscious choice to serve their communities and thereby create a source of lasting joy for other Black women. Such celebration of women's service operates comfortably within the boundaries of respectable womanhood while reframing Black womanhood as a public identity. The lyrics thus encourage female readers to take action and invest in their Black communities.

The sketches in *Homespun Heroines* cultivate feelings of joy and gratitude by narrating how Black women enjoyed their own lives while also bringing pleasure to those around them and providing a source of delight for future readers.[93] Randall Burkett observed that the women profiled in this collection were "extraordinarily talented" and that most used their talents in multiple fields.[94] To capture the range of excellence, therefore, this final section focuses on Black women's achievements in four broad categories: as performers, teachers, artists and craftswomen, and community figures.

The enjoyment of writing and reading about the achievements of Black women comes across clearly in M. M. Marshall's sketch of singer and music teacher Madam Emma Azalia Hackley. At six pages, it is one of the longer sketches. The author communicated her admiration for Hackley even in the subtitle, which reads, "Mme. E. Azalia Hackley, Singer, Musician, Humanitarian; *a Woman who has made her Life a Masterpiece*."[95] The use of such language suggests that Marshall presented Hackley as worthy of admiration in part because her life itself was a kind of work of art, a thing of beauty. Along the same lines, the word "love" appears frequently—twelve times—in the sketch, in most cases either professing Hackley's love for her work and her race or people's love for Hackley. The narrator tells us that, even before birth, Hackley's mother bequeathed to her daughter a "love of music and faith in the Negro's voice as a medium and power for good," as well as a "love of duty" and "love of service."[96] In her adulthood, the narrator explains, Hackley was presented with the "tantalizing temptation" to pass for White, yet this "loyal race woman" firmly rejected this temptation. The narrator immediately frames this example as a sound justification for admiration, saying "This is one reason why we loved her." The sketch continues, "She loved her race, and has proven it, time and again."[97] Hackley's love for her race also expressed itself specifically in her love of "Negro folk songs," the appreciation and teaching of which she made the focus of her later career. According to the narrator, Hackley was "a pioneer teaching the masses to love their folk songs."[98] The sketch claims that her commitment to this educational vision also brought her enjoyment: "She was so dead in earnest about musical social uplift that sacrifices and total self-effacement were a pleasure to her."[99] Throughout this sketch, Marshall characterized her subject as a person who derived great joy from her work, and her mode of representing Hackley also communicates that remembering her life can bring joy, as can the appreciation of a beautiful musical performance.

As perhaps the most common (and often only) professional pursuit for educated women during this time, teaching became an important source of joy both for women engaged in it and for women remembering these inspiring instructors. Burkett observed that one-third of the women profiled were identified as teachers.[100] Two separate profiles illustrate how remembering the work of great teachers can be enjoyable and encouraging. At ten and eleven pages, respectively, the profiles of Victoria Earle Matthews and Maria Louise Baldwin are two of the longest sketches in the collection. Frances Keyser's profile of Matthews, for instance, recalls her own visits to the "little mission rooms" where Matthews taught, saying "it was a joy and an inspiration to see the enthusiasm with which this attractive young woman . . . gave herself to the work of teaching these neglected little ones."[101] Her firsthand observation further enabled her to describe the "pleasing picture" of Matthews "surrounded by these little ones, each clamoring for a place next to her."[102] Keyser's account throughout the sketch draws attention to her own eyewitness position, first during her visits to Matthews's schools then in her position as the assistant superintendent of Matthews's White Rose Home.[103]

In a similar fashion, Brown's sketch of Baldwin utilizes the tributes of parents and colleagues to provide firsthand accounts of this woman's remarkable career as a teacher. For much of her career, Baldwin served as a teacher, principal, and finally "master" of the Agassiz School in Cambridge,

Massachusetts, which was populated by five hundred students, mostly White.[104] Baldwin died suddenly, leaving the school community bereft. The tributes quoted by Brown demonstrated that Baldwin occupied a treasured place in the hearts of her students, their parents, and her colleagues. Both the tributes and the sketch itself repeatedly use words such as "gratitude," "debt," and "appreciation" to capture community members' feelings toward Baldwin.[105] Like Brown's other sketches, this one uses carefully selected language (even that of others) to evoke feelings of gratitude as readers learn about another remarkable and yet familiar woman of their race.

The sketch of Baldwin also illustrates how authors crafted layered, textured meditations on Black female excellence rather than rosy paeans. For instance, one tribute shares a poignant story that illustrates what the anonymous author described as Baldwin's "deep feeling" and "her sensitiveness to the wrong done to those to whom she belonged and loved."[106] The author explained that it occurred when the film *The Birth of a Nation* premiered in Boston, presumably sometime between its 1915 release and Baldwin's death in 1922. The author explained that Baldwin felt that the screening was "an insult . . . to the race itself."[107] The narrator of the original anecdote (presumably White) reported that they had gathered "some of the colored race" to express goodwill toward them during that trying time, and the author asked them to "read from Paul Dunbar's poems" and "sing 'My Country, 'Tis of Thee.'" Baldwin declined, saying, "Please do not sing that then for it would break my heart when I know of the feeling of so many in Boston and throughout the country, who do not recognize truly the fact that this is our country. I might sing it another time, but not now."[108] This anecdote is striking and significant in its ability to represent Baldwin as a multidimensional human being who experienced both moments of "high idealism" and "depression."[109] By including these many tributes, Brown insisted on remembering Baldwin in the fullness of her humanity as a Black woman—a revolutionary choice for this moment, yet one also aligned with practices of Black women's memory work.

In addition to achieving excellence in specialized fields and success in teaching, the Black women profiled in this collection were gifted craftswomen. The most affecting story illustrating this area of expertise appears in the profile of Mrs. Jane Roberts, wife of Joseph Jenkins Roberts, the "first African President of Liberia."[110] Although the profile is ostensibly focused on Jane Roberts, a quarter of the text is devoted to a story about Martha Ann Ricks. The sketch notes that Mrs. Roberts met Queen Victoria twice: once with her husband and a second time when accompanying Liberian citizen Ricks. The narrator explains that Ricks, who was "famous for her patch work quilts,"[111] had been working on a quilt for the Queen for 25 years.[112] Although others laughed at her insistence that she would present the finished product to the Queen, "Mrs. Roberts saw and admired the quilt, heard the story and the way was found."[113] According to this account, Mrs. Roberts was captured not only by the fine handiwork but also by Ricks's determination and confidence in her abilities, as evinced in her "story." The sketch includes a vividly detailed description of the quilt to illustrate and emphasize Ricks's skill: It "showed a complete coffee tree all in green and yellow on white ground—its branches and leaves perfectly formed, the flowers at the root of the leaves and its berries—exquisite in traces and workmanship."[114] This concise yet rich imagery supplies a prime example of what Aristotle described as "bringing before the eyes," a rhetorical technique with which sketch author Brown would have been well acquainted. The sketch then continues by imagining the emotional outcome of the trip to England: "On reaching London a meeting was arranged and Aunt Martha stood in a palace and had the joy, after years of patience and perseverance, to present in person her quilt which was graciously accepted by that noblest of sovereigns, the Queen of Great Britain and Empress of all India, Victoria Regina."[115] By explaining that Ricks had "stood in a palace," presented the quilt "in person," and had the opportunity to have her quilt "graciously accepted" by this respected ruler, the passage demonstrates that the Queen welcomed Ricks—a formerly enslaved Black woman—as an embodied person into her home. Using the Queen's official title underscores the dignity and significance of the situation. As if anticipating the objections to this fanciful scene, Brown offered readers evidence of the event, saying, "Today the workmanship of this humble African woman adorns a niche in the art collections of Windsor Castle."[116] This story of Martha Ricks elevates the skilled handiwork practiced by many Black women, presenting it as a source of joy and pride for intimates and sovereigns alike.

Finally, sketches in this collection highlight the individual, everyday excellence enacted by community figures. These individuals did not exhibit achievements that the White patriarchal society would accept as notable. Rather, they exhibited virtuous behavior oriented toward their communities. Sketches of such women provide further evidence of the blurred line between extraordinary and ordinary women throughout the collection. Although this can be seen in several sketches about the lives of respected community members such as "Granny Gross," "Grandma Pyles," and "Aunt Mac," I focus on the sketch of Hannah MacDonald ("Aunt Mac"), as it provides the best illustration of the approach.[117] Moreover, the account exemplifies Hallie Quinn Brown's signature rhetorical style—rich description, vivid imagery, and a sentimental tone. Brown divided this narrative into three "chapters": The first focuses on childhood and young adulthood, the second describes her time in Wilberforce, and the third relates the days after Aunt Mac's death. Like many other sketches, this one begins by describing the hardships faced by the subject as a child. Young Hannah Morris had moved from Virginia to Kentucky with her family. Her parents died when she was still young, and the children's care and inheritance were not executed fairly. Having been deprived of an education and "defrauded of thirty thousand dollars," the children were "thrown upon their own responsibilities."[118] Even in the midst of these difficulties, the narrator insists that "each attained honorable manhood and womanhood."[119] Hannah married in 1833 but was widowed after only seven years. At that point, Hannah went to live with her sister in Cincinnati and finally in Wilberforce, Ohio.[120]

The second chapter begins with a lush description: "We find ourselves standing in a large grove where tall symmetrical trees nod and wave to each passing breeze. Nicely-kept paths intersect each other, winding here and there and leading to the neat cottages that stand in orderly rows on either side of the campus."[121] At the end of her description, the narrator declares, "What an enchanted spot is this!"[122] Then, directly engaging with the reader, she asks, "Can you not recognize the place, dear friend? Ah! yes, you say, 'tis the name so dear to many, the oft-repeated name of Wilberforce."[123] In 1856, Wilberforce, Ohio, became the site of Wilberforce University, the first historically Black college owned and operated by Black Americans. By inviting readers to imagine or recall this place, the passage locates them within a rich site of African-American memory. The core of the sketch then focuses on Aunt Mac, who was so closely associated with that place in the community's memory. These two central paragraphs describe Hannah MacDonald's place within the community as "everybody's Aunt Mac."[124] Brown used her characteristic homespun metaphors and sentimental language to evoke the feelings that this woman fostered in her community. The following passage illustrates Brown's choices: "All the little ones for miles around knew and loved her. She had a kind word for Willie and a caress for Jennie, and when in the height of their childish sports her laugh would ring out and mingle with theirs in innocent glee. And such a laugh! I wish you might have heard it! It was like the rippling of some happy stream, so cheery its sound and so full of hearty good will. She was the very providence, too, of the whole neighborhood."[125] Specific names such as Willie and Jennie ground the description, and direct address invites readers further into Brown's recollection. As if anticipating reader objections that this person is too good to be true, Brown concluded the "chapter" by saying, "This, dear reader, is no fiction, but a glimpse only of one of the most beautiful, Christian characters that was ever perfected for immortality."[126] The lofty, sentimental phrasing brings Aunt Mac—an "ordinary" woman—into the orbit of immortality.[127] Although the language strongly implies that the sketch was based on an eyewitness account, nowhere did Brown explicitly draw attention to her source of information.

The final chapter describes the community's mourning after their beloved Aunt Mac's death. Brown yielded to high melodrama in these final paragraphs, concluding with the declaration that the community will "miss her forever" yet can take comfort in being able to "set up a tablet in the heart" with a loving inscription to the "sacred" memory of Aunt Mac.[128] Although a similar account by a White author might evoke images of the "mammy," Brown's narrative conveys a sense of deep love and respect that dignifies rather than diminishes its subject. By firmly grounding Aunt Mac's story in the place of Wilberforce, Brown revealed the magnitude of a life that brought joy and encouragement to Black communities. Aunt Mac is connected to no major figures, no historical events or social movements, but her memory is embedded in and shapes a community that celebrates Black love and Black excellence.

Collected Memories, Collective Feelings

Homespun Heroines is both a representative and an exemplary instance of the unique genre of women's collective biography. It is also a unique case for advancing the study of Black women's community memory work in the 1920s—a time when the New Negro Movement celebrated African-American arts and literature and the Nineteenth Amendment opened new opportunities for women. Often an afterthought in advancements of "the race" as well as "their sex," Black women in the interwar period needed more than ever to create commemorative space for their intersectional identities. To understand how Black women created such space, we must look past the formidable memorials and monuments to the humbler "homespun" memories that Black women produced for their own communities.

A collection of such diverse lives invites myriad feelings, from despair to delight. In this chapter, I focused on the feelings of gratitude and joy, specifically, to demonstrate how Black women used the common, even mundane, rhetorical form of the multibiography to uplift their communities while also acknowledging their shared struggles. Initially, it might appear that highlighting positive feelings like gratitude and joy constitutes a Pollyanna-ish approach to traumatic experiences such as enslavement and racial discrimination. However, as scholars such as Ahad-Legardy, Brock, and others argue, it can be misleading and even detrimental for storytellers and scholars to focus exclusively on trauma when considering the history of Black Americans. Referring to the pronounced ambivalence about Southern Blackness, Stewart observes, "In our haste to rid the public sphere of southern Black joy, we miss the danger in confining our stories to racial sorrow."[129]

Focusing on the positive communal feelings invited by this collection yields several important insights about Black American women's community memory work. First, it shows how these Black women writers marshaled their rhetorical skills to acknowledge both the deep pain and the great joy in the lives of their foremothers. They thereby rejected simplistic accounts of Black lives as either doomed to despair or blissfully free of suffering. This is important not only as a historical claim about rhetorical activity of the period but also because it attests to the long history that grounds contemporary efforts to honor Black joy. Second, examining this collection's evocation of gratitude and joy supplies evidence of the rhetorical skill and savvy of Black women in the face of numerous constraints, including the politics of respectability. The politics of respectability, according to historian Evelyn Brooks Higginbotham "emphasized reform of individual behavior and attitudes as a goal in itself and as a strategy for reform of the entire structural system of American race relations."[130] As Higginbotham and other scholars have noted, the discourse of respectability enabled middle-class Black women of the period to enact traditional feminine morals while also advancing more radical forms of protest. Celebrating and expressing gratitude for the lives of virtuous Black women would have been, at the time, an acceptable activity for upstanding African-American women. Yet doing so also provided these authors and their audiences the space to preserve their own memories and to build a supply of stories from which they could build powerful critiques of White public memories, if they later chose to do so. Third, foregrounding gratitude reveals the rhetorical power of feelings to connect women of different time periods. Exhorting readers to feel gratitude toward their foremothers can seem like an empty piety, but in this instance, it cultivates a sense of historical continuity for women of a race purported to have no history. This expression of gratitude also participates in the Black cultural practice of ancestor acknowledgment, as described by Temple.[131] Just as Black women speakers acknowledged exemplary women, the creators of *Homespun Heroines* gave thanks for lives that continued to inspire. Finally, attending to joy, as Brown put it in the introduction, both in the writing and in the reading of these lives shows how this volume may have served to develop affiliative resources among contemporaries, which, in turn, would enable them to act politically on behalf of their communities. In *Homespun Heroines,* we see the joy of community memory work.

Epilogue

Abundance, Memory, Risk

It was 1863, in the depths of the US Civil War and the dawn of emancipation. Sarah Woodson addressed fellow educators assembled for a meeting of the Ohio Colored Teachers' Association. An Ohio native and 1856 graduate of Oberlin College, Sarah Woodson (later Early) taught at Wilberforce University and would eventually address the crowds at the 1893 World's Congress of Representative Women. Her 1863 speech, "Address to the Youth," exhorted young people to pursue education and intellectual development. As I described in chapter 3, Woodson regularly addressed White audiences and cooperated with White women in her national temperance work, yet the lion's share of her advocacy invested in Black communities—especially schools and churches. Moreover, Woodson inherited a commitment to Black nationalism from her parents and older siblings (she was the youngest of eleven) that powerfully shaped her approach to her communities.

Woodson's reflections on history in this 1863 speech manifest her Black nationalist commitments and attest to the significance of community memory work. Although she lamented the lack of historical records featuring the "brave and noble" of her people, she theorized how education might reveal great deeds of the past and produce great deeds in the present:

> If you take a retrospect of the past, you perceive that in the darkest periods, when truth and virtue appeared to sleep, when science had dropped her telescope and philosophy its torch, when the world would have seemed to be standing still, the inscrutable wisdom of Divine

> Providence was preparing new agents, and evolving new principles, to aid in the work of individual and social improvement.
>
> It would appear as if the world, like the year, had its seasons; and that the seed disseminated in spring time, must first die before it can vegetate and produce the rich harvests of autumn. The developments of one period seem obscured for a season, by the unfolding of the great mysterious curtain, by which to disclose the glories of the next.[1]

Woodson reassured her audience that "new agents," "new principles," and "developments" were waiting to be revealed as the years unfolded. Using familiar farming and light–dark metaphors, Woodson reasoned that deeds done in the past and yet unknown may emerge at some future time, just as deeds done in obscurity in the present may also emerge in their season of fruitfulness. She recognized that stories from the past may be stored like seeds in some other place, by some previous people (or Providence), waiting for a time when they might blossom again. Although she did not speak explicitly of Black communities here, Woodson's audience and record indicate that she had them in mind.

Woodson's words also seem to reach out from the past and point to those of another Black woman writer, Maya Angelou:

> You may write me down in history
> With your bitter, twisted lies,
> You may trod me in the very dirt
> But still, like dust, I'll rise [. . .]
>
> I rise
> Bringing the gifts that my ancestors gave,
> I am the dream and the hope of the slave [. . .][2]

In her poem "And Still I Rise," Angelou deployed the same seed and soil metaphors to communicate her vision of persistence and flourishing. Angelou's poem also weaves together both community memory ("the gifts that my ancestors gave") and critical memory ("your bitter, twisted lies"), showing their intimate connections. Both Woodson and Angelou perceived the potentialities of Black memory and its ability to persist through time. Utilizing cultivation metaphors, both women also emphasized the patience and care required of those tending to memory work.

While I was working on this book, journalist and scholar Nikole Hannah-Jones became the face of Black women's critical memory work.

Hannah-Jones has often been reduced to a lone figure seeking to correct whitewashed historical narratives, but her work has been collective, both within her temporal moment and across historical periods. Referring to herself in her social media profiles as "Ida Bae Wells," Hannah-Jones pays homage to the journalistic pioneer Ida B. Wells, a Black woman who likewise used her role to advance a cause significant to Black people: changing public opinion and laws about lynching. Hannah-Jones's work on the *New York Times*'s "1619 Project" garnered her the 2020 Pulitzer Prize. The landing page of her website prominently features this statement: "I see my work as forcing us to confront our hypocrisy, forcing us to confront the truth that we would rather ignore." Using the words "forcing" and "confront" twice each in this short sentence communicates Hannah-Jones's commitment to critical memory work. Her investigative journalism, opinion writing, speaking, podcasting, and social media engagement likewise evinces this approach. Both Hannah-Jones and her collaborators perform critical memory work that, to borrow Houston Baker's words, "judges severely, censures righteously, renders hard ethical evaluations."[3] Her projects directly and deliberately seek to correct mainstream—typically White and male—narratives about the past. She intentionally invokes the memory of Black women who preceded her, including activist journalists such as Wells.

Women such as Hannah-Jones have made incredible strides in shifting Black people toward the center of the conversation about public memory in the United States. Without downplaying the work of such women, we can also note that White discourse in the United States frames them primarily as critics. They are consistently typecast (and sometimes caricatured) in that role, portrayed as brash debunkers of false histories. Such a position can be rhetorically expedient, as it goads opponents and rallies sympathetic allies to the cause. However, it also dramatically limits the public legibility of the other forms of building and theorizing that contemporary Black women memory workers do. Hannah-Jones's transition to the professoriate supplies a notable example. After being offered a position at the University of North Carolina, Chapel Hill (UNC), Hannah-Jones was not granted tenure upon hire. UNC subsequently reconsidered their decision and offered tenure to Hannah-Jones, who then turned it down in favor of a position in the journalism department at Howard University.[4] Hannah-Jones has noted of her time at the prominent historically Black university, "I feel like we come from a collective community that understands that our own individual success is insignificant if everyone else around us is suffering." The Howard *Hilltop* student newspaper article went on to note that Hannah-Jones "credits all of her success to her community and people who came before her and fought for the rights that she now benefits from."[5] Hannah-Jones' critical memory work is most visible to the US public, but her community work is equally significant.

I draw together these two examples of Woodson and Hannah-Jones to highlight the historical continuity of Black women's memory work from the nineteenth century into the twenty-first century. Both of these women were driven to public address and activism by a desire to serve Black communities and advance their interests through education—in particular, historical education. Both of these women were also cognizant of the power of dominant memories and the necessity of challenging them. I read them together, just as I read the case studies in this book in conversation, to explore how certain features of Black women's memory work have persisted and evolved over time. I also read these cases through the Black feminist tradition to explore and, as Ashley Hall put it, "identify a certain kind of continuity between the rhetorical strategies that Black women employ in the past and the present, collapsing linear configurations of time and space predicated on white humanity and Black death."[6] I view the memory work of Black women like Woodson, Anna Julia Cooper, Hallie Quinn Brown, Maude Nooks Howard, Beatrice Cannady, Nikole Hannah-Jones and many others as a continuous, evolving tradition nourished by the similarly evolving tradition of Black feminist thought. By bringing these rhetorical practices together across time, the analysis in this book also responds to Kent Ono's call for enriched intersectional rhetorical analyses. Ono argued that, in addition to intersectional rhetorical analyses that examine multiple identities and axes of marginalization, "There is a need [. . .] for diachronic and vertical thinking in intersectional analysis, as well—that is, chronicling a group and groups across time and era."[7] This book has chronicled the memory work of Black American women from Reconstruction into the New Negro Movement, showing a coherent yet far from monolithic set of rhetorical practices attuned to these Black women's own intersectional experiences.

This book deepens understanding of the memory work of Black American women by developing a more robust representation of their rhetorical efforts in that field. Rather than focus only on critique, this book has examined memory work that builds community, advances critique, and combines the two. I have also shown how rhetorical efforts to shape our shared memories constitute a form of activism. In some cases, Black women's memory work lays the groundwork for future activism—whether by providing clubwomen experience in organizing or by theorizing about the role that history ought to play in the work of liberation. Memory work also provides a respite from activism by sustaining Black communities through positive stories about their ancestors or cultivating affiliative community feelings. In other cases, the memory work *is* activism—as when leaders such as Mary Church Terrell and the members of the PWYWCA published their written protests of the proposed "Mammy" monument. The cases examined in this book thus demonstrate that memory work can serve as a key feature of the rhetoric of social movements. The remainder of this epilogue outlines some of the things I learned while writing this book, which I believe holds value for readers who are interested in Black women's rhetoric, memory, history, and related fields. Specifically, I focus on what this book taught me about rhetoric's abundance, memory's meanings, and the critic's risk.

Rhetoric's Abundance

This book is nourished by rhetoric's abundance and pluralism, seeking to integrate theory, criticism, and historical research. I undertook this book from an understanding of the rhetorical critic's work that resonates with Kirt Wilson's "functionalist" approach to what he calls "theory/criticism."[8] Wilson argues that, in such an approach, "the purity of a theory or the authority of any critical practice is less important than what they do and how they accomplish what they do."[9] Rather than reduce the work of rhetorical criticism or the rhetors themselves, this understanding expands both by framing rhetorical criticism as the process of *opening* a text or set of texts. Angela G. Ray articulated something similar in a 2016 essay on the "state of the art" of rhetorical criticism. She described the field to which she was initially attracted as "riotously profligate in its object focus," and she further noted that specialization within that field "is the basis for abundance in a pluralistic enterprise."[10] These conceptualizations of rhetorical criticism envision the work of the critic as expansive, abundant, creative—all values I have worked to inhabit as I wrote this book.

Completing this project convinced me that a functionalist understanding of rhetorical theory and criticism can open our perspective to the creative use of rhetoric in various contexts. A functionalist perspective is beneficial for those interested in expanding understanding of the rhetorical activities of marginalized rhetors, such as Black women in the United States. As Ronisha Browdy reminds us, "Black Women's Rhetoric(s) is disruptive, resistant, alternative, and creative because it has to be."[11] I examine "traditional" texts of public address, such as speeches; I also look to less studied examples such as biographical sketches. Drawing on this variety of texts expands the range of what might be considered rhetorical activities, especially when engaged by less dominant groups. Examining a body of texts including public speeches, opinion pieces, petitions, biography collections, and even fictionalized newspaper editorials demonstrates the myriad ways that Black women used the rhetorical tools at their disposal to advocate for the kinds of memories that they believed would nourish their communities and fuel their public advocacy.

Examining a variety of texts also demonstrates the abundance of Black women's rhetorics more generally. Although they have not often seemed abundant, Black women's rhetorics have "been here," as scholars such as Olga Idriss Davis and Browdy have shown, whether or not the broader field of rhetorical studies has acknowledged them.[12] This book is not a project of recovery or inclusion but an effort to center Black women as agents of knowledge, as skillful rhetors, as powerful theorists, and as sophisticated memory workers. This book contributes to the field of Black women's rhetoric(s) that Browdy has staked out, as well as to the field of rhetorical studies more broadly. Although I have sometimes been encouraged to do so, my primary goal is not to show how Black women have used the same strategies as White rhetors or to show, through sustained comparison, how their rhetoric contrasts with that of rhetors who are not Black women. Rather, it is to read Black women's rhetorics within their own theoretical and historical contexts, relying on methods derived from Black feminist thought and Black women's experiences. Doing so secondarily enhances our understanding of humanity in all its complexity. As Browdy has explained, "Multiple awareness of the truths of Black womanhood, as well as awareness of the hateful acts and reasoning for destroying those truths, are often vocalized within Black Women's Rhetoric(s). These multi-conscious and multi-voiced representations are a part of what allows this work to speak across, and be useful to, multiple and mixed audiences."[13] Learning about Black women's memory work can benefit people across social positions and categories. The pluralism of rhetoric here intersects with the multivocality of Black feminist thought to yield an abundance of insight.

Memory's Meanings

This book also advances scholarship on rhetoric and public memory by (re) introducing the concept of memory work and developing the supporting concepts of community and critical memory work. I have found memory work to be a more capacious and critically generative term than *public memory*, which can be both naggingly nebulous and oddly exclusive of nondominant rhetorical forms. Although the unique contours of community and critical memory work emerged from examining Black women's rhetorics, I believe that these concepts may also be applicable in other contexts, with some adjustment.

Four additional insights on memory have continued to return to me as I've worked on this project. First, studying this variety of texts through the lens of Black feminist thought enabled me to see the equal importance of community memory work and critical memory work. Although I think that examining one or the other is certainly a valid and sometimes necessary intellectual choice, it seemed that the texts themselves and the rhetorical efforts of Black women required that any analysis acknowledge their equal commitment to nourishing Black communities and advancing critiques of Whiteness. Indeed, as Hine and Squires (among others) have noted, often those two goals work together.[14] Thinking about both community and critical memory work also provides an opportunity to consider the role of the audience. The texts examined in this project addressed fellow Black women, White women, Black men, and interracial audiences. These rhetors astutely adjusted their claims and arguments to disarm preexisting prejudices, which were numerous. The texts in this book show both the individual rhetorical skill and collective rhetorical activism that Black women were engaging in during this time period. The fact that these women presented their memory work differently, depending on the audience, furthermore demonstrates how their rhetorical savvy not only applied to traditional rhetorical aims but also was animated by broader purposes.

Second, reading these rhetorical texts alongside Black studies treatments of memory and Black feminist scholarship enabled me to think more holistically about the affective dimensions of Black women's memory work. The rhetoric of Black women examined in this book makes it clear that they understood that their representations of the past were shot through with important, sometimes conflicting, feelings. They lamented how they could be "disheartened" by history's "seasons of darkness," and they celebrated the "pleasure" that could be had when reading about the lives of "self-sacrificing heroines."[15] They did not eschew negative or positive emotion but embraced affective tension, and they did so in ways as varied as the women themselves. Thus, reading these texts also supports the claims advanced by contemporary scholars such as Badia Ahad-Legardy and Christel N. Temple that Black memories include traumatic experiences but are not defined by them.[16]

Third, reading these texts revealed how Black women memory workers theorize their relationship to and experience of time. Across the speeches, biographies, and petitions, Black women in the United States exhibited a keen awareness that time could and should be rhetorically manipulated to better reflect their reality. Black women during Reconstruction, for example, spoke of the importance of education to reconstruct a Black past that had been obscured by enslavement and White supremacy. Black women during the 1890s redefined "progress" to account for both the deprivations of enslavement and the inestimable potential of educated and organized Black womanhood. Black women during the early twentieth century—the height of lynching and anti-Black violence—saw their present as intimately connected to their future, which positioned the audience for their memory work as not only their contemporaries but also generations to come. Much of the memory work described in this study insists on the right of Black women to determine their own temporalities and, often, to do so in ways that emphasize connections among past, present, and future. Through these rhetorical manipulations of time, Black women theorize about temporality in ways that resonate with the arguments of philosopher Charles Mills and rhetoric scholars Ersula Ore and Matthew Houdek.[17] Mills calls for an "oppositional racial chronopolitics" that contests White time by identifying itself with "historical narratives that also seek to explain the present and stake particular claims on the future."[18] Ore and Houdek specifically highlight the "role of Black women as those who push the countertemporalities of Black life, healing, and struggle into the public arena, and in doing so demonstrate what it means to breathe in times of suffocation."[19] Listening to the voices of these Black women of the past demonstrates how they, too, participated in articulating new temporalities that centered themselves and, in some cases, countered "suffocating" White time. Black women memory workers are theorists of time.

Fourth, Black women used these self-defined temporalities to theorize that collecting memories could combat erasure and serve as a storehouse from which future generations could draw to enable their activism. Although much memory scholarship emphasizes that public or collective memory is driven by present concerns, attention to Black women's rhetorical activities demonstrates that memory work is also animated by futurity. Many of these women seemed to recognize that their rhetoric would not find a large sympathetic audience in their present; indeed, some of them clearly stated that their rhetorical efforts were primarily oriented toward the future, as Hallie Quinn Brown did in her sketch about Harriet Tubman in *Homespun Heroines and Other Women of Distinction.*[20] In a sense, the storehouse of memory built by Black women inverts what Paul Ricoeur described in *Memory, History, Forgetting* as "forgetting held in reserve."[21] His analysis does not attend closely to the power dynamics inherent in this particular memory process. However, if we were to do so, we might think of this process from two perspectives: from those enforcing the "forgetting" and from those stewarding the "forgotten" memory so that it will not be completely erased. At the risk of oversimplifying, in this case, White America forgets the Black past; Black women remember it. It is important to remember that this storehouse of Black memory is not always primarily a critique of White hegemonic memory but a tool for survival and thriving in Black communities.

A Critic's Risks

Finally, I want to reflect on how writing this book has changed me, as a critic and as a person. Only a few short years after the murders of Breonna Taylor and George Floyd and the summer of 2020, many of us White Americans put away the Black Lives Matter signs we carried in protests, left behind the little black boxes and hashtags in our social media feeds, returned to our segregated spaces, and became consumed once again with our individual lives and the work of processing the trauma of a global pandemic. I, too, have struggled with the desire to give up the pursuit of justice and instead give in to despair and exhaustion. However, writing this book enabled me to persist in both risk and reflection, challenging me and fortifying me during this singular historical moment. It expanded my thinking about how we in the United States engage with African-American history, Black feminism, and the struggle for racial justice more broadly.

This book has been, for me, a continual invitation to the risks inherent in collective learning and collective struggle. It is a risk for me—a tenured White female scholar working at a predominantly White institution in a city where almost forty percent of my neighbors are Black—to write a book about the rhetorics of Black women.[22] The ethical demands of this book have obligated me to venture into new "contextual fields," as Kent Ono calls them and which I outlined in the introduction. Ono explains that "a contextual field may be the theory or theoretical field one uses to understand a text, the synchronic social-cultural context surrounding a text, or the diachronic history or genealogy that either anchors or situates the text temporally in some way."[23] This study has required me to engage with the Black feminist tradition more deeply, including reflecting on how I, as a White feminist scholar, should learn from this intellectual tradition and thereby do greater justice to the texts and voices of Black women. I have wrestled with the concept of intersectionality to understand what it might mean for a White feminist scholar to engage in intersectional analysis without performing something akin to what Michelle Colpean and Rebecca Dingo called "drive-by" race scholarship.[24] I have learned about womanist biblical interpretation and Afrocentric perspectives on memory and mythology. I have confronted the unsettling idea of a politics of refusal while interrogating my own education in a politics of recognition. Spending more time in these contextual fields is a risk as an "outsider," as a graduate student once described me in relation to my work. For as Ono reminds us, "doing deeply contextual work requires risks, risks of being found naïve, risks of offending members of groups about which one has no expertise."[25] Try as I might to avoid such outcomes, I cannot eliminate them. Such risks are, admittedly, different in both degree and kind from those faced by my colleagues of color, queer colleagues, disabled colleagues; yet they are risks, nonetheless. I have learned that doing this work "means opening oneself up to being evaluated by others and possibly being found to be inferior. Doing such research means being vulnerable; in being vulnerable in the face of others, a tremendous change in the world is possible."[26] In the midst of this imperfect and vulnerable work, I take heart from bell hooks' exhortation in *Teaching to Transgress*: "If we really want to create a cultural climate where biases can be challenged and changed, all border crossings must be seen as valid and legitimate."[27] I am certain that I have done this work imperfectly, and I am grateful for those willing to engage it in its imperfection.

More than anything, this book has been an opportunity for me to think through how we as human beings contextualize—but do not erase—traumatic experiences as we renarrate our pasts so that they do not paralyze us but, rather, enable us to continue acting. At times, the grief of the world and its relentless injustice felt like too much piled upon my own personal grief. I have also felt buried beneath heartache upon personal heartache, even as I, alongside others, have navigated the larger lamentations of environmental degradation and rising authoritarianism and collective pandemic trauma and racial injustice. While I was working on this book, I faced the death of a close friend, the loss of a child through a disrupted adoption, ongoing infertility, a confrontation with yet more broken systems through the adoption of our second child, and the separation from my local faith community. However, I didn't lose any close friends or family to COVID-19. I had housing, work, food, a support system, and access to health care. Writing this book has been, in many ways, an exercise in hope that has kept me afloat in the midst of grief, both personal and global. Although writing this book has buoyed me, I hope even more that the stories and voices amplified here will challenge and lift others as well, whether directly or indirectly. This book is about rhetoric and memory work; it's also about much more.

ACKNOWLEDGMENTS

A favorite picture book in our family is *Last Stop on Market Street*, rhythmically written by Matt de la Peña and memorably illustrated by Christian Robinson. The book follows a little boy, CJ, and his grandmother as they move through their city one Sunday. As they approach their final destination, CJ looks around him and wonders aloud, "How come it's always so dirty over here?" His nana responds, "Sometimes when you're surrounded by dirt, CJ, you're a better witness for what's beautiful." When my older daughter and I attended an author reading of the book in our then-home of Las Vegas, the author inscribed our copy of the book, "To Phoebe—Be a witness."

Although this book isn't explicitly about "witnessing" in a theoretical sense, my experience of writing it felt like bearing witness to the beauty of Black American women's memory work, past and present. It's an honor and a privilege to witness this work, and I'm grateful to all of the people who have done that work and helped me to see and better understand and appreciate it. As Christel N. Temple put it in her book *Black Cultural Mythology*, "Witnesses offer a testimony of remembrance." I offer this book as a testimony to the power of Black women's memory work.

First, some specific words of gratitude for assistance that folks offered me on particular aspects of research for this book. For chapter 1, I thank the editors, reviewers, and readers who gave me opportunities to conceptualize the community and critical memory work framing: Simone Drake, who invited me to write about memory for the *Oxford Handbook on African American Women's Writing*; the 2023 leadership of the Central States Communication Association Women's Caucus, for the encouragement they provided at that year's conference; and my colleagues and friends Leslie Harris and Shevaun Watson, who read versions of the chapter draft. For chapter 2, I thank my University of Nevada–Las Vegas graduate students Kacey

Ballard and Gabriella Tscholl for their work as research assistants during the initial stages of my work on this chapter, when I actually thought it was going to be part of an entirely different book. For chapter 3, I again thank Leslie Harris for her careful reading of a draft, the University of Wisconsin–Milwaukee (UWM) Department of African and African Diaspora Studies for inviting me to present this work at their symposium, and Karrin Vasby Anderson and my anonymous reviewers from the *Quarterly Journal of Speech* for their incisive comments on an earlier version of this chapter. For chapter 4, I'm grateful to Megan Fitzmaurice, whose 2016 National Communication Association paper helped me to better understand the rhetorical dynamics of Black women's responses to the proposed "Mammy" monument. For chapter 5, I thank Allyson Farzad-Phillips and Carly Woods for organizing a 2019 conference panel on feminist rhetorical memory, during which I was able to present the initial research for this chapter.

Now, for some more general thanks to the many people who have supported and encouraged me in my work on this book.

In October of 2023, I was able to convene a workshop to receive additional feedback on my book manuscript. Thanks to the generous startup funds I received from UWM, I was able to compensate the expert readers who carefully reviewed my manuscript, took time out of their schedules to travel to Milwaukee, shared their insightful commentary both verbally and in writing, and enthusiastically engaged with one another and the workshop attendees. This book was greatly enriched by the feedback of scholars Natasha Barnes, Kimberly Alecia Singletary, and Tracy Vaughn-Manley. I am especially grateful to Kim, who has shared with me her friendship, intelligence, humor, and incomparable editing skills for more than fifteen years. I appreciate everyone who attended the workshop—and a special nod to Sabrina Fuller Muñiz, who kept the trains running, as usual.

I'm grateful for my UWM colleagues, both in the Department of Communication and across the university. I am especially grateful for the colleagues and friends in my writing accountability group. There is no way that I could have persisted in writing this book through a global pandemic and after the death of one of my closest friends without their support. Over the past six years, various permutations of the following incredibly smart and savvy human beings participated in the group: Rachel Bloom-Pojar, Leslie Harris, Katie Vater, Shevaun Watson, and Lia Wolock. They have cheered me when my energy was flagging, challenged me when I needed a nudge, and laughed with me over innumerable beverages in various coffee shops across Milwaukee.

Scholars like me who do historical research are also dependent on archivists and librarians. I appreciate all of the painstaking and often progressive work done by these experts, especially UWM archivist Abigail Nye and Alexandra Villaseran at the US National Archives and Records Administration.

Thank you to all of the students who have taken my courses on African-American public discourse at the University of Nevada–Las Vegas and UWM. These students asked critical questions and urged me to articulate implicit theories and choices (in some cases, very directly: "Why do you teach so many speeches given by Black women?"). Moreover, they encouraged me to persist in this area of study and scholarship when I was sometimes tempted to abandon it. I also thank Derek Handley for partnering with me in an ongoing collaborative experiment to teach African-American rhetorics across the graduate and undergraduate curriculum at UWM and for being a great colleague and friend on "the other side" of rhetoric.

I am grateful to graduate advisees who have become friends and colleagues, especially Josh Miller, Scarlett Harrington, Darrian Carroll, the deeply missed Misti Yang, Alisa Hardy, Kristin Gates, Jessica Gehrke, Jillian Schemenauer, Cassandra Hightower, Carly Parr, and honorary advisee Alex Parr Balaram. I continue to learn from all of these folks. Thanks to all of the incredible graduate students I've had the pleasure to know and learn from.

I thank my own teachers and mentors, always Angela Ray most of all.

Thank you to my University of South Carolina Press editor Aurora Bell and series editor Vicki Gallagher for believing in this project and helping me shepherd it along its path to becoming a real book. I greatly appreciate their encouragement and advice and their wisdom in selecting thoughtful readers. Many thanks go to those anonymous readers also—reviewing book manuscripts is a time-consuming and often thankless task. I am very grateful for the energy, care, and attention to detail they invested in this project. These folks made this a richer, stronger book. Any errors or shortcomings of the work are entirely my own.

I could not do any of this without the support of community, friends, and family. I thank the Milwaukee Public Schools staff who nurture and teach my children. I thank my neighbors who make our corner of Milwaukee a hopeful and welcoming place to live. I thank friends far and near: my Milwaukee book group, Susan Sytsma Bratt, Jessica Bratt Carle, Kyla Ebels-Duggan, Kim Singletary (again) and the whole Kjersti Knox and Garrett Bucks family. My academic work is supported (and sometimes even read!) by people in both my family of origin and family of experience: my parents,

Ric and Julie VanderHaagen, and Phoebe Dobrowski; and my sister, Laura Gustafson; and our extended family through adoption, the Lamer-Davis family. Most of all, I thank my husband, Chris Verkaik, who has cared for our children, done our laundry, kept us fed, and performed the lion's share of household tasks so that I could focus on my work. I'm so very grateful for our two decades of partnership. Our children, Phoebe and Joanna, teach me daily about what it means to be a witness to beauty in our complex and messy human lives. I'm forever glad I get to witness their lives up close.

Speaking of other beauties, finally: I thank my gardens and all the beings who live there, both in Las Vegas and Milwaukee, for giving me work for my hands, delight for my senses, and wonder for my spirit.

NOTES

CHAPTER 1: "TO EMBALM HER MEMORY IN SONG AND STORY"

1. Genesis 1:2, New International Version.
2. Matthews, "The Awakening of the Afro-American Woman," in *Lift Every Voice*, 836.
3. Matthews, "The Awakening of the Afro-American Woman," in *Lift Every Voice*, 838.
4. Cox, *Dixie's Daughters*; McElya, *Clinging to Mammy*; Wallace-Sanders, *Mammy*.
5. See Cooper, *Beyond Respectability*, 10; O. I. Davis, "A Black Woman as Rhetorical Critic," 77–89; O. I. Davis, "Theorizing African American Women's Discourse," in *Centering Ourselves*, 35–51; S. Davis, "Taking Back the Power," 303; Gittens, "'What If I Am a Woman?'" 311; Houston and Davis, "Introduction," in *Centering Ourselves*, 3–4; Stanback, "Feminist Theory and Black Women's Talk," 188.
6. Campbell, "Style and Content in the Rhetoric of Early Afro-American Feminists," 434.
7. Davis, "A Black Woman as Rhetorical Critic," 77–89; Davis, "Theorizing African American Women's Discourse," 35–51.
8. Walker, *The Rhetoric of Struggle*; Logan, *We Are Coming*.
9. Although these books have had the most impact in rhetorical studies, monographs and collections about individual Black women rhetors have also advanced understanding in this area. Prominent examples include Marilynn Richardson's work on Maria W. Stewart, Maegan Parker Brooks's work on Fannie Lou Hamer, and Susan Pullon Fitch and Roseann Mandziuk's work on Sojourner Truth. See Richardson, ed. *Maria W. Stewart*; Brooks and Houck, eds. *The Speeches of Fannie Lou Hamer*; Brooks, *A Voice that Could Stir an Army*; Brooks, *Fannie Lou Hamer*; Fitch and Mandziuk, eds., *Sojourner Truth as Orator*. Scholars continue to add to these monographs; in no way should this list be considered exhaustive.
10. Browdy, "Black Women's Rhetoric(s)," n.p.
11. Eves, "A Recipe for Remembrance," 280–97; P. G. Davis, "The *Other* Southern Belles," 308–31.
12. Erll, "Travelling Memory," 4.
13. Olick, Sierp, and Wüsterberg, "Introduction: Taking Stock of Memory Studies," 1399.
14. Houdek and Phillips, "Public Memory," 3. For instance, representative recent books in the field on this subject include Aden, *Upon the Ruins of Liberty*; P. G. Davis, *Laying Claim*; Dunn, *Queerly Remembered*; Haskins, *Popular Memories*; and Tell, *Remembering Emmett Till*.

15. Yates, *The Art of Memory.*
16. VanderHaagen, *Children's Biographies of African American Women*, 23–34.
17. VanderHaagen, *Children's Biographies of African American Women*, 11.
18. Phillips, "Introduction," *Framing Public Memory*, 2.
19. Houdek and Phillips, "Public Memory," 3.
20. Blair, Dickinson, and Ott, "Introduction: Rhetoric/Memory/Place," *Places of Public Memory*, 6.
21. See, for instance, Toi Derricotte's 2018 poem "Joy is an act of resistance," 23; artist Kleaver Cruz's ongoing Black Joy Project (https://kleavercruz.com/the-black-joy-project); and 2021 videos by *The Root* editorial staff (https://www.theroot.com/you-get-some-black-joy-and-you-get-some-black-joy-eve-1846347970; and https://www.theroot.com/black-and-jubilant-unpacking-black-joy-from-the-revolu-1846288040).
22 Glymph, "'Liberty Dearly Bought,'" *Time Longer Than Rope*, 111–39; Brand, Inwood, and Alderman, "Truth-Telling and Memory-Work in Montgomery's Co-Constituted Landscapes," 468–83; Ohito, "Remembering My Memories," 1856–75. Mary E. Triece's *Memory Work: White Ignorance and Black Resistance in Popular Magazines, 1900–1910*, the only book in rhetorical studies that I am aware of that uses this concept, was published in late 2024, after this book was in press.
23. Kuhn, "A Journey Through Memory," *Memory and Methodology*, 186.
24. Scott, "The Evidence of Experience," 773–97.
25. Notable exceptions to this pattern are the few PhD dissertations focused on Black women's commemorative practices, including Russell, "Sites Seen and Unseen."
26. Blight, *Race and Reunion*. This omission is especially evident in chapter 9, "Black Memory and the Progress of the Race," in which Blight focused overwhelmingly on the efforts of prominent Black men like Frederick Douglass and Alexander Crummel to shape memories of slavery during the end of the nineteenth century. Although Frances E. W. Harper and Ida B. Wells both make brief appearances, their rhetoric was not substantively analyzed; nor did Blight cite any of the numerous speeches that Black women gave on "progress" during this period, many of which directly addressed the question of how Americans remember slavery.
27. Romano and Raiford, eds., *The Civil Rights Movement in American Memory.*
28. Kachun, *First Martyr of Liberty;* Hamilton, *Booker T. Washington in American Memory*; Dyson, *Making Malcolm.*
29. Sernett, *Harriet Tubman.*
30. Dickinson, Blair, and Ott, *Places of Public Memory*; P. G. Davis, *Laying Claim*; Tell, *Remembering Emmett Till.*
31. Ono, "Contextual Fields of Rhetoric," 266.
32. Saad, "Gallup Vault: Black Americans' Preferred Racial Label."
33. I capitalize "Black" or "African American" as well as "White" throughout this book. I do so to highlight "White" as a socially constructed racial identifier and "Whiteness" as a system of racialized hierarchy. My reasons for this choice echo those articulated in this statement from the MacArthur Foundation: Mack and Palfrey, "Capitalizing Black and White."
34. Temple, *Black Cultural Mythology*, 14.
35. Baker, "Critical Memory and the Black Public Sphere," 3.
36. Baker, "Critical Memory and the Black Public Sphere," 3.
37. Baker, "Critical Memory and the Black Public Sphere," 31. Emphasis in original.

38. Temple, “The Emergence of Sankofa Practice in the United States,” 127–50; Temple, *Black Cultural Mythology*.
39. Temple, “The Emergence of Sankofa Practice in the United States,” 130.
40. Temple, “The Emergence of Sankofa Practice in the United States,” 127.
41. Temple, “The Emergence of Sankofa Practice in the United States,” 129.
42. Temple, *Black Cultural Mythology*, 23.
43. Temple, *Black Cultural Mythology*, 1.
44. Temple identifies fifteen attributes of Black cultural mythology: hero dynamics, ancestor acknowledgment, historical re-enactment of worldview, resistance-based cognitive survival, hyperheroic actions, epic intuitive conduct, immortalization sensibility, sacred observation, ritual remembrance, commemoration philosophy, mythological structure, sacrificial inheritance, aesthetic memorialization, reconciliation and renewal, and antiheroics (23, 84).
45. Ahad-Legardy, *Afro-Nostalgia*, 3.
46. Ahad-Legardy, *Afro-Nostalgia*, 3.
47. Ahad-Legardy, *Afro-Nostalgia*, 8.
48. VanderHaagen, *Children's Biographies of African American Women*, 25–34.
49. See, for example, Ahad-Legardy's claim that nostalgia is not just passive or unconscious but an active form of “memory work that can be called on and self-induced for the purpose of feeling good in the now,” *Afro-Nostalgia*, 10; Baker's discussion of the need for “agential, black imaginative work” in “Critical Memory,” 12; and Temple's formulation of heroics or “past models of Black agency” as a centerpiece of Black cultural mythology, *Black Cultural Mythology*, 60.
50. Ronisha Browdy, among others, has described “the contentious relationship that Black women for decades have had with the word ‘feminism,’ opting out of such labeling of their writings, stories, music, and other modes of expression and communication as ‘feminist’ because of its connection to white feminism.” Browdy, “Black Women's Rhetoric(s),” n.p.
51. Collins, *Black Feminist Thought*, 298.
52. This is also closely aligned with Karlyn Kohrs Campbell's articulation of agency in her 2005 essay “Agency,” 1–19.
53. In *Feminism is for Everybody*, bell hooks characterized women's agency as “the power to be self-defining” (95). Philosopher Alisa Bierria developed a particularly compelling explication of the roles that self-definition and self-determination play in Black feminist conceptions of agency. She explained that “racist authoring of black agentic action evacuates black agents' self-generated explanation from their actions, replacing it with intentions and explanations constructed through the living archive and sanctioned by institutional racism.” Black agents, Bierria concluded, thus become “missing in action,” and the only remedy is self-definition (134). See also O. I. Davis, “Theorizing African American Women's Discourse,” 38–9; S. Davis, “Taking Back the Power,” 302.
54. Nash, “Practicing Love,” 14, 19.
55. Madison, “‘That Was My Occupation,’” 230. See also Allen, “Black Womanhood and Feminist Standpoints,” 577; S. Davis, “Taking Back the Power,” 302–4; Gittens, “‘What If I Am a Woman?’” 310.
56. Collins, “No Guarantees,” 2350.
57. Houston and Davis, “Introduction,” in *Centering Ourselves*, 13; Stanback, “Feminist Theory and Black Women's Talk,” 188. Having described the emphasis on self-definition in Black feminist thought, I also acknowledge the tension

produced when a scholar who identifies as a White woman, such as myself, advances an interpretation of Black women's words and actions. Lacking what Bierria described as "self-generated explanation" (134) from the historical Black women featured in this analysis, I look to implicit theorizing in their discourses and rely on the explanation of contemporary Black feminist thinkers to guide this analysis. This analysis attempts to treat Black women as "active agents who interpret their own and others' discourse."

58. Allen, "Goals for Emancipatory Research on Black Women," in *Centering Ourselves*, 24.
59. The few existing works include Schwalm, "Emancipation Day Celebrations," 291–332; Eves, "A Recipe for Remembrance"; Johnson, "'Ye Gave Them a Stone,'" 62–86; Griffiths, *Traumatic Possessions*; Davis, "The Other *Southern* Belles"; and Russell, "Sites Seen and Unseen."
60. Nash, *Black Feminism Reimagined*, 5.
61. Nash, *Black Feminism Reimagined*, 57.
62. Anderson, *Imagined Communities*, 6.
63. Baker, "Critical Memory and the Black Public Sphere," 3.
64. Hine, "African American Women and Their Communities in the Twentieth Century," 2.
65. Squires, "Rethinking the Black Public Sphere," 446.
66. Squires, "Rethinking the Black Public Sphere," 446. Drawing on the work of Margaret S. Boone, Carla Peterson formulated a similar taxonomy of African-American social spheres. She identified the following spheres as locations for Black women's activism: domestic, ethnic community, ethnic public, and national public spheres. See *"Doers of the Word,"* 8.
67. Wherever possible, I use the adjective "enslaved" to denote a potentially temporary, externally imposed condition rather than the word "slave," which defines the person so named primarily by their enslavement rather than their humanity. This choice follows that of many journalists and historians who write about this time period, and it is guided by the ideal of "people-first" language promoted by contemporary advocates for people with disabilities.
68. Wheatley, "On Recollection," in *The Collected Works of Phillis Wheatley*, 62–64.
69. Gates, *The Trials of Phillis Wheatley*, 49–82.
70. Walker, *In Search of Our Mothers' Gardens*, 237.
71. Woodson, "Address to the Youth," in *Lift Every Voice*, 386.
72. Remond, Letter to the *National Anti-Slavery Standard*, 2.
73. The concept of a "usable past" appears to stem from a 1918 article by US literary critic Van Wyck Brooks. In this essay, Brooks advocated for a "usable past" through applicable literary criticism. His commentary begins with literature, but he extended it to history as well. He said of creating a usable past: "The past is an inexhaustible storehouse of apt attitudes and adaptable ideals; it opens of itself at the touch of desire; it yields up, now this treasure, now that, to anyone who comes to it armed with a capacity for personal choices. If, then, we cannot use the past our professors offer us, is there any reason why we should not create others of our own?" Brooks, "On Creating a Usable Past," 339.
74. Glymph, "'Liberty Dearly Bought,'" 115.
75. "NAACP: A Century in the Fight for Freedom. The New Negro Movement," Library of Congress.
76. Watts, *Hearing the Hurt*, 3.

77. Notably, Glymph argued that "the Lost Cause movement stands as an explicit rejoinder to the memory-work of black southerners, not the other way around." Glymph, "'Liberty Dearly Bought,'" 116.
78. Cox, *Dixie's Daughters*, 63–83.
79. "Whose Heritage? Public Symbols of the Confederacy."
80. Several excellent historical treatments of African-American women's diverse forms of public activism during this time period have been published, including Brown, *Private Politics and Public Voices*; Higginbotham, *Righteous Discontent*; Logan, *We Are Coming*; and Terborg-Penn, *African American Women in the Struggle for the Vote, 1850–1920.*
81. Fauset, "Looking Backward," 126. Fauset also theorized memory in an August 1921 essay in *The Crisis* titled "Nostalgia." Although not widely known, Fauset was a significant figure in the New Negro Movement, or the Harlem Renaissance. She was a writer, editor, and teacher—most notably, the literary editor of *The Crisis* from 1919 until 1926. She supported and advocated for many young writers, including poet Langston Hughes.
82. Hine and Thompson, *A Shining Thread of Hope*, 39.
83. Hine and Thompson, *A Shining Thread of Hope*, 27.
84. Peterson, *"Doers of the Word,"* 223.
85. For more detail about this contentious period in American memory, see Blight, *Race and Reunion*, 98–139.
86. Glymph, "'Liberty Dearly Bought,'" 124.
87. Bailey, "Days of Jubilee," 353–73; Kachun, *Festivals of Freedom*; Kerr-Ritchie, *Rites of August First*; Schwalm, *Emancipation's Diaspora.*
88. Historian Rayford Logan first characterized this period as the "nadir" in his 1954 book *The Negro in American Life and Thought: The Nadir, 1877–1901.*
89. Gilmore, "Somewhere in the Nadir of African American History."
90. Hine and Thompson, *A Shining Thread of Hope*, 181; Russell, "Sites Seen and Unseen," 17–47.
91. Luckerson, "The Women Who Preserved the Story of the Tulsa Race Massacre"; Tolson, "Making Books Available," 9–16.
92. Dagbovie, "Black Women Historians from the Late 19th Century to the Dawning of the Civil Rights Movement," 241–44; Massenburg, "Documenting the Contributions Made by Black Women to Carter G. Woodson's Early Black History Movement," 28–34.
93. In fact, this special collection named for writer and activist James Weldon Johnson accomplished two goals of memory work: It corrected racist memories of Black people, and it commemorated the life of Johnson. Although this collection was primarily for Black children, Baker also noted its significance for White children. The fact that she prioritized Black children in her Harlem neighborhood leads me to describe this act as "community memory"; Baker, *Books About the Negro for Children*, n.p.
94. Baker, *Books About the Negro for Children*, n.p.
95. Although the critique of the "Great Man" approach has gained traction since the late twentieth century, scholars disagree about exactly how to avoid the "Great Speaker" approach in practice, as an exchange between Barbara Biesecker and Karlyn Kohrs Campbell illustrates. Biesecker and Campbell both identified female tokenism as a particularly tricky problem for scholars working to expand the rhetorical canon, especially because, as Biesecker argued, recovery projects

often reinscribe the very (White male) individualism that excluded people in the first place. See Biesecker, "Coming to Terms," 140–61; Campbell, "Biesecker Cannot Speak for Her Either," 153–59; Biesecker, "Negotiating with our Tradition," 136–41.

96. O. I. Davis, "Theorizing African American Women's Discourse," 38.
97. O. I. Davis, "Theorizing African American Women's Discourse," 38; Nash, *Black Feminism Reimagined*, 5.
98. Collins, "Intersectionality's Definitional Dilemmas"; Nash, *Black Feminism Reimagined*, 5.
99. On the term "race women," see Cooper, *Beyond Respectability*, 11–31.
100. Hall, "Slippin' In and Out of Frame," 344.
101. Flores, "Between Abundance and Marginalization," 5, 17.
102. Ricoeur, *Memory, History, Forgetting*, 414.
103. Parts of chapter 1 were adapted from "Memory Work and Rhetorical Activism," in *Oxford Handbook on African American Women's Writing*, edited by Simone C. Drake. Published online February 2, 2025. https://doi.org/10.1093/oxfordhb/9780197647424.013.0001. Reproduced with permission of the Licensor through PLSclear. This content is excluded from all forms of open access license, including Creative Commons, and the content may not be reused without the permission of Oxford University Press. Details of how to obtain permission can be found at https://global.oup.com/academic/rights/permissions/.

CHAPTER 2: "TO STRIVE BY THEIR EXAMPLE"

1. Stewart, "What If I Am a Woman?" in *Lift Every Voice*, 139.
2. Nash, *Black Feminism Reimagined*, 5. It is important to point out that Nash views Black feminism not as singular but as "a varied project with theoretical, political, activist, intellectual, erotic, ethical, and creative dimensions; black feminism is multiple, myriad, shifting, and unfolding" (5).
3. Mann, "Theorizing 'What Could Have Been,'" 581–82.
4. Nash, *Black Feminism Reimagined*, 5.
5. Nash, *Black Feminism Reimagined*, 116.
6. Collins, "No Guarantees," 2350.
7. Welter, "The Cult of True Womanhood," 152.
8. For more detailed discussions of these ideologies, their time frame, and how Black women negotiated them, see Weir-Soley, *Eroticism, Spirituality, and Resistance in Black Women's Writings*, 21–31; and Carby, *Reconstructing Womanhood*, 3–7.
9. Weir-Soley, *Eroticism, Spirituality, and Resistance in Black Women's Writings*, 24; Hine, "Rape and the Inner Lives of Black Women in the Middle West," 912–20; Higginbotham, *Righteous Discontent.*
10. Higginbotham, *Righteous Discontent*, 187.
11. Isocrates, "To Demonicus," in *Isocrates I*, 19–21; Hampton, *Writing from History*, 1–30; McCormick, "Mirrors for the Queen," 273–96.
12. Herdt, "Exemplarity Between Tradition and Critique," 553.
13. Hampton, *Writing from History*, 3.
14. Wilson, "The Racial Politics of Imitation in the Nineteenth Century," 89–108; Temple, *Black Cultural Mythology*.
15. McCormick, "Mirrors for the Queen," 274. McCormick used the word "example" in this passage, but he is referring to the same rhetorical strategy that I am.

16. Ceccarelli, "Polysemy," 404.
17. McCormick, "Mirrors for the Queen," 275.
18. McCormick, "Mirrors for the Queen," 292.
19. Ceccarelli, "Polysemy," 405.
20. Ambiguity can also have cultural import. In her book on Martin Luther King Jr., Trudier Harris noted an "inherent ambiguity of African American heroic folk traits" that actively resist simplification of King as a hero. Trudier Harris, *Martin Luther King Jr., Heroism, and African American Literature*, 2.
21. McCormick, "Mirrors for the Queen," 275.
22. See, for example, Hauser, "The Example in Aristotle's Rhetoric," 78–90; Benoit, "Aristotle's Example," 182–92; Hauser, "Aristotle's Example Revisited," 171–80; Benoit, "On Aristotle's Example," 261–67; Hauser, "Reply to Benoit," 268–73.
23. Arthos, "Where There Are No Rules," 321.
24. Arthos, "Where There Are No Rules," 321.
25. Arthos, "Where There Are No Rules," 322.
26. For a discussion of some of the problems inherent in a "mere imitation" approach to moral exemplars in character education, see Kristjánsson, "Emulation and the Use of Role Models in Moral Education," 40.
27. McCormick, "Mirrors for the Queen," 275.
28. Vos, "Learning from Exemplars," 21.
29. Vos, "Learning from Exemplars," 21–22.
30. See Herdt, "Exemplarity Between Tradition and Critique," 560; and Vos, "Learning from Exemplars," 22–23.
31. Both Kristjánsson and Vos were keen to distinguish between simplistic, uncritical copying and something more reflective, which they typically refer to as "emulation." However, neither made a sharp distinction between emulation and imitation—rather, they were advancing understanding of that more engaged form of audience/student uptake. Kristjánsson, "Emulation and the Use of Role Models in Moral Education," 40; Vos, "Learning from Exemplars," 22.
32. Wilson, "The Racial Politics of Imitation," 90.
33. Wilson, "The Racial Politics of Imitation," 97, 99.
34. Wilson, "The Racial Politics of Imitation," 102.
35. Temple, *Black Cultural Mythology*, 23. Temple conceptualizes this Afrocentric philosophy of heroes not as defined essentially by certain "African" features or ideology but rather characterized historically as a commitment of diasporic people to center their thinking on stories, people, and beliefs that originated with their ancestors on the African continent.
36. Temple, *Black Cultural Mythology*, 18.
37. Temple, *Black Cultural Mythology*, 31.
38. An initial survey turned up fourteen speech texts given between 1833 and 1928 that cited female exemplars. My research assistant at the University of Nevada, Las Vegas, Kacey Ballard, and I looked for published speeches that invoked women as examples, whether in a passing reference or a sustained narrative. This initial search drew mainly from published collections and other publicly accessible sources such as *BlackPast.org*. Subsequent searches of other databases and digital archives have produced three additional speeches for a total of seventeen. While this set is not exhaustive, it is large enough to be representative of Black middle-class women's public discourse during the period. I opted to include some rhetors from before the stipulated time period for this book, such as

Stewart, because their speeches aligned with and even set the stage for later uses of exemplars.

39. Maria W. Stewart, "What If I Am a Woman?" (1833) in *Lift Every Voice*, 138; Mary Ann Shadd, "Break Every Yoke and Let the Oppressed Go Free" (1858) in *Lift Every Voice*, 321; Sojourner Truth, "Equal Rights for All, Three Speeches" (1867) in *Lift Every Voice*, 465–66; Mary V. Cook, "Woman's Place in the Work of the Denomination" (1887) in *Lift Every Voice*, 668.
40. Shadd simply invoked sisters Martha and Mary as women with whom Christ associated and thereby demonstrated that he "heald [*sic*] the sexes indiscriminately thereby implying an Equal inheritance." See "Break Every Yoke," 321.
41. There are several women named Mary identified in the Gospels, which can lead to some confusion in identifying the speakers' precise references. All four Gospels identify Mary Magdalene by name as one of the first people (if not the first person) to witness the resurrected Christ. Some traditions have conflated Mary Magdalene and Mary of Bethany, who is the sister of Martha and Lazarus. In this case, it is possible that Shadd's and Cook's references to Mary could have been invoking the same person. For more information on the traditions behind the Marys of the Gospels, see Beavis, "Who is Mary Magdalene?"
42. Truth, "Equal Rights for All," 465–66.
43. Truth thus participates as a "forerunner" of what is now characterized as womanist biblical interpretation. See Junior, *An Introduction to Womanist Biblical Interpretation*, 39–53.
44. Lanham, *A Handlist of Rhetorical Terms*, 1.
45. Stewart, "What If I Am a Woman?" 137.
46. The elimination of religious "middle men" in this fashion illustrates Stewart's Black radical (and, anticipatorily, Black feminist) interpretation of central Reformation tenets.
47. Stewart, "What If I Am a Woman?" 140, 139.
48. Cook, "Woman's Place," 666–68.
49. Cook, "Woman's Place," 665.
50. Cook, "Woman's Place," 665. This focus on a "pure and undefiled Christianity" clearly exhibits the virtues of purity and piety upheld in the cult of True Womanhood. Although such comments reveal Cook's reliance on certain conservative feminine ideals, they are also in line with the reasoning of Black female contemporaries like Frances Ellen Watkins Harper, who argued for a more holistic approach to Black women's rights. Black women who had previously been denied the safety and dignity of domestic life and religious practice in enslavement often expressed a very different perspective on political solutions to sexism than did White middle-class women.
51. Cook, "Woman's Place," 665–66.
52. Cook, "Woman's Place," 666.
53. Cook, "Woman's Place," 666. Sarah, in fact, twice doubted God's covenant with her husband Abraham: In the book of Genesis, chapter 16 recounts the story of how a barren Sarah forced her slave Hagar to sleep with Abraham to produce an heir, and chapter 18 narrates her laughter at God's promise of a son.
54. Cook, "Woman's Place," 667. Emphasis added.
55. Cook, "Woman's Place," 668.
56. Cook, "Woman's Place," 675.

57. Cook, "Woman's Place," 666.
58. Cook, "Woman's Place," 666.
59. Cook, "Woman's Place," 668.
60. Speeches invoking historical women from a source other than the Bible included the following: Cook, "Woman's Place"; Victoria Earle Matthews "The Awakening of the Afro-American Woman," in *Lift Every Voice*, 834–40; Lucy Wilmot Smith, "The Future Colored Girl," in *Minutes and Addresses of the American National Baptist Convention,* 68–74; Stewart, "What If I Am a Woman?"
61. On the predominance of such texts, see Booth, *How to Make It as a Woman*, 1–47.
62. Stewart, "What If I Am a Woman?" 140.
63. Cook, "Woman's Place," 671, 672.
64. Cook, "Woman's Place," 672.
65. Cook, "Woman's Place," 667.
66. Smith, "The Future Colored Girl."
67. Smith, "The Future Colored Girl."
68. Matthews, "The Awakening of the Afro-American Woman," 837.
69. Examples from Cook, "A Woman's Place," 667; Stewart, "What If I Am a Woman?" 140; Matthews, "The Awakening of the Afro-American Woman," 837.
70. Terrell, "The Progress of Colored Women."
71. Cook, "Woman's Place," 672.
72. Cook, "Woman's Place," 673.
73. Laney, "The Burden of the Educated Colored Woman," in *Lift Every Voice*, 886.
74. Laney, "The Burden of the Educated Colored Woman," 889.
75. Papers of the NAACP, Part I, 1909–1950: Meetings of the Board of Directors, Records of Annual Conferences, Speeches, and Special Reports, xi.
76. Cannady, "Address to the NAACP."
77. Although Cannady's treatment of Ovington here suggests that her praise is sincere, it is possible that she is also flattering Ovington, who would have been present in the audience. Both things could be true, and both purposes would contribute to Cannady's rhetorical goals. Of course, as with any speech, the motivations remain ambiguous.
78. Ovington was also a suffrage advocate, but that is not the work for which Cannady recognizes her.
79. Temple, *Black Cultural Mythology*, 31.
80. Cook, "Woman's Place," 672.
81. These eleven speeches are, in chronological order: Elizabeth Jennings, "On Improvement of the Mind" (1837); Frances Ellen Watkins Harper, "We Are All Bound Up Together" (1866); Olivia A. Davidson, "How Shall We Make the Women of Our Race Stronger?" (1886); Mary V. Cook, "Woman's Place in the Work of the Denomination" (1887); Hallie Quinn Brown, "Discussion of the Same Subject" (1893); Anna Julia Cooper, "Women's Cause Is One and Universal" (1893); Mary Church Terrell, "The Progress of Colored Women" (1898); Lucy Craft Laney, "The Burden of the Educated Colored Woman" (1899); Rosetta Douglass Sprague, "My Mother as I Recall Her" (1900); Mary McLeod Bethune, "President's Address to the 15th Biennial Convention of the National Association of Colored Women" (1926); and Beatrice Morrow Cannady, "Beatrice Morrow Cannady Speaks to the NAACP" (1928).

82. As noted in chapter 1, such views are explicitly expressed in speeches by Sarah J. Woodson and Victoria Earle Matthews. See Woodson, "Address to the Youth," in *Lift Every Voice*, 386; and Matthews, "The Awakening of the Afro-American Woman," in *Lift Every Voice*, 836.
83. Temple, *Black Cultural Mythology*, 85.
84. Speeches by Cook (1887), Brown (1893), and Laney (1899) identify Harper for recognition. Harper died in 1911, near the end of the period under examination.
85. Harper, "We Are All Bound Up Together," 460. For more on the uniquely powerful role that Tubman has played as an African-American hero, see Temple, *Black Cultural Mythology*, 137–53.
86. Speeches that name Wheatley include Brown (726), Laney (886), and Terrell; those that cite Truth include Brown (727), Laney (886), Cannady.
87. Elizabeth Jennings, "On Improvement of the Mind," in *Lift Every Voice*, 168.
88. Mikorenda, "Beating Wings in Rebellion."
89. Jennings, "On Improvement of the Mind," 168.
90. Jennings, "On Improvement of the Mind," 168. This transcript spells Mathews's surname with two "t"s, whereas most historical sources indicate that it was spelled with only one. See Porter, "The Organized Educational Activities of Negro Literary Societies, 1828–1846," 555–76.
91. Davidson, "How Shall We Make the Women of our Race Stronger?" 649.
92. Davidson, "How Shall We Make the Women of our Race Stronger?" 651.
93. Davidson, "How Shall We Make the Women of our Race Stronger?" 652.
94. Davidson, "How Shall We Make the Women of our Race Stronger?" 649.
95. Bethune, "President's Address to the 15th Biennial Convention of the National Association of Colored Women, Civic Auditorium, Oakland, California," 2–3.
96. Bethune, "President's Address," 3.
97. Emphasis added.
98. Sprague, "My Mother as I Recall Her," 898–99. Sprague's published, illustrated version of this speech, along with newspaper clippings, is also available through the Library of Congress at https://www.loc.gov/resource/mss11879.02007/?st=gallery.
99. Sprague, "My Mother as I Recall Her," 899.
100. Sprague, "My Mother as I Recall Her," 899, 900, 901, 904, 902.
101. Sprague, "My Mother as I Recall Her," 901, 902.
102. Sprague, "My Mother as I Recall Her," 903, 905.
103. Sprague, "My Mother as I Recall Her," 905.
104. Logan, *We Are Coming*, 47.
105. Harper, "We Are All Bound Up Together," 460.
106. Harper, "We Are All Bound Up Together," 460. The "Montgomery" referred to here is Colonel James Montgomery of the Union Army, with whom Tubman conducted the Combahee River Raid that freed several hundred enslaved people.
107. Temple also uses the language of survival in her analysis of Tubman, saying that she is "one of the most recognized survivors of enslavement." Temple, *Black Cultural Mythology*, 137.
108. For more on how Tubman might function in the practice of ancestor acknowledgment, see Temple, *Black Cultural Mythology*, 140.
109. Harper, "We Are All Bound Up Together," 460.

110. Brown, "Discussion of the Same Subject," 725–27.
111. Brown, "Discussion of the Same Subject," 725.
112. Brown, "Discussion of the Same Subject," 729.
113. Terrell, "The Progress of Colored Women."
114. Burke, *Grammar of Motives*, xix.
115. Arthos, "Where There Are No Rules," 322.
116. Nora, "Between Memory and History," 12; Ricoeur, *Memory, History, Forgetting*, 414.
117. Amponsah, "Towards a Black Cultural Memory," 33.

CHAPTER 3: "SELF-EMANCIPATING WOMEN"

1. Early, "The Organized Efforts of the Colored Women of the South to Improve Their Condition," in *World's Congress of Representative Women*, ed. Sewall, 2:720. Hereinafter in the notes, this compilation is referred to as "*WCRW*."
2. Although Florence Lewis was scheduled to speak on May 18, as the last of three respondents to Williams's address, Sewall's proceedings record neither a speech nor any other appearance by Lewis. It is possible that when Frederick Douglass gave his impromptu speech after Coppin, he preempted or at least overshadowed Lewis's speech. Douglass's speech, unlike Lewis's speech (if it was given at all), is recorded in the proceedings. See *WCRW*, ed. Sewall, 1:76, 2:717. See also Maddux, *Practicing Citizenship*, 86.
3. Truman, *History of the World's Fair*, 23.
4. "Announcement," in *WRCW*, 1:v.
5. Logan, "Frances E. W. Harper, 'Woman's Political Future,'" 46. Hazel Carby saw the invitation somewhat differently from Logan: "The fact that six black women eventually addressed the World's Congress was not the result of a practice of sisterhood or evidence of a concern to provide a black political presence but part of a discourse of exoticism that pervaded the fair." Carby, *Reconstructing Womanhood*, 5. Although I have not been able to locate evidence documenting exactly how these women were selected or invited, I think it most likely that they were selected by the Board of Lady Managers because they were already prominent figures. Williams was well known and likely deemed acceptable to White Chicago socialites; she was the first Black speaker invited. In inviting the other speakers, it is possible that the Board took inspiration from a widely dispersed circular that Black women crafted to express their disappointment with the lack of representation at the Fair. The circular "earnestly solicited" several "representative colored women" to be present at the Fair, including Early, Harper, Brown, and Coppin. "Of Great Interest to Colored Women," *The Freeman*, 8.
6. For the schedule of the general congresses, see Sewall, *WCRW*, 1:76–84.
7. Much as she argued in 1866, Harper here held that suffrage was not a "panacea" but one political tool among many: Harper, "Woman's Political Future," in *WCRW*, ed. Sewall, 1:434. See also Logan, "Frances E. W. Harper, 'Woman's Political Future,'" 48–49. Suffrage was the primary concern addressed by discussant Margaret Windeyer. Her brief response to Harper's speech focused almost exclusively on arguing that women should prioritize the franchise. See Windeyer, "Discussion of the Preceding Address by Margaret Windeyer of Australia, Representative of the Womanhood Suffrage League of New South Wales," in *WCRW*, ed. Sewall, 1:437–38.

8. S. W. Logan, "Frances E. W. Harper, 'Woman's Political Future,'" 43; see also Kachun, *Festivals of Freedom*, 175; and R. Logan, *The Negro in American Life and Thought*.
9. Carby, *Reconstructing Womanhood*, 96.
10. Previous scholarship examined the speeches in different configurations. Shirley Wilson Logan analyzed Williams's and Cooper's speeches, as well as Harper's ("Woman's Political Future"). Laura L. Behling examined only Williams, Cooper, and Coppin. I build on the work of both Logan and Behling, but my analysis offers an alternative to Behling's interpretation, which, in my view, overemphasized the speakers' objectification as "exhibits" at the expense of considering how they acted as agents. Kristy Maddux framed these speeches as part of the project of "racial uplift" and examined them alongside ten others, including speeches by White women. Maddux's analysis, although appropriate to her purpose, does not closely examine the Black women's unique positionalities and rhetorical strategies. See Logan, *We Are Coming*; Behling, "Reification and Resistance," 173–96; and Maddux, *Practicing Citizenship*, 86–120.
11. For an example of research that examines the significance of the collective in interpersonal spaces, see S. Davis, "The 'Strong Black Woman Collective,'" 20–35. For a more detailed explanation of why it is important to account simultaneously for individual speech and collective rhetorical action, see VanderHaagen, "'A Grand Sisterhood,'" 15–18.
12. Allen, "Goals for Emancipatory Research on Black Women," in *Centering Ourselves*, 24.
13. Collins, *Black Feminist Thought*, 298.
14. See Bierria, "Missing in Action," 134; O. I. Davis, "Theorizing African American Women's Discourse," 38–39; S. Davis, "Taking Back the Power," 302; hooks, *Feminism is for Everybody*; and Nash, "Practicing Love," 14. See also Campbell, "Agency," 1–19.
15. Massa, "Black Women in the 'White City,'" 319; Rydell, "World's Columbian Exposition."
16. Speakers variously used the Emancipation Proclamation (1863) and the Thirteenth Amendment (1865) to mark emancipation.
17. Reed, *"All the World is Here!"* xxii; 52–53. Quoting St. Clair Drake and Horace R. Cayton.
18. See Carby, *Reconstructing Womanhood*, 3–6; Harris and Werner, "Forensic Rhetoric and Racial Justice," 618–33; Maddux, *Practicing Citizenship*, 99–104; Paddon and Turner, "African Americans and the World's Columbian Exposition," 19; and Reed, *"All the World,"* xi–xiv.
19. Massa, "Black Women," 331; Weimann, *The Fair Women*, 103–24; Reed, *"All the World,"* 26–30.
20. Reed, *"All the World,"* 27.
21. Massa, "Black Women," 329. Reed claimed that Palmer's decision was opportunistic and political, and Weimann believed that it was influenced by the need to appease the powerful Southern White women; Reed, *"All the World,"* 29; Weimann, *The Fair Women*, 104. See also Paddon and Turner, "African Americans and the World's Columbian Exposition," 22.
22. Quoted in Tsenes-Hills, *I Am the Utterance of My Name*, 193. For the full text, see Hallie Q. Brown, "A Great Slight to the Race," *The Indianapolis Freeman*, April

30, 1892, 4. Although the Board viewed Brown's decision as petty, Brown could have perceived the small position as both inadequate to her aspirations and woefully undercompensated. See Massa, "Black Women," 333; Weimann, *The Fair Women*, 117–19.

23. Reed, *"All the World,"* 30. At the state level, Joan Imogen Howard nearly single-handedly orchestrated the substantive inclusion of African-American work in the New York state exhibit. Harper served in a nominal role on the WCRW "Home Advisory Council." See Sewall, *WCRW*, 2:934.
24. African-American women were visible elsewhere: Williams also spoke at the Congress on Africa, and Brown performed at "Colored American Day"; Reed, *"All the World,"* 17, 102, 138. The first "Aunt Jemima," Nancy Green, also appeared in an advertising campaign at the Fair; see Wallace-Sanders, *Mammy*, 63–67. Unlike the WCRW speakers, Ida B. Wells wrote her critique from an external position, as she boycotted the Fair's events. This position rendered her statement quite different—although no less significant—in its rhetorical function.
25. Karlyn Kohrs Campbell and Cindy Koenig Richards have noted that women have often had to cloak radical arguments in conventional garb; see Campbell, "Gender and Genre," 479–95; Richards, "Inventing Sacagawea," 1–22.
26. Cooper, *Beyond Respectability*, 11. The few book-length studies of nineteenth-century African-American women's rhetoric from the field of rhetorical studies and communication have also attested to the significance of some or all of these six women. See Atwater, *African American Women's Rhetoric*, 3; Royster, *Traces of a Stream*, 289–93; Logan, *We Are Coming*.
27. Royster, *Traces of a Stream*, 178.
28. Foster, "Harper, Frances Ellen Watkins," in *Black Women in America*, ed. Hine, 2:22–25.
29. Perkins, "Coppin, Fannie Jackson," in *Black Women in America*, ed. Hine, 1:312–14. Most sources, including publications authored by Coppin, spell her first name "Fanny."
30. Reed, *"All the World,"* 17.
31. Lemert, "Cooper, Anna Julia," in *Black Women in America*, ed. Hine, 1:308–12.
32. Fisher, "Brown, Hallie Quinn," in *Black Women in America*, ed. Hine 1:168–70.
33. Cooper, *Beyond Respectability*, 18.
34. Maddux, *Practicing Citizenship*, 87.
35. Maddux, *Practicing Citizenship*, 86.
36. Blight, *Race and Reunion*, 332. Blight provides a nuanced overview of the controversies over progress in the Black community, but his account is limited by its near-exclusive focus on Black men. An examination of Black women's speeches provides an important correction and addition to Blight's argument.
37. Blight, *Race and Reunion*, 319, 321.
38. Maddux, *Practicing Citizenship*, 111.
39. "Not Lost Sight Of. The Afro-American is Gradually Being Brought into the Fair," *Plaindealer* (Detroit), March 24, 1893, 1.
40. Fannie Barrier Williams, "The Intellectual Progress of the Colored Women of the United States Since the Emancipation Proclamation," in *WCRW*, ed. Sewall, 2:696.
41. Williams, "Intellectual Progress," in *WCRW*, ed. Sewall, 2:696.
42. Williams, "Intellectual Progress," in *WCRW*, ed. Sewall, 2:697, 704.

43. Williams, "Intellectual Progress," in *WCRW*, ed. Sewall, 2:704.
44. Williams, "Intellectual Progress," in *WCRW*, ed. Sewall, 2:704.
45. Williams, "Intellectual Progress," in *WCRW*, ed. Sewall, 2:697.
46. Here, Williams offered a subtle critique of White women, but in other sections, she praised them as "saintly" (697) and compared Black women with them. Such passages illustrate Williams's investment in respectability politics. We can also see Williams's class prejudice in passages lamenting White Americans' inability to differentiate between the Black elite and what she described as the "non-progressive peasants of the 'black belt' of the South" (705). Behling (2010) interpreted such choices as Williams denying her racial identity in favor of identification with her White female audiences. Although I agree that this is quite problematic, I contend that Williams did this strategically to gain the trust of White women and thus utilized her position to become a more amenable messenger for radical ideas. For further discussion of the issue of the social distinctions among Black Americans in the Gilded Age, see Reed, *"All the World,"* 37–53.
47. Cooper's characterization of the process of progress resonates strongly with Nash's description of work in Black feminist love-politics (2011).
48. A. J. Cooper, "Discussion of the Same Subject," in *WCRW*, ed. Sewall, 2:712.
49. A. J. Cooper, "Discussion," in *WCRW*, ed. Sewall, 2:712.
50. A. J. Cooper, "Discussion," in *WCRW*, ed. Sewall, 2:713. Cooper's language alludes to a parable of Jesus, recounted in the Gospels of Matthew (13:33) and Luke (13:21) (King James Version).
51. Coppin, "Discussion Continued," in *WCRW*, ed. Sewall, 2:716.
52. Coppin, "Discussion," in *WCRW*, ed. Sewall, 2:715.
53. Coppin, "Discussion," in *WCRW*, ed. Sewall, 2:715.
54. Frederick Douglass, who had been seated on the platform during the session, followed Coppin's address with a brief impromptu response. He articulated a strong break between past and present and appropriated the apocalyptic biblical language of the books of Ecclesiastes and Revelation to herald the arrival of a new order; see *WCRW*, ed. Sewall, 2:717. Reed noted that Douglass's statement would have had particular impact, as he was the only man to address the Congress since the opening remarks. Reed, *"All the World,"* 124.
55. Early, "Organized Efforts," in *WCRW*, ed. Sewall, 2:723.
56. Early, "Organized Efforts," in *WCRW*, ed. Sewall, 2:723.
57. Early, "Organized Efforts," in *WCRW*, ed. Sewall, 2:723.
58. I counted six references to specific amounts of time (e.g. "thirty years") and twelve general references (e.g., "centuries," "the age"). This enumeration is inspired by Allison Prasch's "rhetorical theory of deixis," which "is concerned with how a speaker defines his/her rhetorical act within both senses of time (*chronos* and *kairos*), place, and space-time while also attending to the ways a discourse might change over time in accordance with historical events, moments that often define, and are defined by, their placement"; Prasch, "Toward a Rhetorical Theory of Deixis," 174.
59. Brown, "Discussion of the Same Subject," in *WCRW*, ed. Sewall, 2:725.
60. Brown, "Discussion," in *WCRW*, ed. Sewall, 2:726.
61. Brown, "Discussion," in *WCRW*, ed. Sewall, 2:728.
62. Brown, "Discussion," in *WCRW*, ed. Sewall, 2:729.
63. Harper, "Woman's Political Future," in *WCRW*, ed. Sewall, 1:434.

64. Kachun, *Festivals of Freedom*, 168.
65. Blight, *Race and Reunion*, 313.
66. Schwalm, "'Agonizing Groans of Mothers' and 'Slave-Scarred Veterans,'" 291.
67. See Blight, *Race and Reunion*, 311–19; Johnston, "Freedom and Slavery in the *Voice of the Negro*," 30–34; Kachun, *Festivals of Freedom*, 148; Schwalm, "Emancipation Day Celebrations," 293.
68. I thank Ashley R. Hall for a conversation that helped me to conceptualize the idea of the negative in these speeches.
69. Williams, "Intellectual Progress," in *WCRW*, ed. Sewall, 2:703.
70. Williams, "Intellectual Progress," in *WCRW*, ed. Sewall, 2:698, 701.
71. Williams, "Intellectual Progress," in *WCRW*, ed. Sewall, 2:701.
72. Williams, "Intellectual Progress," in *WCRW*, ed. Sewall, 2:703.
73. Maddux, *Practicing Citizenship*, 95.
74. It is important to note that Williams's elite position may have hindered her ability to recognize enslaved Black women as survivors rather than mere victims.
75. Cooper, "Discussion," in *WCRW*, ed. Sewall, 2:712.
76. Cooper, "Discussion," in *WCRW*, ed. Sewall, 2:712.
77. Cooper, "Discussion," in *WCRW*, ed. Sewall, 2:712.
78. Cooper, "Discussion," in *WCRW*, ed. Sewall, 2:711, 713. The language of heroism that Cooper used here also strongly resonates with Christel N. Temple's claims about the philosophy of heroism in Black cultural mythology: "defined organically from diasporic experiences with survivalist impact, achievement against the odds, and the extension of human capacity beyond the ordinary." Temple, *Black Cultural Mythology*, 18.
79. Early, "Organized Efforts," in *WCRW*, ed. Sewall, 2:719.
80. Early, "Organized Efforts," in *WCRW*, ed. Sewall, 2:719.
81. Early, "Organized Efforts," in *WCRW*, ed. Sewall, 2:720.
82. Coppin, "Discussion," in *WCRW*, ed. Sewall, 2:716; Harper, "Woman's Political Future," in *WCRW*, ed. Sewall, 1:435.
83. Brown, "Discussion," in *WCRW*, ed. Sewall, 2:724.
84. Brown, "Discussion," in *WCRW*, ed. Sewall, 2:724.
85. Brown, "Discussion," in *WCRW*, ed. Sewall, 2:724.
86. Brown, "Discussion," in *WCRW*, ed. Sewall, 2:724.
87. Brown, "Discussion," in *WCRW*, ed. Sewall, 2:725.
88. Cooper, *Beyond Respectability*, 144.
89. S. Davis, "Taking Back the Power," 302.
90. Nash, "Practicing Love," 16.
91. Williams's use of the phrase "slight tinge" may also betray her color prejudice and accommodation to White beauty norms.
92. Williams, "Intellectual Progress," in *WCRW*, ed. Sewall, 2:706.
93. Cooper, "Discussion," in *WCRW*, ed. Sewall, 2:711.
94. Brown, "Discussion," in *WCRW*, ed. Sewall, 2:728.
95. Brown, "Discussion," in *WCRW*, ed. Sewall, 2:728.
96. Cooper, "Discussion," in *WCRW*, ed. Sewall, 2:712.
97. Williams, "Intellectual Progress," in *WCRW*, ed. Sewall, 2:700.
98. Williams, "Intellectual Progress," in *WCRW*, ed. Sewall, 2:699.
99. Early, "Organized Efforts," in *WCRW*, ed. Sewall, 2:719; Williams, "Intellectual Progress," in *WCRW*, ed. Sewall, 2:700; Cooper, "Discussion," in *WCRW*, ed. Sewall, 2:714. Although the language of self-help can be problematic if it blames

the oppressed for their oppression, in these instances, the women use it as a means of focusing on Black women's action as an engine for progress.

100. As Kirt Wilson has shown, the "racial politics of imitation" during this time period were complex, with many Whites (and some people of color) viewing Black Americans as "natural" mimics but unable to internalize imitated virtues. Black Americans, on the other hand, saw imitation of good qualities as a means of uplifting their race. This latter enactment of imitation by Black people, Wilson notes, became threatening to Whites, revealing the progressive potential in a seemingly regressive idea. See Wilson, "The Racial Politics of Imitation in the Nineteenth Century," 89–108.
101. Coppin, "Discussion," in *WCRW*, ed. Sewall, 2:716.
102. Early, "Organized Efforts," in *WCRW*, ed. Sewall, 2:719.
103. Early, "Organized Efforts," in *WCRW*, ed. Sewall, 2:719.
104. Early, "Organized Efforts," in *WCRW*, ed. Sewall, 2:720.
105. Early, "Organized Efforts," in *WCRW*, ed. Sewall, 2:720.
106. Nash, "Practicing Love," 18.
107. Williams, "Intellectual Progress," in *WCRW*, ed. Sewall, 2:700.
108. Williams, "Intellectual Progress," in *WCRW*, ed. Sewall, 2:700–01.
109. Early, "Organized Efforts," in *WCRW*, ed. Sewall, 2:723.
110. Harper, "Woman's Political Future," in *WCRW*, ed. Sewall, 1:433.
111. Harper, "Woman's Political Future," in *WCRW*, ed. Sewall, 1:435.
112. Harper, "Woman's Political Future," in *WCRW*, ed. Sewall, 1:437.
113. Harper, "Woman's Political Future," in *WCRW*, ed. Sewall, 1: 437; Wells, "Lynch Law in All Its Phases," in *Lift Every Voice*, 759.
114. Collins, "Intersectionality's Definitional Dilemmas," 8.
115. Collins, "No Guarantees," 2350.
116. Weimann, *Fair Women*, 523–32.
117. Rev. D. A. Graham, "World's Fair Glances." Graham's article is the only substantive Black newspaper account of these speeches that I was able to locate. My reading of White newspapers' accounts of the speeches confirms Graham's report.
118. "The 1619 Project," *New York Times Magazine*, August 14, 2019; Schuster, *Teaching Hard History*, January 31, 2018. https://www.splcenter.org/20180131/teaching-hard-history.
119. Silverstein, "Why We Published The 1619 Project," *New York Times*, December 20, 2019. It is no accident or coincidence that a Black woman thought leader, Nikole Hannah-Jones, has become the scapegoat of right-wing narratives vilifying what they classify as critical race theory in "The 1619 Project," in which Hannah-Jones has played a pivotal role. This case clearly demonstrates how Black women who dare to use their rhetorical skills to change public memory continue to face dangerous consequences meted by the powers of White supremacy.
120. Hall, "Slippin' In and Out of Frame," 344.
121. Nash, "Practicing Love," 19.

CHAPTER 4: "THE SHADOWS OF THE PAST"

1. McElya, *Clinging to Mammy*, 120.
2. McElya, "Monumental Citizenship," 110.
3. "Charlotte Hawkins Brown Speaks at Oberlin," 1; Phyllis Wheatley Young Women's Christian Association, "Petition to Congress," 1; Terrell, "The Black

Mammy Monument," 6; Howard, "'Mammy' Gets 'Em Told," 7; H. Q. Brown, "The Black Mammy Statue," 3.

4. Most contemporary historians and scholars use the "Phillis" spelling, but historical sources vary, with "Phillis" and "Phyllis" being most prominent. I will use the spelling preferred by the historical source. Elsewhere in this book, I use "Phillis." Alexandria Russell addresses this usage in a helpful note in her doctoral dissertation: Russell, "Sites Seen and Unseen," 18; See also Carretta, *Phillis Wheatley*; Shields, "Wheatley, Phillis," in *Black Women in America*, ed. Hine, 3: 344–47.
5. "Fourteenth Census of the United States, 1920."
6. Catherine Squires outlined the concept of Black "enclave publics" in her essay "Rethinking the Black Public Sphere," 446–68.
7. Black men such as Neval Thomas were also publicly opposed to the monument. However, Black men as a group were much less publicly unified in this view than were Black women. Individual men and groups led by men issued statements in support of the monument, as I detail later.
8. McElya, *Clinging to Mammy*, 124–28.
9. Joan Marie Johnson addressed some of these influences in her essay "'Ye Gave Them a Stone,'" 62–86.
10. Neu, *The Wilson Circle*, 4.
11. Biographical information summarized from Neu, *The Wilson Circle*, 3–32.
12. O'Reilly, "The Jim Crow Policies of Woodrow Wilson," 117.
13. Du Bois, "My Impressions of Woodrow Wilson," 453.
14. O'Reilly, "The Jim Crow Policies of Woodrow Wilson," 117.
15. O'Reilly, "The Jim Crow Policies of Woodrow Wilson," 119.
16. Information drawn from Flexnor and Fitzpatrick, *Century of Struggle*, 136–48.
17. Terborg-Penn, *African American Women in the Struggle for the Vote*, 108.
18. Terborg-Penn, *African American Women in the Struggle for the Vote*.
19. Stillion Southard, *Militant Citizenship*, 121.
20. Stillion Southard, *Militant Citizenship*, 83–86.
21. Palczewski, "The 1919 Prison Special," 107.
22. Flexnor and Fitzpatrick, *Century of Struggle*, 300–17.
23. Terborg-Penn, *African American Women in the Struggle for the Vote*, 160.
24. Terborg-Penn, *African American Women in the Struggle for the Vote*, 165.
25. Equal Justice Initiative, *Lynching in America*.
26. Messer, *The 1921 Tulsa Race Massacre*, 8.
27. Glymph, "'Liberty Dearly Bought,'" 127.
28. Glymph, "'Liberty Dearly Bought,'"116.
29. "Whose Heritage?" 33.
30. Hine and Thompson, *A Shining Thread of Hope*, 181; Russell, "Sites Seen and Unseen," 17–47.
31. Johnson, "'Ye Gave Them a Stone,'" 64.
32. "House Applauds Carolinian's Plea to Honor Mammy," *Washington Evening Star*, January 11, 1923, 40.
33. "That Responsive Racial Feeling," *Richmond Planet*, January 13, 1923, 4; "House Gives Ovation to Plea for Statue of Negro Mammy," *The Monitor*, January 19, 1923, 1; B.B. Cowan, "Balsam of Gilead," *The Monitor*, January 19, 1923, 2.
34. Notably, the mainstream White newspaper the *Washington Evening Star* reported on February 6 that a group of "ministers and deacons representing all of

the colored churches in Washington" had voted to endorse the monument (9). The *Richmond Planet* also provided an interesting "Southern" perspective on the monument with a decidedly conservative flavor to several of the opinion pieces published there. See especially articles from January 13 (4) and February 3 (4).

35. Cowan, "Balsam of Gilead," 2.
36. See the *Monitor*, February 16, 1923, 2; *Appeal*, February 17, 1923, 1; *Colorado Statesman*, February 17, 1923, 1; *Baltimore Afro-American*, February 23, 1923, 1.
37. See, for instance, Kelly Miller, "Kelly Miller Says," *Baltimore Afro-American*, February 23, 1923, 9; "Senate OK's Bill for Monument to 'Black Mammy,'" *The Northwestern Bulletin* (St. Paul, MN), March 17, 1923, 1; Cowan, "Balsam of Gilead."
38. *Baltimore Afro-American*, March 2, 1923, 9.
39. John Bodnar's conceptualization of vernacular and official memories has been influential; Bodnar, *Remaking America*, 13–20. For an example focused on rhetoric, memory, and race, see P. G. Davis, *Laying Claim*, 17.
40. Quoted in McElya, *Clinging to Mammy*, 118, 123.
41. Johnson, "'Ye Gave Them a Stone,'" 63.
42. VanderHaagen, "(Mis)Quoting King," 91.
43. Good character, good sense, and goodwill are the three features of appeals to ethos, according to Aristotle's original formulation of the concept in his *Rhetoric*. See *On Rhetoric*, 120–21.
44. VanderHaagen, "(Mis)Quoting King," 96.
45. VanderHaagen, "(Mis)Quoting King," 98.
46. Glymph, "'Liberty Dearly Bought,'" 116.
47. Quoted in McElya, *Clinging to Mammy*, 123.
48. Lowenthal, "Stewardship, Sanctimony and Selfishness," in *History and Heritage*, 169.
49. Stedman, *A Monument in Commemoration of the Faithful Colored Mammies of the South*, 2.
50. Stedman, *Monument in Commemoration of the Faithful Colored Mammies of the South*, 3.
51. "Charlotte Hawkins Brown," *New York Age*, 1.
52. PWYWCA, "Petition to Congress," 1.
53. H. Q. Brown, "The Black Mammy Statue," 3.
54. "Charlotte Hawkins Brown," *New York Age*, 1.
55. In 1923, the use of dialect in general, and "Black" dialect in particular, was much more common among writers of all racial backgrounds. However, the reasons for using dialect would have diverged quite dramatically, depending on the identity and position of the author. Whereas White writers and performers infamously used such dialect to portray derogatory images of the "darky" in minstrel shows and the like, Black artists and authors deployed this dialect in much more complex and potentially positive ways. Black writers of the late nineteenth and early twentieth centuries often used exaggerated "Black" dialect to connect with working-class Black audiences and, significantly, to make fun of White people's interpretations of Blackness. The complexity of these layers of parody parallels the history of the cakewalk. Although I cannot confirm Howard's intentions, it appears that her use of dialect in Mammy Lou's speech in a fictional story published in a prominent Black newspaper is not intended to be derogatory. It is much more likely to have been viewed within the context of her satirical purposes

in the essay, as a means of using Mammy's "improper" English to shame clueless Whites. This "mammy" speaks truths and makes arguments—she is not to be dismissed because she speaks in Southern Black dialect. I thank readers Natasha Barnes, Kim Singletary, and Tracy Vaughn-Manley for suggesting and clarifying this interpretation. On Black dialect poetry, see Harris, "'The Sole Province of the Public Reader,'" 36–55; Nurhussein, *Rhetorics of Literacy*. On the history of the cakewalk, see Shrum, "Who Takes the Cake? The History of the Cakewalk."

56. Howard, "'Mammy' Gets 'Em Told," 7.
57. Terrell, "The Black Mammy Monument," 6.
58. Kimberly Wallace-Sanders argued that assumptions about motherhood—both biological and surrogate—were central to the image of the "mammy" during the early twentieth century. Although she did not discuss this monument in detail, her analysis poses important questions about the complicated and difficult experience of motherhood for enslaved women. She also emphasized the way in which the image of the "mammy" came to operate as a "coercive force" in public discourse (93); see Wallace-Sanders, *Mammy*, 93–117.
59. Howard, "'Mammy' Gets 'Em Told," 7.
60. Brown, "The Black Mammy Statue," 3.
61. PWYWCA, "Petition to Congress," 1.
62. "Charlotte Hawkins Brown," *New York Age*, 1.
63. "Charlotte Hawkins Brown," *New York Age*, 1.
64. PWYWCA, "Petition to Congress," 1.
65. PWYWCA, "Petition to Congress," 1.
66. Terrell, "The Black Mammy Monument."
67. Quoted in McElya, *Clinging to Mammy*, 12.
68. PWYWCA, "Petition to Congress," 1.
69. Terrell, "The Black Mammy Monument."
70. H. Q. Brown, "The Black Mammy Statue," 3.
71. Megan Fitzmaurice expanded on this point significantly in her National Communication Association conference presentation, "A Strategic Reversal: The National Association of Colored Women's Narrative Reframing of the Mammy Monument," 2016.
72. "Charlotte Hawkins Brown," *New York Age*, 1.
73. H.Q. Brown, "Black Mammy Statue," 4.
74. This connection among past, present, and future, combined with an insistence on futures of freedom and liberation, is an example of what Charles Mills described in his essay "The Chronopolitics of Racial Time." He described an "alternative vision of racial time, aimed not at racial revenge and the aspiration to a new time of reversed nonwhite domination, but of racial equality." Such visions "demanded alternative futures of independence and freedom quite different from those mapped out for them by their colonial masters." See Mills, "The Chronopolitics of Racial Time," 312–13.
75. Young, *Embodying Black Experience*, 19–20.

CHAPTER 5: "PLANTING GOOD AND JOY INSTEAD"

1. Brown, 1926 introduction to *Homespun Heroines*, vii.
2. Brown, *Homespun Heroines*, 55.
3. Here again are echoes of Paul Ricoeur's idea of forgetting "kept in reserve." In the case of racialized memories in the United States, White supremacy has broadly

suppressed or "forgotten" the presence of Blackness. This erasure, although pervasive and devastating, has not been complete, thanks in large part to Black Americans themselves. Although White America has forgotten, Black America has kept in reserve its stories, long advocating for more just memories. See Ricoeur, *Memory, History, Forgetting*, 414.

4. Burkett, introduction to *Homespun Heroines*, xxix.
5. Booth, *How to Make It as a Woman*, 23.
6. *Bits and Odds*, which was originally published in 1884 and reprinted in 1910, was a reciter text including forty selections for performance, opened by a fourteen-page introduction on theories and practices of elocution written by Brown. Brown there detailed the theory of imitation that undergirded her performance and teaching. These ideas are further enacted in *Homespun Heroines.*
7. Bethune, "Oswald Garrison Villard and Hallie Quinn Brown," 6.
8. See also Burkett, introduction to *Homespun Heroines*, xxix.
9. Burkett, introduction to *Homespun Heroines*, xxix.
10. Margo, *Race and Schooling in the South*, 6–9.
11. VanderHaagen, *Children's Biographies of African American Women*, 35–57.
12. Watts, *Hearing the Hurt*, 3.
13. Booth, *How to Make It as a Woman*, 214–18.
14. VanderHaagen, "Black Heroes and 'The Jury,'" in *A Centennial Celebration of* The Brownies' Book *Magazine*, eds. Johnson-Feelings and McNair, 56–77.
15. Booth, *How to Make It as a Woman*, 12.
16. Booth, *How to Make It as a Woman*, 197.
17. Booth, *How to Make It as a Woman*, 10, 9–10. References to selection criteria are often present in the works' peritextual material, such as prefaces and forewords. For more on the rhetorical analysis of peritextual material in collective biographies for children, see Bloomfield and VanderHaagen, "Where Women Scientists Belong."
18. Burkett, introduction to *Homespun Heroines*, xxxiv.
19. Brown, *Homespun Heroines*, vii.
20. In her chronological catalog of women's multibiographies, Booth recorded between eight (1921) and forty-two (1900) published per year between 1865 and 1940 (390–92). She noted that 1894, the year after the World's Fair, was a high point with thirty-seven texts (213–14). Although some of these texts included token women of other racial groups, such as Harriet Tubman and Pocahontas, the vast majority were focused on women of European descent. These numbers highlight just how unusual were the texts devoted to Black women.
21. Eves, "A Recipe for Remembrance," 280–97; P. G. Davis, "The *Other* Southern Belles," 308–31.
22. Eves, "Recipe for Remembrance," 295.
23. Davis, "The *Other* Southern Belles," 309.
24. Davis, "The *Other* Southern Belles," 310.
25. Houdek and Phillips, "Public Memory," 11.
26. Blair, Dickinson, and Ott, "Introduction: Rhetoric/Memory/Place," in *Places of Public Memory*, 7.
27. Cvetkovich, "Public Feelings," 459–68.
28. Cvetkovich, "Public Feelings," 461.
29. Corrigan, *Black Feelings*, xxiii.

30. Lisa M. Corrigan explains that "in the case of social movements, expressions of new feelings become political action." Brown and her coauthors may not be producing new feelings, necessarily, but their volume nonetheless clearly highlights the potential connection among memories, feelings, and political action. See Corrigan, *Black Feelings*, xv.
31. "Joy," *Dictionary of Psychology*.
32. Dunn and Love, "Antiracist Language Arts Pedagogy Is Incomplete without Black Joy," 191.
33. For a few notable examples, see Toi Derricotte's 2018 poem "Joy is an act of resistance," artist Kleaver Cruz's ongoing Black Joy Project (https://kleavercruz.com/the-black-joy-project), and 2021 videos by *The Root* editorial staff.
34. Johnson, "Black Joy in the Time of Ferguson," 180.
35. Stewart, *The Politics of Black Joy*, 9.
36. Hunter, *To 'Joy My Freedom*, 168–86.
37. Hunter, *To 'Joy My Freedom*, 172.
38. See especially Stewart, *The Politics of Black Joy*, 1–25, 27–44.
39. Stewart's argument in *The Politics of Black Joy* centers around the complex politics of Black joy as manifested in the work and art of Hurston (and Beyoncé), which differs from that of the creators of *Homespun Heroines*, who appear to have been more invested in feminine virtue, Christian piety, and racial uplift. Stewart argues that Hurston's insistence on Black joy struck a posture of refusal rather than resistance. Stewart explains: "Instead of directly protesting oppression, Hurston's emphasis on Black joy was more like a refusal to entertain the white gaze. That is, she strove to maintain an emotional indifference toward whites, relegating them to the periphery of a Black world. Rather than actively fight against whites, she refused to pay them attention" (9). Although the politics of Hurston and the creators of *Homespun Heroines* differ significantly, I see resonances in their shared effort to celebrate the lives and joys of Black women outside of the White gaze, in their own communities.
40. For a summary of studies on gratitude in the field of positive psychology, see "Giving Thanks Can Make You Happier," *Harvard Health Publishing*.
41. Emmons and McCullough, introduction to *The Psychology of Gratitude*, 5, 6.
42. Emmons and McCullough, introduction to *The Psychology of Gratitude*, 5.
43. Emmons and McCullough, introduction to *The Psychology of Gratitude*, 7.
44. Komter, "Gratitude and Gift Exchange," in *Psychology of Gratitude*, eds. Emmons and McCullough, 204.
45. Quoted in Edward J. Harpham, "Gratitude in the History of Ideas," in *Psychology of Gratitude*, eds. Emmons and McCullough, 20.
46. Temple, *Black Cultural Mythology*, 85.
47. On the dark side of gratitude in unjust scenarios, see Jackson, "Why Should I Be Grateful?" 277–79; Rodríguez-Silva, "Abolition, Race, and the Politics of Gratitude in Late Nineteenth-Century Puerto Rico," 622–23.
48. See Ahad-Legardy, *Afro-Nostalgia*; Brock, *Distributed Blackness*; Lu and Steele, "'Joy is Resistance,'" 823–37; Stewart, *The Politics of Black Joy*; and Temple, *Black Cultural Mythology*.
49. Brock, *Distributed Blackness*, 229.
50. Ahad-Legardy, *Afro-Nostalgia*, 3.
51. Ahad-Legardy, *Afro-Nostalgia*, 4.

52. On "eavesdropping audiences," see Leff and Utley, "Instrumental and Constitutive Rhetoric in Martin Luther King Jr.'s 'Letter from Birmingham Jail,'" 47.
53. Brown, *Homespun Heroines*, vii.
54. Brown, *Homespun Heroines*, vii.
55. Brown, *Homespun Heroines*, vii.
56. Burkett, introduction to *Homespun Heroines*, xxix. On other biographical collections published during the late nineteenth and early twentieth centuries, see Booth, *How To Make It as a Woman*, 213–23.
57. Brown, *Homespun Heroines*, 104.
58. Brown, *Homespun Heroines*, 105.
59. Brown, *Homespun Heroines*, 31. Brown reported that Cox was involved in a case that went to the Supreme Court, which she called the "Famous Randolph Will Case" (31). For additional history on the 1917 Supreme Court decision, see Mathias, "John Randolph's Freedman," 263–72.
60. Brown, *Homespun Heroines*, 119.
61. Brown, *Homespun Heroines*, 55.
62. As I noted in chapter 3, the Black women speakers at the 1893 World's Congress of Representative Women used the same argument to enlighten audiences about the remarkable accomplishments of their community.
63. For instance, the sketches report that both Catherine S. Delany (wife of Martin Delany) and Mary Shadd Cary were said to have fled the United States for Canada after the passage of the Fugitive Slave Act (90–91; 93).
64. Mary Catherine Windsor and Sarah J. S. Tompkins Garnet.
65. Brown, *Homespun Heroines*, 119.
66. Brown, *Homespun Heroines*, 121.
67. Brown, *Homespun Heroines*, 63.
68. Brown, *Homespun Heroines*, 23.
69. Brown, *Homespun Heroines*, 169.
70. Brown, *Homespun Heroines*, 170.
71. Temple, *Black Cultural Mythology*, 18, 86.
72. Historical significance is, of course, rhetorically constructed. Moreover, "traditional standards" at the time would have been dictated by White patriarchal definitions of history, which inherently exclude all but the most exceptional European women, let alone Black women.
73. Brown, *Homespun Heroines*, 6, 13, 14.
74. Brown, *Homespun Heroines*, 53, 145, 188.
75. Brown, *Homespun Heroines*, 55.
76. Brown, *Homespun Heroines*, 55.
77. Brown, *Homespun Heroines*, 64.
78. Brown, *Homespun Heroines*, 23.
79. Brown, *Homespun Heroines*, 24.
80. Brown, *Homespun Heroines*, 28.
81. Brown, *Homespun Heroines*, 28.
82. Brown, *Homespun Heroines*, 169.
83. Brown, *Homespun Heroines*, 171.
84. Brown, *Homespun Heroines*, 171.
85. Brown, *Homespun Heroines*, 169.
86. Brown, *Homespun Heroines*, 169.
87. Brown, *Homespun Heroines*, 170.

88. Brown, *Homespun Heroines*, 204.
89. Brown, *Homespun Heroines*, vii. In the individual sketches, the word "gratitude" or "grateful" is used five times to report feelings toward the subjects (53, 145, 182, 184, and 188); the word "appreciation" appears six times (61, 115, 155, 171, 180, and 218). These terms are applied to both prominent and lesser-known figures.
90. Brown, *Homespun Heroines*, 22.
91. Brown, *Homespun Heroines*, vii.
92. Brown, *Homespun Heroines*, 207. While the text references the tune as "Glory, Glory, Hallelujah," the more familiar title associated with this tune is "The Battle Hymn of the Republic," whose words were written by Julia Ward Howe during the Civil War. The original tune written by William Steffe gained popularity as a Union marching song called "John Brown's Body."
93. I am not talking about these women's lives as mere entertainment here but rather showing how the text is oriented toward producing pride and pleasure in certain readers (i.e., Black women) who view the women profiled not as passive objects to be gazed at but as active subjects like themselves.
94. Burkett, introduction to *Homespun Heroines*, xxx.
95. Brown, *Homespun Heroines*, 231; emphasis added.
96. Brown, *Homespun Heroines*, 231.
97. Brown, *Homespun Heroines*, 233.
98. Brown, *Homespun Heroines*, 236.
99. Brown, *Homespun Heroines*, 235.
100. Burkett counted nineteen out of sixty women profiled. Burkett did not indicate how he arrived at this total. The collection includes profiles of fifty-five individual women and one joint profile of "California Colored Women Trailblazers," which names seven specific women. Burkett, introduction to *Homespun Heroines*, xxx.
101. Brown, *Homespun Heroines*, 212.
102. Brown, *Homespun Heroines*, 213. In both of these examples, Keyser draws attention to her appearance, saying she is "attractive" (212) and "pale" (213). These references to appearance, although not atypical in the collection, raise difficult questions about Black women as objects to be enjoyed and, in particular, favoring light-skinned women as more worthy of admiration.
103. Brown, *Homespun Heroines*, 216.
104. Brown, *Homespun Heroines*, 183. Notably, in 2002, the name of the school was changed to honor Baldwin rather than Louis Agassiz, whose racial views were judged out of alignment with the community. In 2024, a young Black former student from the school successfully completed a years-long effort to similarly rename the Cambridge neighborhood in which the school is located. See Dorgan, "Committee Renames Local Agassiz School," *Harvard Crimson*; and Mitchell, "The Renaming of a Neighborhood," *Harvard Gazette.*
105. Brown, *Homespun Heroines*, 182–93.
106. Brown, *Homespun Heroines*, 186.
107. Brown, *Homespun Heroines*, 186.
108. Brown, *Homespun Heroines*, 187.
109. Brown, *Homespun Heroines*, 186–87.
110. Brown, *Homespun Heroines*, 46.
111. Brown, *Homespun Heroines*, 47.
112. Although the sketch does not specify the date, a report from the "BBC World

News" notes the date as July 16, 1892. See Dale, "How a Former Slave Gave a Quilt to Queen Victoria," *BBC Africa.*

113. Brown, *Homespun Heroines,* 48.
114. Brown, *Homespun Heroines,* 48.
115. Brown, *Homespun Heroines,* 48.
116. Brown, *Homespun Heroines,* 48.
117. Although familial terms such as "Granny" or "Aunt" have been used by White society to diminish Black women, in this Black-woman-focused context the titles have positive valence. Recent discussions of the various views on these terms can be found in Dahleen Glanton, "Is 'Auntie' a Term of Endearment for African American Women or Does It Promote an Aunt Jemima Stereotype?" *Chicago Tribune*; and Perry, "The Crucial Legacy of the Black Aunt," *Jezebel.*
118. Brown, *Homespun Heroines,* 51.
119. Brown, *Homespun Heroines,* 51.
120. Brown, *Homespun Heroines,* 51. The sketch notes in passing that Aunt Mac was the sister of "Mrs. D. A. Payne" (52) and, therefore, the sister-in-law of Daniel A. Payne. He was a bishop in the African Methodist Episcopal Church and the president of Wilberforce, among other roles. Aunt Mac's connection with the Paynes perhaps enhanced her prominence among Wilberforce residents, but that fact is not emphasized in the sketch.
121. Brown, *Homespun Heroines,* 51.
122. Brown, *Homespun Heroines,* 51.
123. Brown, *Homespun Heroines,* 51–52.
124. Brown, *Homespun Heroines,* 52.
125. Brown, *Homespun Heroines,* 52.
126. Brown, *Homespun Heroines,* 53.
127. Brown's reference resonates with the feature of Black cultural mythology that Temple calls "immortalization sensibility." Temple notes Maria W. Stewart as an exemplar of this practice, which is elaborated as "the Africana iteration of cultural eternal life, of never forgetting, of never being defeated." Temple, *Black Cultural Mythology,* 23, 28, 86.
128. Brown, *Homespun Heroines,* 54.
129. Stewart, *The Politics of Black Joy,* 6.
130. Higginbotham, *Righteous Discontent,* 187.
131. Paying ritual homage to one's ancestors was a key feature of West African spiritual practice that has been adapted and continued in African-American communities, as in the observance of Kwanzaa and the pouring of libations. See Temple, *Black Cultural Mythology,* 54, 71.

EPILOGUE: ABUNDANCE, MEMORY, RISK

1. Woodson, "Address to the Youth," in *Lift Every Voice,* 386–87.
2. Angelou, "And Still I Rise," in *And Still I Rise,* 41–42.
3. Baker, "Critical Memory and the Black Public Sphere," 3.
4. Jaschik, "Hannah-Jones Turns Down UNC Offer," *Inside Higher Ed.*
5. Seabrooks, "The People's Professor," *The Hilltop.*
6. Hall, "Slippin' In and Out of Frame," 344. Temple expands this perspective on death by describing how certain Black cultural traditions perceive continuity, even at the end of life, through proper community remembrance: "The life cycles

that we remember are retained and recycled in oral and written traditions because the death transitions represent the culmination of sacrifice on behalf of others. At life's end, one's deeds should be honorable and worthy of remembrance." Temple, *Black Cultural Mythology*, 196.

7. Ono, "Contextual Fields of Rhetoric," 272.
8. Wilson, "Theory/Criticism," 281–82. Angela G. Ray also articulates what is essentially a functionalist definition of rhetorical criticism in a 2016 essay: "Rather than offering a definition of the term rhetorical criticism and assessing an instance of scholarship based on its proximity to that stipulated definition, we will instead assume, for the purposes of assessing the state of the art, that scholarship identified by authors, editors, reviewers, and readers as rhetoric is, in fact, that." See Ray, "Rhetoric and the Archive," 45.
9. Wilson, "Theory/Criticism," 281.
10. Ray, "Rhetoric and the Archive," 45.
11. Browdy, "Black Women's Rhetoric(s)," n.p.
12. Browdy, "Black Women's Rhetoric(s)." See also O. I. Davis, "A Black Woman as Rhetorical Critic," 78.
13. Browdy, "Black Women's Rhetoric(s)."
14. Hine, "African American Women and Their Communities in the Twentieth Century," 2; Squires, "Rethinking the Black Public Sphere," 446.
15. Woodson, "Address to the Youth," 386; Brown, introduction to *Homespun Heroines*, vii.
16. Ahad-Legardy, *Afro-Nostalgia*, 3; Temple, *Black Cultural Mythology*, 88.
17. Mills, "Chronopolitics"; Ore and Houdek, "Lynching in Times of Suffocation," 443–58.
18. Mills, "Chronopolitics," 312.
19. Ore and Houdek, "Lynching in Times of Suffocation," 456.
20. Brown, *Homespun Heroines*, 55.
21. Ricoeur, *Memory, History, Forgetting*, 414.
22. *U.S. Census Bureau Quick Facts.*
23. Ono, "Contextual Fields of Rhetoric," 265. Ono defines contextual fields as "the situating elements used to make sense of the rhetorical text, texts, intertexts, transtexts, paratexts, or even 'discourse formations' under study."
24. Colpean and Dingo, "Beyond Drive-By Race Scholarship," 306.
25. Ono, "Contextual Fields of Rhetoric, 274.
26. Ono, "Contextual Fields of Rhetoric," 276.
27. hooks, *Teaching to Transgress*, 131.

WORKS CITED

"The 1619 Project." *New York Times Magazine*. August 14, 2019, https://www.nytimes.com/.

Aden, Roger C. *Upon the Ruins of Liberty: Slavery, The President's House at Independence National Historical Park, and Public Memory.* Philadelphia: Temple University Press, 2019.

Ahad-Legardy, Badia. *Afro-Nostalgia: Feeling Good in Contemporary Black Culture*. Urbana: University of Illinois Press, 2022.

Allen, Brenda J. "Black Womanhood and Feminist Standpoints." *Management Communication Quarterly* 11, no. 4 (1998): 575–86.

Amponsah, Emma-Lee. "Towards a Black Cultural Memory: Black Consciousness and Connectivity in the Online-Offline Continuum." *African Diaspora* 15, no. 1 (June 13, 2023): 28–54.

Anderson, Benedict Richard O'Gorman. *Imagined Communities: Reflections on the Origin and Spread of Nationalism*. New York: Verso, 2006.

Angelou, Maya. "And Still I Rise." In *And Still I Rise*, 41–42. New York: Random House, 1978.

Aristotle. *On Rhetoric: A Theory of Civic Discourse*. Translated by George Kennedy. New York: Oxford University Press, 1991.

Arthos, John. "Where There Are No Rules or Systems to Guide Us: Argument from Example in a Hermeneutic Rhetoric." *Quarterly Journal of Speech* 89, no. 4 (November 2003): 320–44.

Atwater, Deborah F. *African American Women's Rhetoric: The Search for Dignity, Personhood, and Honor.* Lanham, MD: Lexington Books, 2009.

Bailey, Amber. "Days of Jubilee: Emancipation Day Celebrations in Chicago, 1853 to 1877." *Journal of the Illinois State Historical Society* 109, no. 4 (2016): 353–73.

Baker, Augusta. *Books About the Negro for Children*. The James Weldon Johnson Collection: New York Public Library, 1944. HathiTrust. https://digital-research-books-beta.nypl.org/read/4440245.

Baker, Houston A. "Critical Memory and the Black Public Sphere." *Public Culture* 7, no. 1 (January 1, 1994): 3–33.

Beavis, Mary Ann. "Who is Mary Magdalene?" *Center for Christian Ethics at Baylor University* (2013): 23–29. https://ifl.web.baylor.edu/sites/g/files/ecbvkj771/files/2024-03/WomenintheBibleStudyGuides.pdf.

Behling, Laura L. "Reification and Resistance: The Rhetoric of Black Womanhood at the Columbian Exposition, 1893." *Women's Studies in Communication* 25, no. 2 (2002): 173–96.

Benoit, William Lyon. "Aristotle's Example: The Rhetorical Induction." *Quarterly Journal of Speech* 66 (1980): 182–92.

Benoit, William Lyon. "On Aristotle's Example." *Philosophy and Rhetoric* 20, no. 4 (1987): 261–67.

Bethune, Mary McLeod. "Oswald Garrison Villard and Hallie Quinn Brown." *Chicago Defender*. October 15, 1949, 6.

Bethune, Mary McLeod. "President's Address to the 15th Biennial Convention of the National Association of Colored Women, Civic Auditorium, Oakland, California." August 2, 1926.

Bierria, Alisa. "Missing in Action: Violence, Power, and Discerning Agency." *Hypatia* 29, no. 1 (2014): 129–45.

Biesecker, Barbara. "Coming to Terms with Recent Attempts to Write Women into the History of Rhetoric." *Philosophy and Rhetoric* 25, no. 2 (1992): 140–61.

Biesecker, Barbara. "Negotiating with our Tradition: Reflecting Again (Without Apologies) on the Feminization of Rhetoric." *Philosophy and Rhetoric* 26, no. 3 (1993): 136–41.

Blight, David W. *Race and Reunion: The Civil War in American Memory*. Cambridge, MA: Belknap Press, 2001.

Bloomfield, Emma Frances, and Sara C. VanderHaagen. "Where Women Scientists Belong: Placing Feminist Memory in Biography Collections for Children." *Women's Studies in Communication* 45, no. 2 (2022): 187–209.

Bodnar, John. *Remaking America: Public Memory, Commemoration, and Patriotism in the Twentieth Century*. Princeton, NJ: Princeton University Press, 1992.

Booth, Alison. *How to Make It as a Woman: Collective Biographical History from Victoria to the Present*. University of Chicago Press, 2004.

Brand, Anna Livia, Joshua Inwood, and Derek Alderman. "Truth-Telling and Memory-Work in Montgomery's Co-Constituted Landscapes." *ACME: An International E-Journal for Critical Geographies* 21, no. 5 (September 2022): 468–83.

Brock, André, Jr. *Distributed Blackness: African American Cybercultures*. New York University Press, 2020.

Brooks, Maegan P. *Fannie Lou Hamer: America's Freedom Fighting Woman*. Library of African American Biography Series. Lanham, MD: Rowman & Littlefield, 2020.

Brooks, Maegan P. *A Voice that Could Stir an Army: Fannie Lou Hamer and the Rhetoric of the Black Freedom Movement*. Jackson: University Press of Mississippi, 2014.

Brooks, Maegan P., and Davis W. Houck, eds. *The Speeches of Fannie Lou Hamer: To Tell It Like It Is*. Jackson: University Press of Mississippi, 2011.

Brooks, Van Wyck. "On Creating a Usable Past." *The Dial*. April 11, 1918. 337–41. https://archive.org/details/dialjournallitcrit64chicrich.

Browdy, Ronisha. "Black Women's Rhetoric(s): A Conversation Starter for Naming and Claiming a Field of Study." *Peitho: Journal of the Coalition of Feminist Scholars in the History of Rhetoric and Composition* 23, no. 4 (Summer 2021). https://cfshrc.org/article/black-womens-rhetorics-a-conversation-starter-for-naming-and-claiming-a-field-of-study/.

Brown, Hallie Q. *Bits and Odds: A Choice Selection of Recitations for School, Lyceum, and Parlor Entertainments*. Xenia, OH: Chew Printers. 1884.

Brown, Hallie Q. "The Black Mammy Statue." *National Notes*. April 1923, 3–4.

Brown, Hallie Q. "A Great Slight to the Race." *The Indianapolis Freeman*. April 30, 1892, 4. https://news.google.com/newspapers?nid=FIkAGs9z2eEC&dat=18920430&printsec=frontpage&hl=en.

Brown, Hallie Q. *Homespun Heroines and Other Women of Distinction*. Edited by Henry Louis Gates Jr. The Schomburg Center Library of Nineteenth-Century Black Women Writers. New York: Oxford University Press, 1988.

Brown, Nikki. *Private Politics and Public Voices: Black Women's Activism from World War I to the New Deal*. Bloomington: Indiana University Press, 2006.

Burke, Kenneth. *Grammar of Motives*. Berkeley: University of California Press, 1969.

Campbell, Karlyn Kohrs. "Agency: Promiscuous and Protean." *Communication and Critical/Cultural Studies* 2, no. 1 (2005): 1–19.

Campbell, Karlyn Kohrs. "Biesecker Cannot Speak for Her Either." *Philosophy and Rhetoric* 26, no. 2 (1993): 153–59.

Campbell, Karlyn Kohrs. "Gender and Genre: Loci of Invention and Contradiction in the Earliest Speeches by U.S. Women." *Quarterly Journal of Speech* 81, no. 4 (1995): 479–95.

Campbell, Karlyn Kohrs. "Style and Content in the Rhetoric of Early Afro-American Feminists." *Quarterly Journal of Speech* 72, no. 4 (November 1986): 434–45.

Cannady, Beatrice Morrow. "Address to the NAACP." June 28, 1928. *Black Past.org*. https://www.blackpast.org/african-american-history/1928-beatrice-morrow-cannady-speaks-naacp/#sthash.q7FOVSl4.dpuf.

Carby, Hazel V. *Reconstructing Womanhood: The Emergence of the Afro-American Woman Novelist*. New York: Oxford University Press, 1988.

Carretta, Vincent. *Phillis Wheatley: Biography of a Genius in Bondage*. Athens: University of Georgia Press, 2011.

Ceccarelli, Leah. "Polysemy: Multiple Meanings in Rhetorical Criticism." *Quarterly Journal of Speech* 84, no. 4 (1998): 395–415.

"Charlotte Hawkins Brown Speaks at Oberlin." *New York Age*. February 3, 1923, 1. https://www.newspapers.com/article/the-new-york-age-charlotte-hawkins-brown/21033325/.

Collins, Patricia Hill. *Black Feminist Thought: Knowledge, Consciousness, and the Politics of Empowerment*, 2nd ed. New York: Routledge, 2009.

Collins, Patricia Hill. "Intersectionality's Definitional Dilemmas." *Annual Review of Sociology* 41 (2015): 1–20.

Collins, Patricia Hill. "No Guarantees: Symposium on Black Feminist Thought." *Ethnic and Racial Studies* 38, no. 13 (2015): 2349–54.

Colpean, Michelle, and Rebecca Dingo. "Beyond Drive-By Race Scholarship: The Importance of Engaging Geopolitical Contexts." *Communication and Critical/Cultural Studies* 15, no. 4 (2018): 306–11.

Cooper, Brittney C. *Beyond Respectability: The Intellectual Thought of Race Women*. Urbana: University of Illinois Press, 2017.

Corrigan, Lisa M. *Black Feelings: Race and Affect in the Long Sixties*. Jackson: University of Mississippi Press, 2020.

Cowan, B.B. "Balsam of Gilead." *The Monitor*. January 19, 1923, 2. https://chroniclingamerica.loc.gov.

Cox, Karen L. *Dixie's Daughters: The United Daughters of the Confederacy and the Preservation of Confederate Culture*. Gainesville: University Press of Florida, 2019.

Cruz, Kleaver. *The Black Joy Project*. https://kleavercruz.com/.

Cvetkovich, Ann. "Public Feelings." *South Atlantic Quarterly* 106, no. 3 (2007): 459–68.

Dagbovie, Pero Gaglo. "Black Women Historians from the Late 19th Century to the Dawning of the Civil Rights Movement." *The Journal of African American History* 89, no. 3 (2004): 241–61.

Dale, Penny. "How a Former Slave Gave a Quilt to Queen Victoria." *BBC Africa*. July 6, 2017. https://www.bbc.com/news/world-africa-40500884.

Davis, Olga Idriss. "A Black Woman as Rhetorical Critic: Validating Self and Violating the Space of Otherness." *Women's Studies in Communication* 21, no. 1 (1998): 77–89.

Davis, Patricia G. *Laying Claim: African American Cultural Memory and Southern Identity*. Tuscaloosa: University of Alabama Press, 2016.

Davis, Patricia G. "The *Other* Southern Belles: Civil War Reenactment, African American Women, and the Performance of Idealized Femininity." *Text and Performance Quarterly* 32, no. 4 (October 2012): 308–31.

Davis, Shardé M. "The 'Strong Black Woman Collective': A Developing Theoretical Framework for Understanding Collective Communication Practices of Black Women." *Women's Studies in Communication* 38, no. 1 (2015): 20–35.

Davis, Shardé M. "Taking Back the Power: An Analysis of Black Women's Communicative Resistance." *Review of Communication* 18, no. 4 (2018): 301–18.

Dericotte, Toi. "Joy Is an Act of Resistance, and: Special Ears, and: Another Poem of a Small Grieving for My Fish Telly, and: On the Reasons I Loved Telly the Fish." *Prairie Schooner* 82, no. 3 (2008): 22–27.

Dickinson, Greg, Carole Blair, and Brian L. Ott, eds. *Places of Public Memory: The Rhetoric of Museums and Memorials*. Tuscaloosa: University of Alabama Press, 2010.

Dorgan, Lauren R. "Committee Renames Local Agassiz School." *Harvard Crimson*. May 22, 2002. https://www.thecrimson.com/article/2002/5/22/.

Du Bois, W. E. Burghardt. "My Impressions of Woodrow Wilson." *Journal of Negro History* 58, no. 4 (1973): 453–59.

Dunn, Damaris, and Bettina L. Love. "Antiracist Language Arts Pedagogy Is Incomplete without Black Joy." *Research in the Teaching of English* 55, no. 2 (2020): 190–92.

Dunn, Thomas R. *Queerly Remembered: Rhetorics for Representing the GLBTQ Past*. Columbia: University of South Carolina Press, 2016.

Dyson, Michael Eric. *Making Malcolm: The Myth and Meaning of Malcolm X*. New York: Oxford University Press, 1996.

Emmons, Robert A. and Michael E. McCullough, eds. *The Psychology of Gratitude*. New York: Oxford University Press, 2004.

Equal Justice Initiative. *Lynching in America: Confronting the Legacy of Racial Terror*. 3rd ed. 2017. https://lynchinginamerica.eji.org/report/.

Erll, Astrid. "Travelling Memory." *Parallax* 17, no. 4 (November 2011): 4–18.

Eves, Rosalyn Collings. "A Recipe for Remembrance: Memory and Identity in African-American Women's Cookbooks." *Rhetoric Review* 24, no. 3 (2005): 280–97.

Fauset, Jessie. "Looking Backward." *The Crisis*. January 1922, 125–26.

Fauset, Jessie. "Nostalgia." *The Crisis*. August 1921, 154–58.

Fitch, Susan Pullon, and Roseann Mandziuk, eds. *Sojourner Truth as Orator: Wit, Story, and Song*. Westport, CT: Greenwood Press, 1997.

Fitzmaurice, Megan Irene. "A Strategic Reversal: The National Association of Colored Women's Narrative Reframing of the Mammy Monument." Presentation at the National Communication Association Conference, November 2016.

Flexnor, Eleanor, and Ellen Fitzpatrick. *Century of Struggle: The Woman's Rights Movement in the United States*. Enlarged edition. Cambridge, MA: Harvard University Press, 1996.

Flores, Lisa A. "Between Abundance and Marginalization: The Imperative of Racial Rhetorical Criticism." *Review of Communication* 16, no.1 (2016): 4–24.

Foner, Philip S. and Robert James Branham, eds. *Lift Every Voice: African American Oratory, 1787–1900*. Tuscaloosa: University of Alabama Press, 1998.

"Fourteenth Census of the United States, 1920." *FamilySearch.com*. https://www.familysearch.org/ark:/61903/3:1:33S7-9R6B-QKP?view=index&action=view.

Gates, Henry Louis Jr. *The Trials of Phillis Wheatley: America's First Black Poet and Her Encounters with the Founding Fathers*. New York: Basic Civitas Books, 2003.

Gilmore, Glenda Elizabeth. "Somewhere in the Nadir of African American History, 1890–1920." Research Triangle Park, NC: National Humanities Center, 2010. https://nationalhumanitiescenter.org/tserve/freedom/1865-1917/essays/nadir.htm.

Gittens, Rhana A. "'What If I Am a Woman?': Black Feminist Rhetorical Strategies of Intersectional Identification and Resistance in Maria Stewart's Texts." *Southern Communication Journal* 83, no. 5 (2018): 310–21.

"Giving Thanks Can Make You Happier." *Harvard Health Publishing*. August 14, 2021. https://www.health.harvard.edu/healthbeat/giving-thanks-can-make-you-happier.

Glanton, Dahleen. "Is 'Auntie' a Term of Endearment for African American Women or Does It Promote an Aunt Jemima Stereotype?" *Chicago Tribune*. June 20, 2019. https://www.chicagotribune.com/2019/06/20/column-is-auntie-a-term-of-endearment.

Glymph, Thavolia. "'Liberty Dearly Bought': The Making of Civil War Memory in Afro-American Communities in the South." In *Time Longer Than Rope: A Century of African American Activism, 1850–1950*, edited by Charles M. Payne and Adam Green, 111–39. New York: New York University Press, 2003.

Griffiths, Jennifer L. *Traumatic Possessions: The Body and Memory in African American Women's Writing and Performance*. Charlottesville: University of Virginia Press, 2009.

Hall, Ashley R. "Slippin' In and Out of Frame: An Afrafuturist Feminist Orientation to Black Women and American Citizenship." *Quarterly Journal of Speech* 106, no. 3 (2020): 341–51.

Hamilton, Kenneth M. *Booker T. Washington in American Memory*. Urbana: University of Illinois Press, 2017.

Hampton, Timothy. *Writing from History: The Rhetoric of Exemplarity in Renaissance Literature*. Ithaca, NY: Cornell University Press, 1990.

Harris, Amy Hobbs. "'The Sole Province of the Public Reader': Elocutionist Hallie Quinn Brown's Performances of the Poetry of Paul Laurence Dunbar." *Reception: Texts, Readers, Audiences, History* 9 (2017): 36–55.

Harris, Leslie J., and Jansen B. Werner. "Forensic Rhetoric and Racial Justice: Rhetorical Advocacy in *The Reason Why the Colored American Is Not in the World's Columbian Exposition*." *Communication Studies* 72, no. 4 (September 2021): 618–33.

Harris, Trudier. *Martin Luther King Jr., Heroism, and African American Literature*. Tuscaloosa: University of Alabama Press, 2014.

Haskins, Ekaterina. *Popular Memories: Commemoration, Participatory Culture, and Democratic Citizenship*. Columbia: University of South Carolina Press, 2015.

Hauser, Gerard A. "Aristotle's Example Revisited." *Philosophy and Rhetoric* 18, no. 3 (1985): 171–80.

Hauser, Gerard A. "The Example in Aristotle's Rhetoric: Bifurcation or Contradiction?" *Philosophy and Rhetoric* 1 (1968): 78–90.

Hauser, Gerard A. "Reply to Benoit." *Philosophy and Rhetoric* 20, no. 4 (1987): 268–73.

Haynes, Elizabeth Ross. *Unsung Heroes*. New York: DuBois and Dill, 1921. http://archive.org/details/unsungheroes00haynrich.

Herdt, Jennifer A. "Exemplarity Between Tradition and Critique." *Journal of Religious Ethics* 47, no. 3 (2019): 552–65.

Higginbotham, Evelyn Brooks. *Righteous Discontent: The Women's Movement in the Black Baptist Church, 1880–1920*. Cambridge, MA: Harvard University Press, 1993.

Hine, Darlene Clark. "African American Women and Their Communities in the Twentieth Century: The Foundation and Future of Black Women's Studies." *Black Women, Gender + Families* 1, no. 1 (2007): 1–23.

Hine, Darlene Clark, ed. *Black Women in America*. New York: Oxford University Press, 2005.

Hine, Darlene Clark. "Rape and the Inner Lives of Black Women in the Middle West." *Signs* 14, no. 4 (1989): 912–20.

Hine, Darlene Clark, and Thompson, Kathleen A. *A Shining Thread of Hope: The History of Black Women in America*. 1st ed. New York: Broadway Books, 1998.

hooks, bell. *Feminism Is for Everybody*. Cambridge, MA: South End Press, 2000.

hooks, bell. *Teaching to Transgress: Education as the Practice of Freedom*. New York: Routledge, 1994.

Houdek, Matthew, and Kendell R. Phillips. "Public Memory." *Oxford Research Encyclopedia of Communication*. New York: Oxford University Press, 2017. DOI: 10.1093/acrefore/9780190228613.013.181.

"House Applauds Carolinian's Plea to Honor Mammy." *Evening Star*. Washington, DC, January 11, 1923, 40. https://chroniclingamerica.loc.gov.

"House Gives Ovation to Plea for Statue of Negro Mammy." *The Monitor*. January 19, 1923, 1. https://chroniclingamerica.loc.gov.

Houston, Marsha and Olga Idriss Davis, eds. *Centering Ourselves: African American Feminist and Womanist Studies in Discourse*. Cresskill, NJ: Hampton Press, 2002.

Howard, Maude Nooks. "'Mammy' Gets 'Em Told." In "News of Interest from our Correspondents." *Baltimore Afro-American*. February 23, 1923, 7.

Hunter, Tera W. *To 'Joy My Freedom: Southern Black Women's Lives and Labors after the Civil War*. Cambridge, MA: Harvard University Press, 1997.

Isocrates. "To Demonicus." In *Isocrates I*. Translated by David C. Mirhady and Yun Lee Too, 19–21. Austin: University of Texas Press, 2000.

Jackson, Liz. "Why Should I Be Grateful? The Morality of Gratitude in Contexts Marked by Injustice." *Journal of Moral Education* 45, no. 3 (2016): 277–79.

Jaschik, Scott. "Hannah-Jones Turns Down UNC Offer." *Inside Higher Ed*. July 1, 2021. https://www.insidehighered.com/news/2021/07/07.

Johnson, Javon. "Black Joy in the Time of Ferguson." *QED: A Journal of GLBTQ Worldmaking* 2, no. 2 (2015): 177–83.

Johnson, Joan Marie. "'Ye Gave Them a Stone': African American Women's Clubs, the Frederick Douglass Home, and the Black Mammy Monument." *Journal of Women's History* 17, no. 1 (2005): 62–86.

Johnston, Bethany. "Freedom and Slavery in the *Voice of the Negro*: Historical Memory and African-American Identity, 1904–1907." *Georgia Historical Quarterly* 84, no. 1 (2000): 29–71.

"Joy." *Dictionary of Psychology*. Washington, DC: American Psychological Association, 2020. https://dictionary.apa.org/joy.

Junior, Nyasha. *An Introduction to Womanist Biblical Interpretation*. Lexington, KY: Westminster John Knox Press, 2015.

Kachun, Mitch. *Festivals of Freedom: Memory and Meaning in African American Emancipation Celebrations, 1808–1915*. Amherst: University of Massachusetts Press, 2003.

Kachun, Mitch. *First Martyr of Liberty: Crispus Attucks in American Memory*. New York: Oxford University Press, 2017.

Kerr-Ritchie, Jeffrey R. *Rites of August First: Emancipation Day in the Black Atlantic World*. Baton Rouge: Louisiana State University Press, 2007.

Kristjánsson, Kristján. "Emulation and the Use of Role Models in Moral Education." *Journal of Moral Education* 35, no. 1 (March 2006): 37–49.

Kuhn, Annette. "A Journey Through Memory." In *Memory and Methodology*, edited by Susannah Radstone, 179–96. Milton, UK: Taylor & Francis Group, 2000.

Lanham, Richard A. *A Handlist of Rhetorical Terms*. 2nd ed. Berkeley: University of California Press, 1991.

Leff, Michael, and Ebony A. Utley. "Instrumental and Constitutive Rhetoric in Martin Luther King Jr.'s 'Letter from Birmingham Jail.'" *Rhetoric and Public Affairs* 7, no. 1 (2004): 37–51.

Logan, Rayford. *The Negro in American Life and Thought: The Nadir, 1877–1901*. New York: Dial Press, 1954.

Logan, Shirley Wilson. "Frances E. W. Harper, 'Woman's Political Future.'" *Voices of Democracy* 1 (2006): 43–57.

Logan, Shirley Wilson. *We Are Coming: The Persuasive Discourse of Nineteenth-Century Black Women*. 1st edition. Carbondale: Southern Illinois University Press, 1999.

Lowenthal, David. "Stewardship, Sanctimony and Selfishness—A Heritage Paradox." In *History and Heritage: Consuming the Past in Contemporary Culture*. Edited by John Arnold, Kate Davies, and Simon Ditchfield, 169–79. Shaftesbury, England: Donhead Publishing, 1998.

Lu, Jessica H., and Catherine Knight Steele. "'Joy is Resistance': Cross-platform Resilience and (Re)invention of Black Oral Culture Online." *Information, Communication & Society* 22, no. 6 (2019): 823–37.

Luckerson, Victor. "The Women Who Preserved the Story of the Tulsa Race Massacre." *New Yorker* May 28, 2021. https://www.newyorker.com/.

Mack, Kristen, and John Palfrey. "Capitalizing Black and White: Grammatical Justice and Equity." *MacArthur Foundation*. August 26, 2020. https://www.macfound.org/.

Maddux, Kristy. *Practicing Citizenship: Women's Rhetoric at the 1893 Chicago World's Fair*. University Park: Pennsylvania State University Press, 2019.

Madison, D. Soyini. "'That Was My Occupation': Oral Narrative, Performance, and Black Feminist Thought." *Text and Performance Quarterly* 13, no. 3 (1993): 213–32.

Mann, Regis. "Theorizing 'What Could Have Been': Black Feminism, Historical Memory, and the Politics of Reclamation." *Women's Studies* 40, no. 5 (August 7, 2011): 575–99.

Margo, Robert A. *Race and Schooling in the South, 1880–1950: An Economic History*. University of Chicago Press, 1990.

Massa, Ann. "Black Women in the 'White City.'" *Journal of American Studies* 8, no. 3 (1974): 319–37.

Massenburg, Moses. "Documenting the Contributions Made by Black Women to Carter G. Woodson's Early Black History Movement: Mary McLeod Bethune and Zora Neale Hurston." *Black History Bulletin* 88, no. 1 (2018): 28–34.

Mathias, Frank F. "John Randolph's Freedman: The Thwarting of a Will." *Journal of Southern History* 39, no. 2 (1973): 263–72.

McCormick, Samuel. "Mirrors for the Queen: A Letter from Christine de Pizan on the Eve of the Civil War." *Quarterly Journal of Speech* 94, no. 3 (August 2008): 273–96.

McElya, Michele Paige. "Monumental Citizenship: Reading the National Mammy Memorial Controversy of the Early Twentieth Century." PhD dissertation, New York University, 2003. http://search.proquest.com/docview/305313629/abstract/4A5C8BD5E85342F4PQ/1.

McElya, Micki. *Clinging to Mammy: The Faithful Slave in Twentieth-Century America.* Cambridge, MA: Harvard University Press, 2007.

Messer, Chris M. *The 1921 Tulsa Race Massacre: Crafting a Legacy.* Cham, Switzerland: Springer International Publishing AG, 2021.

Mikorenda, Jerry. "Beating Wings in Rebellion: The Ladies Literary Society Finds Equality." The Gotham Center for New York City History. April 7, 2016. https://www.gothamcenter.org/blog/beating-wings-in-rebellion-the-ladies-literary-society-finds-equality.

Miller, Kelly. "Kelly Miller Says." *Baltimore Afro-American.* February 23, 1923, 9. https://news.google.com/newspapers?nid=UBnQDr5gPskC&dat=19230223.

Mills, Charles. "The Chronopolitics of Racial Time." *Time & Society* 29, no. 2 (2020): 297–317.

Mitchell, Stephanie. "The Renaming of a Neighborhood." *Harvard Gazette.* May 8, 2024. https://news.harvard.edu/gazette/story/2024/05/renaming-of-a-neighborhood.

Mossell, N. F. *The Work of the Afro-American Woman.* The Schomburg Center Library of Nineteenth-Century Black Women Writers. New York: Oxford University Press, 1988.

"NAACP: A Century in the Fight for Freedom. The New Negro Movement." Washington, DC: Library of Congress. February 21, 2009. https://www.loc.gov/exhibits/naacp/the-new-negro-movement.html.

Nash, Jennifer C. *Black Feminism Reimagined: After Intersectionality.* Durham, NC: Duke University Press, 2019.

Nash, Jennifer C. "Practicing Love: Black Feminism, Love-Politics, and Post-Intersectionality." *Meridians* 11, no. 2 (2011): 1–24.

Neu, Charles E. *The Wilson Circle: President Woodrow Wilson and His Advisers.* Baltimore, MD: Johns Hopkins University Press, 2022. http://ebookcentral.proquest.com/lib/uwm/detail.action?docID=29138865.

"Not Lost Sight Of. The Afro-American is Gradually Being Brought into the Fair." *Plaindealer*, Detroit, MI. March 24, 1893, 1.

Nora, Pierre. "Between Memory and History: *Les Lieux de Mémoire.*" *Representations* 26 (Special Issue: Memory and Counter-Memory), 26 (Spring 1989): 7–25.

Nurhussein, Nadia. *Rhetorics of Literacy: The Cultivation of American Dialect Poetry.* Columbus: The Ohio State University Press, 2013.

"Of Great Interest to Colored Women." *The Freeman*, Indianapolis, IN,. October 3, 1891, 8. https://chroniclingamerica.loc.gov.

Ohito, Esther O. "Remembering My Memories: Black Feminist Memory Work as a Visual Research Method of Inquiry." *International Journal of Qualitative Studies in Education* 36, no. 9 (2023): 1856–75.

Olick, Jeffery K., Aline Sierp, and Jenny Wusterberg. "Introduction: Taking Stock of Memory Studies." *Memory Studies* 16, no. 6 (2023): 1399–1406.

Ono, Kent A. "Contextual Fields of Rhetoric." *Western Journal of Communication* 84, no. 3 (June 5, 2020): 264–79.

Ore, Ersula, and Matthew Houdek. "Lynching in Times of Suffocation: Toward a Spatiotemporal Politics of Breathing." *Women's Studies in Communication* 43, no. 4 (November 2020): 443–58.

O'Reilly, Kenneth. "The Jim Crow Policies of Woodrow Wilson." *Journal of Blacks in Higher Education*, no. 17 (1997): 117–21.

Paddon, Anna R. and Sally Turner. "African Americans and the World's Columbian Exposition." *Illinois Historical Journal* 88, no. 1 (1995): 19–36.

Palczewski, Catherine H. "The 1919 Prison Special: Constituting White Women's Citizenship." *Quarterly Journal of Speech* 102, no. 2 (May 2016): 107–32.

"Papers of the NAACP, Part I, 1909–1950: Meetings of the Board of Directors, Records of Annual Conferences, Speeches, and Special Reports." Frederick, MD: University Publications of America, 1982, xi. http://www.lexisnexis.com/documents/academic/upa_cis/1414_PapersNAACPPart11909-1950.pdf.

Perry, Jennifer. "The Crucial Legacy of the Black Aunt." *Jezebel*. February 18, 2021. https://jezebel.com/the-crucial-legacy-of-the-black-aunt-1841672941.

Peterson, Carla L. *"Doers of the Word": African-American Women Speakers and Writers in the North (1830–1880)*. New York: Oxford University Press, 1995.

Phillips, Kendall R., ed. *Framing Public Memory*. Tuscaloosa: University of Alabama Press, 2004.

Phyllis Wheatley Young Women's Christian Association. "Petition to Congress." February 6, 1923. US Center for Legislative Archives. Committee for the Library, 67th Congress (internal ref. 9E4/14/12/3, Box 487).

Porter, Dorothy B. "The Organized Educational Activities of Negro Literary Societies, 1828–1846." *The Journal of Negro Education* 5, no. 4 (1936): 555–76.

Prasch, Allison M. "Toward a Rhetorical Theory of Deixis." *Quarterly Journal of Speech* 102, no. 2 (2016): 166–93.

Ray, Angela G. "Rhetoric and the Archive." *Review of Communication* 16, no. 1 (2016): 43–59.

Reed, Christopher Robert. *"All the World is Here!": The Black Presence at White City*. Bloomington: Indiana University Press, 2000.

Remond, Sarah Parker. Letter to the *National Anti-Slavery Standard*. November 3, 1866, 2.

Richards, Cindy Koenig. "Inventing Sacagawea: Public Women and the Transformative Potential of Epideictic Rhetoric." *Western Journal of Communication* 73, no. 1 (2009): 1–22.

Richardson, Marilyn, ed. *Maria W. Stewart, America's First Black Woman Political Writer: Essays and Speeches*. 2nd edition. Bloomington: Indiana University Press, 1987.

Ricoeur, Paul. *Memory, History, Forgetting*. Translated by Kathleen Blamey and David Pellauer. Chicago: University of Chicago Press, 2004.

Rodríguez-Silva, Ileana M. "Abolition, Race, and the Politics of Gratitude in Late Nineteenth-Century Puerto Rico." *Hispanic American Historical Review* 93, no. 4 (2013): 622–23.

Romano, Renee Christine, and Leigh Raiford, eds. *The Civil Rights Movement in American Memory*. Athens: University of Georgia Press, 2006.

Royster, Jacqueline Jones. *Traces of a Stream: Literacy and Social Change among African American Women*. Pittsburgh, PA: University of Pittsburgh Press, 2000.

Russell, Alexandria. "Sites Seen and Unseen: Mapping African American Women's Public Memorialization." PhD dissertation, University of South Carolina, 2018. https://www.proquest.com/docview/2186915071/abstract/8369DDC1E1D84040PQ/10.

Rydell, Robert W. "World's Columbian Exposition." *Encyclopedia of Chicago*. Chicago Historical Society, 2005. http://www.encyclopedia.chicagohistory.org/pages/1386.html.

Saad, Lydia. "Gallup Vault: Black Americans' Preferred Racial Label." *Gallup*. July 13, 2020. https://news.gallup.com/vault/315566/gallup-vault-black-americans-preferred-racial-label.aspx.

Schuster, Kate. *Teaching Hard History*. Montgomery, AL: Southern Poverty Law Center, January 31, 2018. https://www.splcenter.org/20180131/teaching-hard-history.

Schwalm, Leslie A. "'Agonizing Groans of Mothers' and 'Slave-Scarred Veterans': The Commemoration of Slavery and Emancipation." *American Nineteenth Century History* 9, no. 3 (2008): 289–304.

Schwalm, Leslie A. "Emancipation Day Celebrations: The Commemoration of Slavery and Freedom in Iowa." *The Annals of Iowa* 62 (Summer 2003): 291–332.

Schwalm, Leslie A. *Emancipation's Diaspora: Race and Reconstruction in the Upper Midwest*. 1st edition. John Hope Franklin Series in African American History and Culture. Chapel Hill: University of North Carolina Press, 2009.

Scott, Joan W. "The Evidence of Experience." *Critical Inquiry* 17, no. 4 (1991): 773–97.

Seabrooks, Aaliyah. "The People's Professor: Nikole Hannah-Jones Talks Howard Thus Far And Expanding Her 1619 Project." *The Hilltop*. October 18, 2022. https://thehilltoponline.com/.

"Senate OK's Bill for Monument to 'Black Mammy.'" *Northwestern Bulletin*, St. Paul, MN. March 17, 1923, 1. https://chroniclingamerica.loc.gov.

Sernett, Milton C. *Harriet Tubman: Myth, Memory, and History.* Durham, NC: Duke University Press, 2007.

Sewall, May Wright, ed. *World's Congress of Representative Women: A Historical Résumé for Popular Circulation of the World's Congress of Representative Women, Convened in Chicago on May 15, and Adjourned on May 22, 1893, Under the Auspices of the Women's Branch of the World's Congress Auxiliary*. Chicago: Rand McNally, 1894. https://catalog.hathitrust.org/Record/004399612.

Shields, John, ed. *The Collected Works of Phillis Wheatley*. The Schomburg Library of Nineteenth-Century Black Women Writers. New York: Oxford University Press, 1988.

Shrum, Regan. "Who Takes the Cake? The History of the Cakewalk." *National Museum of American History*. May 18, 2016. https://americanhistory.si.edu/.

Silverstein, Jake. "Why We Published The 1619 Project." *New York Times Magazine*. December 20, 2019. https://www.nytimes.com/.

Smith, Lucy Wilmot. "The Future Colored Girl." (August 22, 1886). In *Minutes and Addresses of the American National Baptist Convention, Held at St. Louis, MO, Aug. 25–29, '86*, 68–74. Jackson, MS: J. J. Spelman, 1887. https://search.alexanderstreet.com/lti/view/work/bibliographic_entity|bibliographic_details|3265640.

Squires, Catherine R. "Rethinking the Black Public Sphere: An Alternative Vocabulary for Multiple Public Spheres." *Communication Theory* 12, no. 4 (November 2002): 446–68.

Stanback, Marsha Houston. "Feminist Theory and Black Women's Talk." *Howard Journal of Communications* 1, no. 4 (1988): 187–94.

Stedman, Charles Manly. *A Monument in Commemoration of the Faithful Colored Mammies of the South: Speech of Hon. Charles M. Stedman of North Carolina on H.R. 13672 in the House of Representatives, January 9, 1923*. Washington, DC: US Government Printing Office, 1923. https://catalog.hathitrust.org/Record/102558120.

Stewart, Lindsey. *The Politics of Black Joy: Zora Neale Hurston and Neo-Abolitionism*. Evanston, IL: Northwestern University Press, 2021.

Stillion Southard, Belinda A. *Militant Citizenship: Rhetorical Strategies of the National Woman's Party, 1913–1920*. College Station: Texas A&M University Press, 2011.

Tell, Dave. *Remembering Emmett Till*. Chicago: University of Chicago Press, 2019.

Temple, Christel N. *Black Cultural Mythology*. Albany: State University of New York Press, 2020.

Temple, Christel N. "The Emergence of Sankofa Practice in the United States: A Modern History." *Journal of Black Studies* 41, no. 1 (September 1, 2010): 127–50.

Terborg-Penn, Roslyn. *African American Women in the Struggle for the Vote, 1850–1920*. Bloomington: Indiana University Press, 1998.

Terrell, Mary Church. "The Black Mammy Monument." *Evening Star*, Washington, DC. February 10, 1923, 6. https://chroniclingamerica.loc.gov.

Terrell, Mary Church. "The Progress of Colored Women: An Address Delivered before the National American Woman Suffrage Association, at the Columbia Theater, Washington, D.C., February 19, 1898, on the Occasion of Its Fiftieth Anniversary." Washington, DC: Smith Brothers Printers, February 18, 1898. https://www.loc.gov/item/90898298.

"That Responsive Racial Feeling." *Richmond Planet*. January 13, 1923, 4. https://chroniclingamerica.loc.gov.

Tolson, Nancy. "Making Books Available: The Role of Early Libraries, Librarians, and Booksellers in the Promotion of African American Children's Literature." *African American Review* 32, no. 1 (1998): 9–16.

Triece, Mary E. *Memory Work: White Ignorance and Black Resistance in Popular Magazines, 1900–1910*. Jackson: University of Mississippi Press, 2024.

Truman, Benjamin Cummings. *History of the World's Fair: Being a Complete and Authentic Description of the Columbian Exposition from its Inception*. Philadelphia: H. W. Kelley, 1893.

Tsenes-Hills, Temple Bryonny. "I Am the Utterance of My Name: Black Victorian Feminist Discourse and Intellectual Enterprise at the Columbian Exposition, 1893." PhD dissertation, Loyola University Chicago, 2004.

U.S. Census Bureau Quick Facts. Milwaukee, WI, 2024. https://www.census.gov/quickfacts/fact/table/milwaukeecitywisconsin/PST045222.

VanderHaagen, Sara C. "Black Heroes and 'The Jury': *The Brownies' Book* Biographies as Counter-Memories for Child Readers." In *A Centennial Celebration of* The Brownies' Book *Magazine*. Edited by Dianne Johnson-Feelings and Jonda C. McNair, 56–77. Jackson: University of Mississippi Press, 2022.

VanderHaagen, Sara C. *Children's Biographies of African American Women: Rhetoric, Public Memory, and Agency*. Columbia: University of South Carolina Press, 2018.

VanderHaagen, Sara C. "'A Grand Sisterhood': Black American Women Speakers at the 1893 Congress of Representative Women." *Quarterly Journal of Speech* 107, no. 1 (2021): 1–25.

VanderHaagen, Sara C. "(Mis)Quoting King: Commemorative Stewardship and Ethos in the Controversy over the Martin Luther King Jr. Memorial." *Argumentation and Advocacy* 55, no. 1–2 (June 22, 2019): 91–115.

Vos, Pieter H. "Learning from Exemplars: Emulation, Character Formation and the Complexities of Ordinary Life." *Journal of Beliefs & Values*, 39, no. 1 (2018): 17–28.

Walker, Alice. *In Search of Our Mothers' Gardens*. New York: Harcourt Brace Jovanovich, 1983.

Walker, Robbie Jean, ed. *The Rhetoric of Struggle: Public Address by African American*

Women. Critical Studies on Black Life and Culture; vol. 20. New York: Garland, 1992.

Wallace-Sanders, Kimberly. *Mammy: A Century of Race, Gender, and Southern Memory*. Ann Arbor: University of Michigan Press, 2008.

Watts, Eric King. *Hearing the Hurt: Rhetoric, Aesthetics, and Politics of the New Negro Movement*. Tuscaloosa: University of Alabama Press, 2012.

Weimann, Jeanne Madeline. *The Fair Women*. Chicago: Academy Chicago, 1981.

Weir-Soley, Donna Aza. *Eroticism, Spirituality, and Resistance in Black Women's Writings*. Gainesville: University Press of Florida, 2017.

Welter, Barbara. "The Cult of True Womanhood, 1820–1860." *American Quarterly* 18, no. 2 (1966): 151–74.

"Whose Heritage? Public Symbols of the Confederacy," 3rd edition. Montgomery, AL: Southern Poverty Law Center, 2022. https://www.splcenter.org/sites/default/files/whose-heritage-report-third-edition.pdf.

Williams, Robert V. "Oral History Interview with Augusta Baker." May 7, 1989. South Carolina Library Heritage Project. https://digital.tcl.sc.edu/digital/collection/abaker/id/766.

Wilson, Kirt H. "The Racial Politics of Imitation in the Nineteenth Century." *Quarterly Journal of Speech* 89, no. 2 (May 2003): 89–108.

Wilson, Kirt H. "Theory/Criticism: A Functionalist Approach to the 'Specific Intellectual' Work of Rhetorical Criticism." *Western Journal of Communication* 84, no. 3 (2020): 280–96.

Yates, Frances A. *The Art of Memory*. Chicago: University of Chicago Press, 1966.

"You Get Some Black Joy! And You Get Some Black Joy! Everybody Gets Some Black Joy! Love, *The Root*." *The Root.com*. February 25, 2021. https://www.theroot.com/.

Young, Harvey. *Embodying Black Experience: Stillness, Critical Memory, and the Black Body*. Ann Arbor: University of Michigan Press, 2010.

INDEX

Page numbers in *italics* refer to figures.